Collective Vision

Collective Vision

Igniting District and School Improvement

Nancy Gordon and Dianne Turner

ROWMAN & LITTLEFIELD
Lanham • Boulder • New York • London

Published by Rowman & Littlefield
An imprint of The Rowman & Littlefield Publishing Group, Inc.
4501 Forbes Boulevard, Suite 200, Lanham, Maryland 20706
www.rowman.com
86-90 Paul Street, London EC2A 4NE

Copyright © 2025 by Nancy Gordon and Dianne Turner

All rights reserved. No part of this book may be reproduced in any form or by any electronic or mechanical means, including information storage and retrieval systems, without written permission from the publisher, except by a reviewer who may quote passages in a review.

British Library Cataloguing in Publication Information available

Library of Congress Cataloging-in-Publication Data

Names: Gordon, Nancy, 1959– author. | Turner, Dianne, 1953– author.
Title: Collective vision: igniting school and district improvement / Nancy Gordon and Dianne Turner.
Description: Lanham, Maryland: Rowman & Littlefield, 2024. | Includes bibliographical references and index.
Identifiers: LCCN 2024018456 (print) | LCCN 2024018457 (ebook) | ISBN 9781538195604 (cloth) | ISBN 9781538195611 (paperback) | ISBN 9781538195628 (epub)
Subjects: LCSH: School improvement programs—United States. | School districts—United States—Administration.
Classification: LCC LB2822.82 .G695 2024 (print) | LCC LB2822.82 (ebook) | DDC 371.2/07—dc23/eng/20240521
LC record available at https://lccn.loc.gov/2024018456
LC ebook record available at https://lccn.loc.gov/2024018457

Contents

Foreword	vii
Acknowledgments	ix
Introduction	xiii
Background: The Delta Context	xvii

PART 1: THE DISTRICT AS A LEARNING ORGANIZATION   1

Chapter 1: Focus on a Shared District Vision and Mission	3
Chapter 2: Focus on District Support for the Vision	23
Chapter 3: Focus on Effective Governance	31
Chapter 4: Focus on Learning and Continuous Improvement for All	39
Chapter 5: Focus on Instructional Coherence	45
Chapter 6: Focus on Evidence-Informed Decision Making	53
Chapter 7: Focus on Continuous Professional Learning	59
Chapter 8: Focus on Leadership Learning	71
Chapter 9: Focus on Strong, Collaborative Working Relationships	81
Chapter 10: Focus on Sharing the Learning across Schools and Districts	87
Chapter 11: Connections to Other Research	99

PART 2: SCHOOLS AS LEARNING ORGANIZATIONS   105

Chapter 12: Schools as Learning Organizations	107

PART 3: STRONG LEARNING ENVIRONMENTS   129

Strong Learning Environments   131

PART 4: A SUMMARY OF WHAT MADE A DIFFERENCE   149

A Summary of What Made a Difference   151

PART 5: FULL CIRCLE: WHERE TO NEXT?   165

Full Circle: Where to Next?   167

Chapter 16: Conclusion   177

Appendix A   179

Appendix B   181

References   185

Index   191

Foreword

This is a book about a sustained, long-term inquiry in a school district in British Columbia, Canada. The inquiry began over 10 years ago with a simple question: What impact would a cocreated, shared vision have on learning across a school district? This was a bold question—in order to answer it, patience and time were required, key learning principles of First Peoples.[1,2] In fact, this inquiry would require more than 10 years of time and a strong, unwavering commitment from leaders at all levels, some of whom joined the school district after the inquiry began.

It is quite rare in education to be able to tell the story of educational change and transformation over a sustained period of time. All too often educational initiatives are developed, only to be abandoned a short time later before convincing results are realized. A focused 10-year commitment to a vision was needed to ensure that the goals of the vision had the time required to be realized.

The *Spirals of Inquiry* (Halbert & Kaser, 2013) is a foundational resource to the Delta School District's story. This book describes the school district's 10-year inquiry cycle from *scanning* to *focusing* and *developing a hunch*, through *engaging in new learning, taking action*, and *checking* to see if a difference was made. This account of the first part of the journey ends where the next part of the story begins, with the district scanning and codeveloping a new vision aimed to address the needs of the district through the next 10 years until 2030.

This book is written for school and district leaders who are interested in achieving whole-system transformation and improvement in outcomes for students. Additionally, it speaks to the role of boards of education and district governance in achieving that improvement. It will also appeal to leaders in postsecondary institutions who are responsible for preparing educators for formal leadership roles. This is a book about continuous learning and steadfast determination to make a significant difference for the students who need it the most, and, ultimately, to achieve equity for all learners so that they can contribute their full potential to a future where all learners belong and everyone soars.

Finally, although this book describes a 10-year case study that took place in Canada, we believe that other jurisdictions around the world can learn from this example. As authors, we challenge readers to view this book through the lens of their current context and to reflect on their current practices in order to determine not only areas of strength, but also to ponder areas where further growth may be beneficial. In order to assist with the process of critical reflection, we have included, at the end of each chapter, questions designed to connect the ideas in the book to your own learning.

NOTES

1. The term "First Peoples" refers to Indigenous (First Nations, Métis, and Inuit) peoples in Canada, as well as to Indigenous peoples around the world (FNESC, 2020).

2. The "First Peoples Principles of Learning" articulates an expression of the shared wisdom of Elders and educators within First Peoples communities in BC (FNESC, 2020).

Acknowledgments

The authors would like to acknowledge that this book was written on the traditional, ancestral, and unceded territory of the Coast Salish Peoples, in particular the territories of Tsawwassen First Nations, the Musqueam, Squamish, and Tsleil-Waututh Nations who have been stewards of the land since time immemorial. We are privileged to live, work, and play on these lands. We would like to pay respect to the Elders of the nations, past and present, and are grateful to them for their teachings and for sharing their wisdom and guidance with us on the road to Truth and Reconciliation.

Hay ch q'u

This book would not have been possible without the support and commitment of the educators and staff who work in the Delta School District.[1] Everyone—teachers, educational assistants, support staff, maintenance and facilities workers, school vice-principals and principals, personnel in the school board office, parents, students, and the community—have all played a significant role in the achievements realized in the Delta School District. The district vision would not exist without the thoughtful input of every participant, and not only its creation but also in the deliberate actions that brought the vision to life.

The Delta School District is, in many aspects, unique. It has an energy and a feeling of connectedness that is the result of incredible educators coming together around a common purpose. In Delta, it is believed that everyone is a learner, a teacher, and a leader, and continuous improvement is embraced as a goal for all.

We would especially like to acknowledge the Delta Board of Education[2] for their commitment to the collective vision. This dedication has been continuous and unwavering over multiple elected boards. Delta's senior district leadership team has been instrumental in making sure that the collective visions are leveraged to ensure improved learning outcomes for all. In particular, while he was assistant superintendent, Doug Sheppard took on the responsibility of creating the facilitation process for Vision 2020. As superintendent, in 2021, he gave permission for the two assistant superintendents to take risks and lead the Vision 2030 process. Although Assistant Superintendent Brad Bauman joined the district after Vision 2020 had already been created, he worked tirelessly to help the district achieve the vision, and, in 2021, he co-led the Vision 2030 process. The theme of encouraging others to take risks and to try new approaches to learning runs throughout the district and includes everyone—students, staff, educators, vice-principals, principals, and district leaders. We are privileged to have worked alongside Doug and Brad as team members and are certain the outstanding work toward achieving the vision continues under their leadership.

In addition, a huge thank you goes out to the Delta Principals and Vice Principals Association,[3] whose members play a key role in the leadership of the district. Delta is fortunate to have such capable and forward-thinking leaders in schools. The Delta Teachers Association[4] is to be commended on the support that they have brought to their members and to the efforts of district improvement. Delta teachers are true professionals who engage tirelessly in their learning to improve educational outcomes for students. Another influential and supportive group who made significant contributions to the success of the district are members of the Canadian Union of Public Employees Local 1091, whose members partner with teachers and help keep schools running efficiently for learners.[5] Most importantly, we would like to thank the informal school and district leaders who have contributed to, embraced, and worked toward Vision 2020, and now Vision 2030. There are too many of you to mention individually, but you know who you are.

The Delta School District is one where community members at all levels know each other and recognize the contributions being made by all. There is an understanding that everyone who works in the district is an important part of the whole, and that no matter what their role they exist to enable all learners to succeed and to inspire and nurture future-ready learners.

Sincere appreciation is expressed to Drs. Judy Halbert and Linda Kaser for creating the Network of Inquiry and Indigenous Education and for developing and sharing the *Spiral of Inquiry*. They have been unprecedented in their work in British Columbia and across the world in inspiring networks of inquiry that embrace the goal of improving outcomes for learners. Even more importantly, they have been partners in the learning journey of the Delta School District and this book would not exist without their support and encouragement. In addition, Dr. Louise Stoll has been a valuable friend to the district and her work related to *Schools as Learning Organizations* has played a significant role in the Delta School District's story of improvement.

We would be remiss not to mention the contributions made by Myriam Laberge, Avril Orloff, and Stina Brown who facilitated both collective vision processes. We are especially grateful to Nathan Davidson for his commitment to ensuring this book was published, and to the team at Rowman & Littlefield for their support throughout the publication process.

Finally, we would like to acknowledge our families for believing in us, encouraging us, and for their patience in being there throughout this journey. We are grateful for their love and support.

NOTES

1. British Columbia is divided into 60 school districts which administer publicly funded education until the end of grade 12 in local areas or, in the case of francophone education, across the province.

2. Locally elected school trustees, who make up boards of education in British Columbia, represent a unique form of democratic governance.

3. The BC Principals' & Vice-Principals' Association (BCPVPA) is a voluntary professional association representing school leaders employed as principals and vice-principals in BC's public education system. The Delta Principals and Vice Principals Association is the local chapter of the BCPVPA.

4. The Delta Teachers' Association (DTA) represents the union of school teachers for the School District of Delta. It is the Delta chapter of the British Columbia Teachers' Federation (BCTF), the labor union that represents all public school teachers in the province of British Columbia.

5. The Canadian Union of Public Employees (CUPE) Local 1091 is the Delta chapter of a Canadian trade union serving the public sector.

Introduction

When it comes to district and school improvement, the research is clear. There are key elements that can be leveraged to create stronger districts, schools (Timperley et al., 2013; Leithwood, 2013; Fullan, 2010; Kools & Stoll, 2016), and classrooms or, in current terminology, learning environments (OECD, 2013). As the work of educational researchers evolves, it also begins to align and point to common findings that have a positive impact on schools and districts. Much of the research on school and district leadership in the past focused on the qualities that make leaders effective in their roles. However, many of these qualities could be carried out in isolation, without the need for cross-school and cross-district connections. More recently, researchers have highlighted the need for, as Michael Fullan and Joanne Quinn state, coherence (2016). This suggests a need for common frameworks between schools and districts that provide for organizational alignment, leading to greater coherence and support for student learning. In British Columbia, an example of such a common framework is the Spiral of Inquiry (Halbert and Kaser, 2013) which provides districts with a common approach to professional inquiry yet is open-ended enough to allow for a focus on the unique learning needs of varying jurisdictions.

Through the lens of key current research, this book focuses on the Delta School District's journey of system transformation. Each of the researchers cited in this book has had a strong influence on the work being done in Delta. These researchers have articulated similar findings and although they each present slightly different models and perspectives, the building blocks of their findings are remarkably similar.

Over the past 10 years, the Delta School District has continually examined current educational research as it relates to the unique context and learning needs of the district. Of particular interest is the disconnect between research and practice. Peter DeWitt (2019) cites four major reasons why educators don't use research to help make improvements in their practice:

1. Researchers making their work too complicated and difficult to understand
2. Educators not having enough time to study research
3. Educators failing to see the relevance of research to daily work
4. Educators believing that they are already successful (without evidence to measure success)

Dewitt also expresses four concerns as to why educators do use research:

1. Using research to confirm what they already know (or only reading about topics that they are already passionate about)
2. Relying too much on social media as the only source of research
3. Utilizing only research that is easy to implement
4. Accessing research only when forced to (for example, by the school district or Ministry of Education[1]) (DeWitt, 2019)

Using too small a sample of research or data can be problematic for schools or school districts. If the research being used to provide advice or direction is not broad enough, or credible enough, it might be too easy for educators to head off on tangents, fueled only by their passions or by the "next hot topic," without carefully selecting goals that are based on the actual learning needs of their students, educators, and the system.

How might educators ensure they are accessing research that is truly necessary and impactful within their context? In Delta, the answer to this question can be found in the research of Halbert and Kaser (2013) and the *Spiral of Inquiry* (see figure I.1).

The six stages of the *Spiral of Inquiry* (*scanning, focusing, developing a hunch, new professional learning, taking action,* and *checking*) will be referenced throughout the book but to provide clarity, a quick overview follows.

The first stage of the *Spiral of Inquiry* is the *scanning phase*. During this phase educators are asked to consider "What's going on for our learners?" and "How do we know?" Once educators have done a thorough job of engaging in the *scanning stage*, they will need to consider the question "what do our learners need?" and therefore, it will prevent them from only considering research that is appealing or popular. Instead, they will seek out evidence that ensures the true needs of the learners they serve are met. A critical element of the *scanning phase* is to remain focused on the curricular learning needs of the learner and to not be enticed into focusing on other big ideas that may or may not positively impact student learning. For example, one school's focus on student engagement in mathematical problem solving became confounded by only measuring gains in student engagement. Because it failed to measure

What's going on for our learners?
How do we know?
Why does this matter?

FOCUSING
What does our focus need to be?

SCANNING
What's going on for our learners?

DEVELOPING A HUNCH
What is leading to this situation?

LEARNING
How and where can we learn more about what to do?

CHECKING
Have we made enough of a difference?

TAKING ACTION
What will we do differently?

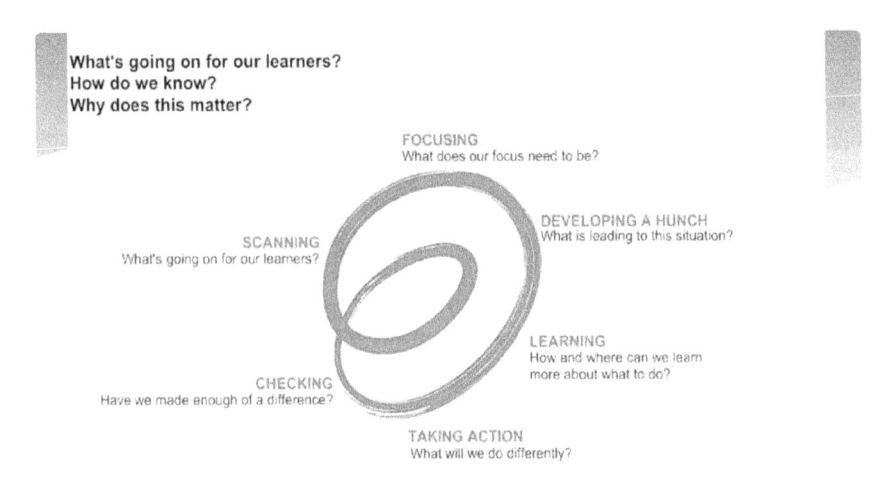

Figure I.1. Spiral of Inquiry (Halbert & Kaser, 2013). Halbert & Kaser, 2013

whether the engagement was actually improving problem-solving skills, no actual improvements were found in students' mathematical ability.

The use of educational research is highlighted throughout the second and third phases of the *Spiral of Inquiry* and in the stages of *focusing* and *developing a hunch*. During the *focusing* stage, the information gathered during the scanning stage is analyzed in order to determine students' strengths and needs and to decide where staff need to concentrate in order to realize the greatest impact on student outcomes. Careful focusing will lead naturally into the fifth phase of the spiral, namely *new professional learning*. Once staff have engaged in the new learning required to shift outcomes, the sixth stage, *taking action*, is required. This is the phase where staff act on what they have learned and take deliberate steps to make a difference in helping students to succeed. It is then that the final stage of the spiral can be realized, *checking*. This is the time when evidence is gathered to see if the desired outcome was achieved: Did the actions of the staff have the desired effect on student learning?

This book describes how Delta School District used the *Spiral of Inquiry* at a systems level to work toward creating not only a strong district, but also toward creating strong schools, and most recently, powerful and inspiring learning environments for all students. The spiral of inquiry used in Delta asked: What does the *district* need to do to be the most powerful learning organization possible? What does the *school* need to focus on to address the needs of its learners? What does this classroom need to focus on in order to meet the needs of *all* students present?

There are five main sections in the book. **Section 1**, *The District as a Learning Organization*, discusses the steps that the Delta School District took to become a strong district—one with a clear, shared vision and the necessary structures in place to achieve the vision. **Section 2**, *Schools As Learning Organizations*, encompasses the work being done to create strong schools—schools with the characteristics that research has shown to be most promising in improving student learning. **Section 3**, *Powerful and Inspiring Learning Environments*, touches upon the district's most recent work. When deliberate attention is paid to all three levels of the learning system, a district will be in the strongest position possible to maximize student learning, to close the learning gap and achieve equity for all, and to create a culture of continuous improvement and collective efficacy. As Halbert and Kaser state, "In a truly transformational learning system, the focus is on high quality and high equity for every learner, regardless of their starting point" (Timperley et al., 2014, p. 3). **Section 4**, *What Made a Difference*, provides a summary of key factors that had a significant impact on the implementation and realization of the vision. This section also shares evidence to show that those powerful changes created improvements in student outcomes. Finally, **Section 5**, *Where to Next*, brings us full circle to the creation of Vision 2030, a renewed vision that will guide the school district's direction for the next 10 years.

In the district's transformed schools, "every learner will cross the stage with dignity, purpose and options" (Timperley et al., 2014, p. 3). In the words of Halbert and Kaser, "Our central argument is that innovation floats on a sea of inquiry and that curiosity is a driver for change. Creating the conditions in schools and learning settings where curiosity is encouraged, developed and sustained is essential to opening up thinking, changing practice and creating dramatically more innovative approaches to learning and teaching" (Timperley et al., 2014, p. 4). These wise words from 2013 have paralleled and been the foundation for the journey that the Delta School District has been on since 2011.

NOTE

1. In British Columbia, the Ministry of Education, under the direction of the Minister of Education, oversees the development of education legislation, regulations, and policies.

Background
The Delta Context

The city of Delta is located in the Lower Mainland region of British Columbia, Canada, and is part of the Greater Metro area of Vancouver. The Delta School District, in the city of Delta, is situated on the traditional territory of the Tsawwassen First Nations and Musqueam Indian Band. The district consists of three distinct geographical areas: North Delta, Ladner, and Tsawwassen. Each community is separated by vast areas of farmland as well as by Burns Bog, which at approximately 3,000 hectares is the largest undeveloped urban landmass in North America. The city of Delta is bordered by the Fraser River to the north, the United States (Point Roberts, Washington) to the south, and the city of Surrey to the east. Bordered by the Pacific Ocean to the west, and the Fraser River with mountains in the distance, it is picturesque and an excellent environment for outdoor learning opportunities. The population of Delta is just over 110,000 people with almost 1,000 living on the lands of the Tsawwassen First Nation (TFN). The student population of the district is nearly 16,000 students, with about 3.5 percent being of Indigenous ancestry. There are 24 elementary schools, seven secondary schools, as well as a farm school site, an adult community college, and an education center. A strong international student program operates within the district, inviting students from more than 30 different countries to study in Delta. A host of unique programs are offered, including International Baccalaureate, HomeQuest (a home-school partnership program), and Delta Access (an online option for grades 10 through 12) to name a few. The district also offers a variety of academies[1] for students, including Hockey, Film Acting, Film Production, and Visual Effects. A variety of unique programs have been offered over the years including a Farm School, and, more recently, a school located on the lands of the Tsawwassen First Nations. These programs are created and evolve based on the needs of students in the school district.

In 2011, the Delta School District underwent a visioning process to establish a collaboratively developed, cocreated, shared Bold Vision. The exercise to create the vision, described in full detail in chapter 1, led the district to adopt professional collaborative inquiry as the framework to help achieve the vision. Although a variety of inquiry frameworks exist, the district chose the *Spiral of Inquiry* because of its strong focus on selecting evidence-based goals that ensure the needs of the students are being met. Additionally, the spiral has a strong focus on new professional learning that is essential for continuous improvement. If educators continue to do what they have always done, they will continue to get the same results. New learning for professionals is a critical step in order to improve student outcomes. Initially, the district used the inquiry cycle that was outlined by Helen Timperley in her book *Realizing the Power of Professional Learning* (2011). When Judy Halbert and Linda Kaser published *Spiral of Inquiry for Equity and Quality* (2013), the district began using the *Spiral of Inquiry* model cited in their publication. This inquiry model appealed to educators because of its simplicity and clear language.

Since the inception of the Delta School District's Bold Vision in 2011, continuous professional learning has been a central goal in the district. The *Spiral of Inquiry* (Diagram 1) has provided the district with a common, coherent framework for learning and decision making at all levels. Staff throughout the district continuously scan their contexts in order to determine the next most imperative learning needs of students, school and district personnel, while engaging in the professional learning required to move learning forward at *all* levels. In addition to Halbert and Kaser (2013), a great deal of research has been published that supports the key foundational principles adopted by Delta, including research by Leithwood (2013), Fullan and Quinn (2016), Istance (OECD, 2013), and Kools and Stoll (2016) to name just a few. The case study, detailed within this book, will describe the deliberate, continuous steps that the Delta School District has taken on its journey to achieve the vision and become *"a leading district for innovative teaching and learner success."*

The book concludes with a chapter describing the most recent visioning process the Delta School District engaged in, beginning in 2021. With the first 10 years of Vision 2020 having served as the North Star for the district from 2011 until 2021, renewing the vision for the next 10 years was seen as both a priority and an expectation within the school district community. The *Spiral of Inquiry* is designed to be a never-ending, continuous improvement process of inquiry and curiosity. Educators and students had engaged in inquiry and research throughout the 10-year term of Vision 2020 and were already beginning to explore more about the future needs of learners in Delta. Throughout the first 10 years of the inquiry journey, educators learned a great deal about the needs of their learners as well as their own professional learning needs. Professional inquiry began to move in a direction that indicated it was time for a new vision. As a framework, the *Spiral of Inquiry* supports educators as learners—immersing them in a culture of continuous learning for all and helping them provide the best possible instructional practices for their learners. Vision 2030 is exciting and forward facing—a worthy new North Star for the Delta School District engaging educators, students, families, and the community in supporting the needs of present and future learners.

CONNECTING YOUR LEARNING

1. In what way does *Spiral of Inquiry* resonate with you? Do you use a different model of inquiry to guide your practice?
2. Compare your context to that of the Delta School District. What similarities might there be? What are the significant differences? What is important for you to pay attention to?

NOTE

1. Academies are focus programs that are fee based and offered within the regular school day.

PART 1

The District as a Learning Organization

Chapter 1

Focus on a Shared District Vision and Mission

Vision without action is merely a dream. Action without vision just passes time. Vision with action can change the world.

Joel Barker

When we began to realize that the Delta School District was lacking a common shared vision, we turned to the work of key researchers to support the idea of creating a *shared* district-wide vision. This research is not new. The importance of visions for organizations has been widely studied for over 30 years. Joel Barker (1991) states that "having a positive vision of the future is the most forceful motivator for *change-for-success* that companies, schools, communities, nations, and individuals possess. It inspires people in an organization to think together, dream together, and act together to make a difference." He suggests there is consensus that a clear vision is central to any transformation process. Barker's research speaks to *why* Delta needed a vision that was embraced by the system, if system transformation and improvement was to be realized.

Additionally, Nanus (1992) stated that a vision serves as "a signpost pointing the way for all who need to understand what the organization is and where it intends to go." Seeley (1992) described having a vision as a "goal-oriented mental construct that guides people's behaviour." He further elaborates that a shared vision can provide a powerful beacon that sets the future direction for individuals who work within a system. Carefully created, it can serve to provide inspiration, motivation, and engagement for educators to work toward the attainment of the vision. A significant factor to the successful outcome of the purpose of creating a vision, however, is in *how* the vision is created. In order to provide the inspiration, commitment, and engagement for a shared vision, there needs to be buy-in and ownership at all levels of the system, and this requires the participation of many community members in the creation of the vision. Nanus provided some clarity as to *how* the vision for the Delta School District would need to be created.

District leaders believed that creating a North Star for Delta would be the first step toward district improvement. Even though Dr. Ken Leithwood's research on the characteristics of strong districts was not published until 2013, Delta had already started taking steps toward achieving the shared vision that had been unveiled in 2011. We were encouraged when Leithwood stated that the first characteristic of a strong district is "a broadly shared mission, vision and goals, founded on ambitious images of the educated person" (Leithwood, 2013, p. 11). His extensive research on strong districts revealed that high-performing school systems have widely shared sets of beliefs about student learning and well-being that have been transparently developed with the engagement of multiple school and system stakeholders. This finding gave the district leadership team and trustees hope for the pathway that we had undertaken.

In his work, Leithwood describes specific practices, with respect to the development of shared beliefs, visions, and goals, that are indicative of strong district leaders. District leaders are tasked with the responsibility to ensure that the visioning process is transparent and direction-setting. Leaders in those strong districts engage the community in an extensive consultation process, providing sufficient time to ensure the mission, vision, and goals of the system are "widely communicated and understood by everyone throughout the school district" (2013, p. 24). It is imperative that the vision, beliefs, and goals are well articulated and demonstrated by system leaders. Furthermore, the importance of the vision is best defined within a district when leaders "regularly and intentionally embed the district vision, directions and improvement plans in principals' meetings and other district processes" (Leithwood, 2013, p. 24). In comparing Leithwood's findings to the steps that had already been taken in Delta, there was optimism that the district was on the right track.

In a search, we discovered that the work of other researchers also supported actions that were being taken within the district. A clear, well-articulated vision sets the stage for the time and effort required to follow through on what might be a long, arduous journey (Sheninger, 2015). Kouzes and Posner (2009) state the only visions that take hold in an organization are shared visions. Furthering the importance of a shared vision, Carmen Gallo (2011), in an article titled "Steve Jobs and the Power of Vision," explained that "Innovation requires a team and you cannot inspire a team of passionate evangelists without a compelling vision: a vision that is bold, simple and consistently communicated." Leadership expert Ken Blanchard (2011) adds that a vision is the vital ingredient for long-term success and without a vision you end up reacting rather than acting. Thus, a vision provides clarity of purpose, with a commitment that helps move an organization forward. Hugh Burkett (2006) adds further to the importance of a compelling shared vision when he states,

> A clear vision . . . that identifies the learning to be achieved can help keep a school (or system) and the efforts of staff on target. A shared vision is critical to an organization's future because it provides the underlying foundation upon which all decisions are made (p. 33).

Fullan, Rincon-Gallardo, and Hargreaves (2015) state, "building professional capital across educational systems requires creating an inspiring and inclusive vision that raises the importance of and sets the direction for education and with teachers in ways that resonates with and inspires a majority of educators, school system leaders, and society as a whole to pursue it" (p. 7).

The book *Start with Why*, written by Simon Sinek (2009), also strongly influenced the thinking of senior district leaders in Delta with respect to the importance of engaging in a visioning process that would include as many people in the school district as possible in order to develop a collective vision, and, ultimately, create stronger ownership of the vision. Sinek's Golden Circle, described later in this chapter, provides a powerful model of the value of finding the "Why," or vision, for an organization.

As seen within the statements from these prominent researchers and authors, the value of incorporating a vision into an organization to support the directions, goals, and planning has often been researched and cited as being foundational to organizational success. These findings further affirmed that the journey toward improvement in the Delta School District was on the right path.

The Delta School District vision, and the subsequent implementation of actions taken to achieve the vision, has raised the importance of the work, inspired the majority of educators in the district, defined the importance of deeper professional learning and collaborative professionalism, and led to greater ownership of the vision and the work by the community as a whole.

DEVELOPING A VISION: DELTA SCHOOL DISTRICT

During the months preceding her 2010 appointment, while working in the role of assistant superintendent, the superintendent of the Delta School District, attended a Canadian Educational Leadership (CEA) conference with a team of principals and students from the district. The main theme of the *What Did You Do in School Today* CEA conference was Student Engagement (Willms et al., 2009). The Canadian Education Association had been conducting a 3-year study on student engagement and the Delta School District was an active participant in the research study during that time period. Researchers from the *What Did You Do in School Today* study visited Delta and met with those who were participants in the study in the district. They were highly impressed with the engagement of the schools and students involved in the study. A group of secondary students from the Delta School District, who had taken part in the district-wide student engagement research project the previous year, were invited to attend the CEA conference and present their findings as a student group.

During a session at the conference, all attendees were asked to describe their school district's vision. While participating in that session, it became immediately apparent to the district team attending the conference that they were not able to describe nor articulate a coherent shared district vision for Delta. After the conference it was further confirmed, through meetings and a few conversations, that there was no clearly understood common vision for the district. Comments described the previous district vision statements in Delta as having been prepared by the board of education, the superintendent, and a small group of staff. Further examination suggested that those vision statements were definitely not very well known by the community, nor was there ownership or buy-in of those previous visions. It was particularly concerning that school principals and vice-principals were not at all clear about a vision existing in the district, and, in fact, they expressed that for some time they had been disappointed regarding the lack of a system-wide district direction.

In the fall of 2010, senior staff and the Delta Board of Education made the decision that the school district would engage in a visioning process. The consensus of the board and senior staff was that the key to this being a success was to find a vision creation process that would be meaningful and provide district direction.

While attending and participating in a strategic-planning event for the Delta Police Department, the superintendent had an opportunity to observe firsthand how a large group process could engage many community members. The police department process included a professional facilitator and a graphic illustrator to document the strategic-planning outcomes. Feedback data about their process indicated the exercise had been well received and was appreciated by those who participated.

Another method of engaging a community in a visioning process was shared by an assistant superintendent on the Delta School District senior team. He described a visioning process he had used a few years earlier when he was principal of a brand-new school in another district. He emphasized how important it was for the new school to have a vision established by the school staff, which would help bring the staff together, create cohesion, set a direction, and create shared values prior to opening the new school.

The superintendent and assistant superintendent invited a professional facilitator to join them to discuss a variety of possible visioning processes that might use a combination of the large-group strategic-planning process the superintendent had witnessed with the Delta Police Department and the smaller-group visioning process the assistant superintendent had described for the new school. Through that discussion they created a template for the visioning process model that would be used in the Delta School District. They contracted and worked closely with the professional facilitator to develop an engaging process and framework for Delta's vision creation, involving as many participants as possible at every school and worksite within the district. Once the visioning process was designed and shared with the board of education, the senior team was hopeful it would provide an opportunity to engage many voices across the district in the creation of a shared vision. The board of education made the decision to begin the visioning process as soon as possible, engaging thousands of people from across the district. Although the visioning process was conducted under a very tight timeline beginning in January 2011 and concluding in April, it afforded the opportunity for Vision 2020 to become the North Star for the district and be highly influential in developing and communicating goals within the district for the following 10 years.

THE VISION DEVELOPMENT PROCESS

The process to create a shared vision for the Delta School District was based on an Appreciative Inquiry (AI) model, with participants engaging in numerous interactive phases along the way. Appreciative Inquiry focuses on appreciation of the best of what already exists in an organization and what can be strengthened, or "What gives life" to the system. Once the definition of the inquiry is clarified, the AI process begins by investigating an organization's potential strength, looking at both the experiences and the potential. When strengths have been identified, an envisioning process starts to surface how a possible future would look, or "What might be," and how the future might be constructed. Using four phases of inquiry, Dr. David Cooperrider developed the Appreciative Inquiry model as a method to build organizational capacity. As seen in figure 1.1, the whole process of Appreciative Inquiry can be visualized as being a cycle of those four phases of activity: *discovery, dream, design and destiny,* which only take place when the clarifying *definition* of the inquiry focus is established.

Definition
"What is the focus of the inquiry?"
Clarifying

Discovery
"What gives life?"
(the best of what is)
Appreciating

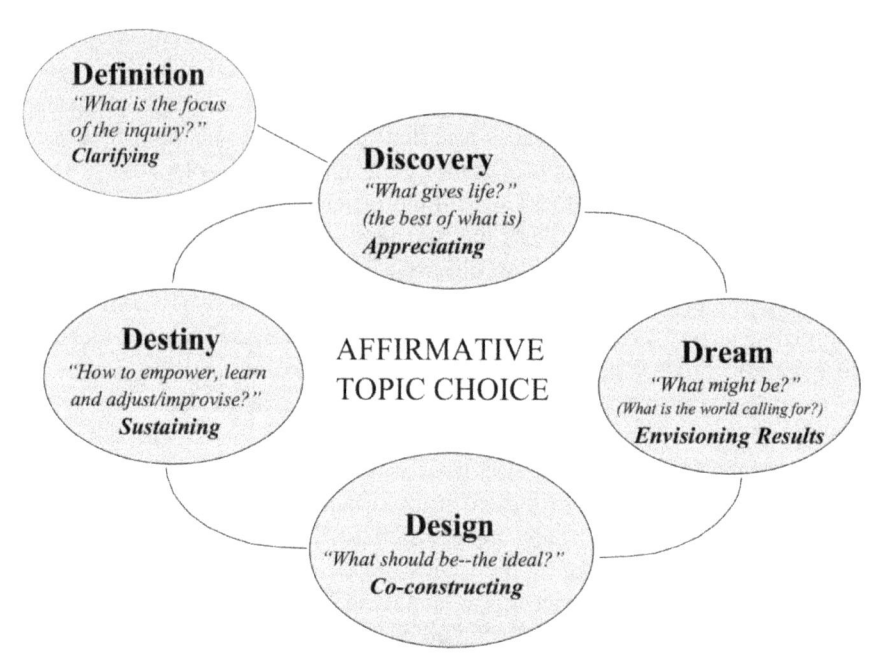

Destiny
"How to empower, learn and adjust/improvise?"
Sustaining

AFFIRMATIVE TOPIC CHOICE

Dream
"What might be?"
(What is the world calling for?)
Envisioning Results

Design
"What should be--the ideal?"
Co-constructing

Figure 1.1. Appreciative Inquiry: A Positive Revolution in Change by David Cooperrider and Diana Whitney (2005). *Cooperrider & Whitney, 2005*

Questions asked during the process of developing the Delta School District shared vision were framed with the positive stance described in the AI model. Clarity about the purpose and the process was established prior to bringing participants together. It was determined that the purpose of the Appreciative Inquiry process was to create a shared vision for the school district. An overarching inquiry question the district was asking was: "Would a collaboratively developed, shared, district-wide vision have an impact on improving outcomes for students and help build capacity across the system?" The *Discovery* phase was designed to surface the core factors for Delta's success. The *Dream* phase helped reveal the most shared images of a preferred future state for the school district. In the *Design* phase participants worked together in teams to create actionable aspirations for the organization. Finally, in the *Destiny* phase of the Appreciative Inquiry process those same teams were asked to commit to actions and projects that would help move the district toward the preferred future.

While using the AI model, participants at every Delta school and worksite were given blank visioning template boards to record and document the outcomes of the visioning inquiry process. As the process began, each participant was asked to individually reflect on the most exciting or amazing learning experience they could possibly recall, during their time of working or learning in the Delta School District. Those memories and reflections were recorded and shared within small groups. From these stories, the common values that resonated in each of the stories were collected and they became the core foundational values of each school and worksite that engaged in the process.

In the next phase of the process, participants were asked to consider "why" the school district existed. What was the purpose of the district? Why did the Delta School District exist as an organization? Each school and worksite crafted responses into a mission statement. In the final stage of the process, every group was asked to consider their boldest vision for the district. What could the Delta School District look like 10 years from now? Participants were encouraged to "dream big" and imagine a future without barriers. They were asked to imagine what the newspaper headlines might say if Delta was successful in achieving its vision. As seen in figure 1.2, these futuristic captions were captured in the new vision for the district.

Once the process was complete, staff at every school and worksite were asked to record their work on a large poster board template and to submit it to the district working committee. That working committee was tasked with the responsibility of extracting all common values from each site so they were able to compile the core values for the district's vision. Further, they examined each of the individual mission statements and created a synthesis of the responses in order to establish a common mission statement for the whole district. Finally, the working committee collated all the vision statements that had been submitted by participating sites. They worked to develop an overarching bold vision for the Delta School District that incorporated and encompassed all the feedback received. It was a complex and rapidly evolving process:

> When the visioning process was originally announced, I truly wondered how it would unfold. When we reached the point where all stakeholders were gathering together at Sands, it was then that I realized the power of the process. Sharing conversations with students, parents, other educators and partner groups from across the district, understanding their perspectives, was incredibly powerful. Although we generally know that we share similar goals when it comes to schools and learning, the chance to hear it face to face from our partner groups, especially those representing other schools, was confirming. Anyone who was fortunate enough to participate in those sessions definitely could see themselves as part of the vision once it was constructed.
>
> Aaron Akune, secondary principal

What emerged from the working group process was the graphic representation of the values, mission, and Bold Vision for the Delta School District, as seen in figure 1.3.

Figure 1.2. Community forum for Vision 2020 held at Sands Secondary School. *Delta School District*

This graphic represents the compilation of all the individual vision processes that took place across the district. Shown in figure 1.4, the Mission describes the reason why the Delta School District exists or the reason for its being:

The central vision statement, *The Delta School District Is a Leading District for Innovative Teaching and Learner Success*, describes the aspirations of the district (see figure 1.5):

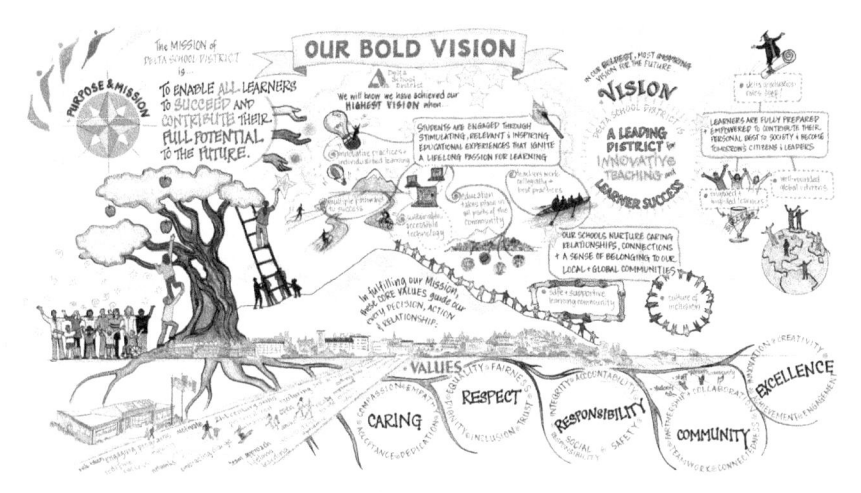

Focus on a Shared District Vision and Mission 11

Figure 1.3. Vision 2020. *Delta School District*

Surrounding the vision statement, in red rectangular boxes, are the three major focused themes that emerged during the visioning process: (1) *students are engaged through stimulating, relevant, and inspiring educational experiences that ignite a lifelong passion for learning;* (2) *our schools nurture*

Figure 1.4. Vision 2020 Mission. *Delta School District*

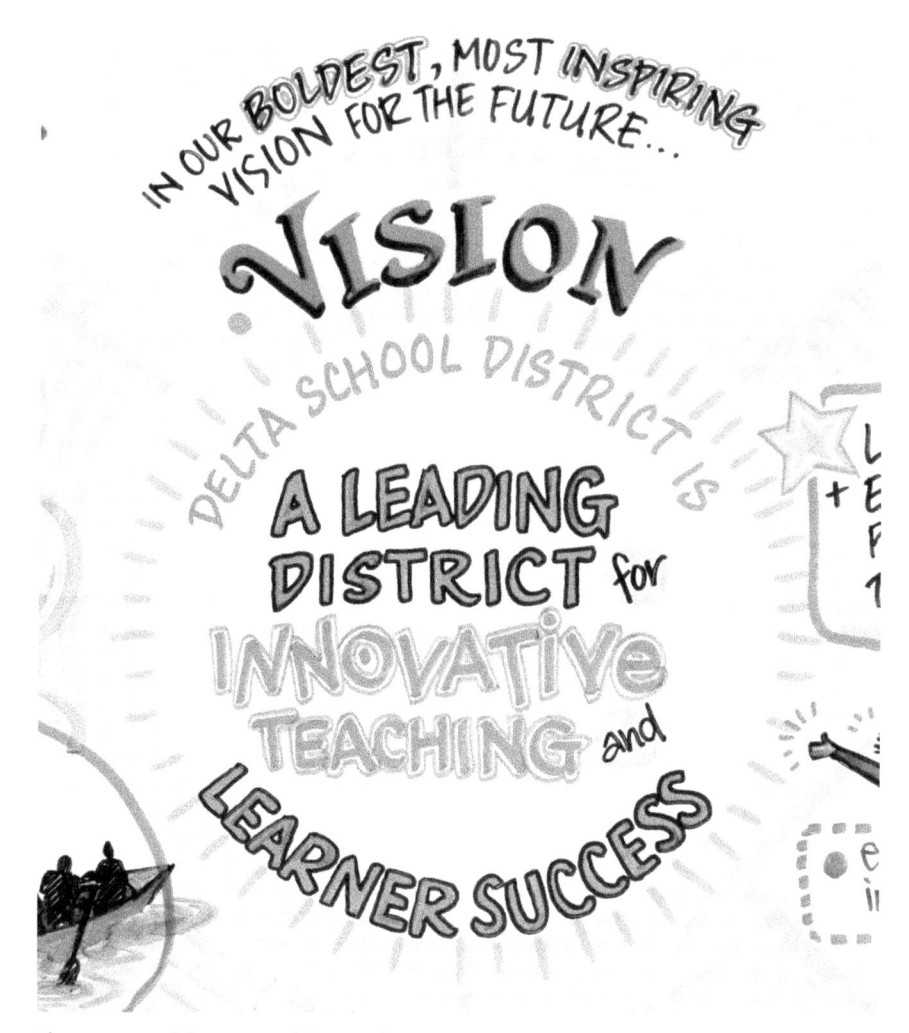

Figure 1.5.   Vision 2020 Vision. *Delta School District*

caring relationships, connections, and a sense of belonging to our local and global communities; and (3) *learners are fully prepared and empowered to contribute their personal best to society and become tomorrow's citizens and leaders* (see figure 1.6).

Adjacent to each of those three major themes there are several subthemes that help to describe the theme in greater detail, and expand on the central shared vision. When actions began to help the district achieve the Vision 2020, these themes and subthemes became the starting point for many district-wide goals and inquiries over the 10 years. They were foundational

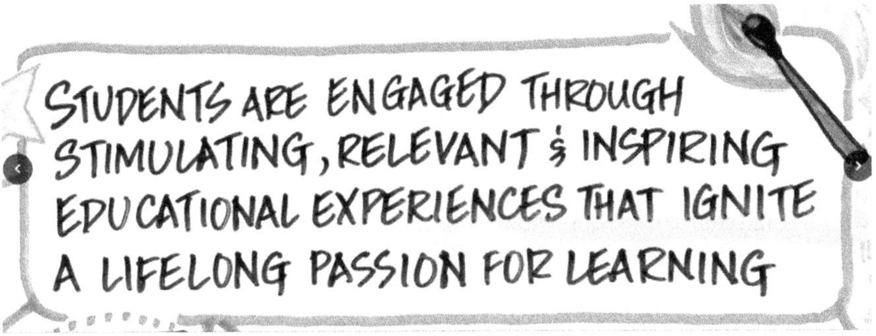

Focus on a Shared District Vision and Mission 13

> STUDENTS ARE ENGAGED THROUGH STIMULATING, RELEVANT & INSPIRING EDUCATIONAL EXPERIENCES THAT IGNITE A LIFELONG PASSION FOR LEARNING

Figure 1.6a.

> LEARNERS ARE FULLY PREPARED + EMPOWERED TO CONTRIBUTE THEIR PERSONAL BEST TO SOCIETY & BECOME TOMORROW'S CITIZENS & LEADERS

Figure 1.6b

> OUR SCHOOLS NURTURE CARING RELATIONSHIPS, CONNECTIONS + A SENSE OF BELONGING TO OUR LOCAL + GLOBAL COMMUNITIES

Figure 1.6c. Vision 2020: Three Themes. *Delta School District*

for every initiative in the district while on the journey to achieving the Bold Vision using the *Spiral of Inquiry*.

At a foundational level, those who were involved in establishing the vision identified five key values, with descriptors encircling each value to further elaborate on the deeper meaning behind what the values meant to the participants. These values represented what many thought the district needed to encourage throughout all of the efforts to achieve the vision. In some schools, the values have become part of the school goals and appear on posters in classrooms. Figure 1.7 shows the five values that were established during the visioning exercises: *caring* (compassion, empathy, dedication, acceptance); *respect* (equality, fairness, dignity, inclusion, trust); *responsibility* (integrity, accountability, social responsibility, safety); *community* (partnership, collaboration, teamwork, connectedness); and *excellence* (innovation, creativity, achievement, engagement).

> Vision 2020 was the beginning of a new direction for the Delta School District. The district has done well academically as increasing graduation rates will attest to but it lacked the cohesiveness of a collective and common purpose and language for all education stakeholders. The process that was utilized to arrive at the final version of Vision 2020, was the first time all education partners felt their voices were heard regarding the future of education in Delta.
>
> With a vibrant graphic of the Bold Vision in all schools and district facilities, it was clear that the district had responded to participants' hopes and dreams for the next decade. As decisions were made at the board level and throughout various district departments and schools, the vision was at the forefront with student success being the goal. A common language around the vision was and is being utilized in Delta schools. Trustees played an important role in ensuring that there would be funding to implement the vision.
>
> Val Windsor, Delta Board of Education trustee

Developing the district-wide vision was not without hurdles. Although most educators and employees of the district participated willingly, and union leaders in Delta helped produce an inspiring video inviting employees to participate in the process to create the vision, there were some individuals, and even a couple of school sites, that were reluctant to engage in the process. Follow-up survey results indicated there were a few reasons for this

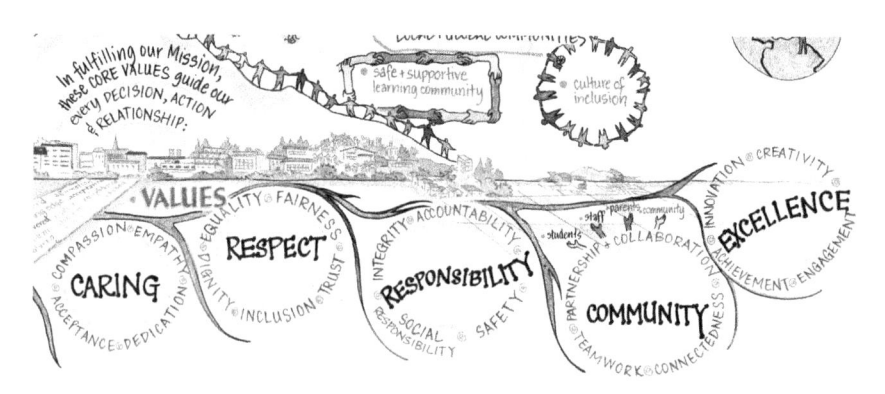

Figure 1.7. Vision 2020: Values. *Delta School District*

reluctance. For some, there was a perception of a lack of trust as previous vision statements had been meaningless to them, while others appeared to be somewhat suspicious of the process. A few expressed that they were reluctant to take part because they felt that the district senior staff and board of education should be the ones to establish the vision, and they commented that they resented giving up their time to engage in a process that they didn't believe was "their job." In the end, all trustees, most employees, and many students and parents did participate in the district process and Vision 2020 was created for Delta. The following quote speaks to the shift from skepticism that took place for many educators who were not a part of the initial visioning process:

> At a community career and postsecondary fair, I had a chance to walk alongside and listen to one of our more senior classroom teachers. He had put in a fair bit of time with the local teacher's union and thus had developed his understanding of education at the district level. He was the one to initiate the conversation and said that he didn't think much of the vision plan at the beginning but three years in he could see we were really standing by it and followed it up with "I get it now!" I believe system-wide change could be put on a bell curve, with early adopters to your later adopters at either end and the majority in between. This teacher's observations reminded me that authentic and meaningful engagement isn't something that just happens at the beginning of the visioning process, but has to involve continuous action to achieve genuine buy-in.
>
> Laura Dixon, Delta Board of Education trustee

A key component of the success of the visioning process was the trust that the board of education placed in the district leaders and the methodology selected to create the vision.

> Our in-person sessions were being facilitated and scribed by our principals who were given some advance training. At our tables we had a mix of support staff, parents, students, and educators but as the principal was trying to capture the vision statement, he checked in with me, the school trustee representative, to ask "Is that right?" I answered to the whole table, "It isn't the vision of the board, but rather *their* vision and that it would be our job as trustees to ensure that we aligned our policy and budgeting decisions based upon their direction." You could feel everyone exhale and I saw more than a few smiles.
>
> Laura Dixon, Delta Board of Education trustee

In April of 2011, once the individual school and worksites had completed their vision process, a district-wide celebration was held at one of the high schools where the Delta School District's Vision 2020 was unveiled to a large gathering. Following the evening event, participants were asked to complete an exit ticket to describe their thoughts on the process and the Vision 2020 itself. It provided rich and important feedback to senior staff and the board of education. One participant described the event as being "very positive and the energy in the room was palpable." Participants who attended that larger district visioning process (including students, parents, teachers, support staff, vice-principals, and principals) said they felt a strong sense of ownership for the vision. During the evening there was a noticeable sense of pride and unity in the gymnasium when the collaboratively created district vision was revealed. Upon reflection a few years later, one Delta teacher stated, "Involving all of our stakeholders in the visioning process enabled us to set a common course for our future. Staff members were invited, but not pressured, to participate and exchange their thoughts and ideas. A positive wave of change has gradually swept across the district."

> We needed a compass for the district. It is so important that we are all on the same page. The district vision is the glue that connects us and it will help us decide what our most important goals are. It will give us a sense of direction and will help us make wise decisions, well thought out for the future of our schools and our students.
>
> Julie Lymburner, secondary school teacher

The morning after the unveiling of the new district vision, as a follow-up to the event, the director of educational programs visited one of the larger high schools in the district, seeking feedback on the unveiling of the district shared vision. When she arrived at the office, the principal and the vice-principals were holding copies of the vision poster handout, discussing the document and sharing their excitement around the possibilities of what could come from the vision. The principal, in his excitement, said, "This is amazing!" He then asked, "How do we get there?" That inquiry question, and others like it, sparked the beginning of a 10-year process of intentional learning in the Delta School District in order to achieve the vision of being *A Leading District of Innovative Teaching and Learner Success.*

There was a shared sense among district leaders that immediate actions were needed to achieve the vision, and it was also understood that the actions would be highly dependent on careful system-wide planning and goal development in order to provide a clear focus for the many change initiatives needed to move from vision to action. District leaders learned together that the planning, goals, and actions would require careful monitoring and evaluation along the way to determine if the district was on the right track to achieve the vision within 10 years. David Taylor (2014) suggests crucial elements are needed to successfully move from vision to actionable change. He says innovation must become a priority and the vision must align with the strategic goals of the organization. There must be communication about what achieving the vision will mean, and leaders must inspire the organization to continually move toward the vision. Taylor further suggests the vision needs to be embraced and supported at all levels of the organization. Pride in the work of the organization moving toward achieving the vision needs to be spoken of often and communicated at every opportunity. Leaders must live the vision and not just pay lip service to it, and they must get involved with the details. Finally, Taylor (2014) says leaders must model the desired practice at all times. The following quote by the superintendent of the Delta School District exemplifies the leadership and commitment that Taylor refers to:

> I believe Vision 2020 answered some fundamental questions for everyone in the district—Who are we? What do we believe in? and What are our hopes/expectations for the next generation? Coming to a shared understanding and set of commitments allowed for a greater sense of purpose and direction for many within the district. It created a tension between where students and staff were in 2011 and where we believed we could be. This tension inspired creative forces throughout the district to pursue methods and strategies that would improve student outcomes for over a decade.
>
> Doug Sheppard, superintendent

WHAT SHAPED OUR THINKING MOVING FORWARD?

Prior to the visioning process, senior district leaders had already engaged in significant research and study about the importance of a shared vision, beliefs, and values through reading books and articles, engaging collaboratively, and sharing their thoughts on how best to undertake the process. More importantly, they discussed and proposed what kinds of actions were needed to help achieve Vision 2020 once it was developed. Several books and articles that contributed to district leaders' initial thinking, and continue to shape their thinking, will be shared throughout this book. It was imperative that district leaders were continually engaged in a learning process, helping them to be adaptive leaders, modeling continuous learning, and keeping decisions focused on achieving the vision and resulting goals.

One book that played a critical role in the development of strategic actions designed to move the visioning process forward was *Start with Why* by Simon Sinek (2009). Sinek's premise, from the Golden Circle model, is that most organizations begin their thinking and planning with a focus on *What* they do. He is clear that although some groups may know *How* they do what they do, very few can clearly state *Why* they do what they do. Few organizations are able to articulate their purpose. In the words of Sinek, "A *Why* is just a belief. That's all it is. The *Hows* are actions you take to realize that belief.

And the *Whats* are the results of those actions" (Sinek, 2009, p. 67). The Bold Vision of the Delta School District became the North Star, providing clarity as to the district's future direction. It provided an almost laser-like focus for every decision and action executed by the district as it became the North Star.

> Before the vision-building process began in Delta back in 2010, it felt like we had many initiatives on the go but no common language, no common threads other than student learning.
>
> Our vision-building process brought together parents, teachers, students, education assistants, and other community partners to talk about what the purpose of education ought to be in Delta. In the end, we created a vision that became our compass, our point of reference for WHY we were doing the things we were doing.
>
> Ted Johnson, district director

According to Sinek, "only when the *Why* is clear and when people believe what you believe can a true loyal relationship develop" (p. 54). Because of the means by which the vision for the Delta School District was developed, with all voices participating in its creation, a clear vision and focus were established for everyone in Delta.

A second influential resource for district leaders that contributed to the process of achieving the vision was a book titled *Building and Connecting Learning Communities* by Steven Katz, Lorna Earl, and Sonia Ben Jaafar (2009). This book had a profound impact on how the vision might unfold in Delta. One of the fundamental concepts in the book relates to the notion that "many can indeed be smarter than the few and networks can be powerful organizational forms for school improvement" (p. 2). When the vision was unveiled in the district, some of the secondary schools in Delta had already begun to build time into their school schedules for educators to engage in collaborative inquiry. At that time, the inclusion of collaboration time appeared to be having a positive impact on teacher professional learning in the secondary schools that had adopted the model. However, as Michael Fullan states, "Collaboration as an end in itself is a waste of time. Groups are powerful, which means that they can be powerfully wrong . . . developing collaborative cultures is careful and precise work and has profound impact when carried out well because increasing social capital improves coherence, which in turn attracts newcomers and feeds forward into better results" (2016). A great deal of effort went into helping staff in the Delta School District ensure that the time set aside for teacher collaboration was connected to continuous improvement.

Secondary schools were able to schedule collaboration time twice a month by changing the start time of the school day for students. Elementary schools, however, were not able to adjust their schedules to include collaboration in the same way as secondary schools. Because it was believed that providing collaboration time was crucial to enable educators to engage in dialogue about their practice, the district focused on finding a way to include collaboration time in every elementary school in Delta. More information on how this inclusion of collaboration time for elementary schools was achieved is elaborated on in the next chapter.

A second key concept in Katz, Earl, and Jaafar's book relates to the importance of lifelong learning and how knowledge is one of the most important resources for social and economic development. We fully concur with the authors when they suggest that "a fundamental challenge for education, then, is to organize working with knowledge in a way that facilitates ongoing knowledge building and sharing among members of the community" (p. 3). The district senior leadership team realized that in order to achieve the Bold Vision of being a *leading district for innovative teaching and learner success*, structures and processes would be required to help promote opportunities for knowledge creation and sharing.

A structure was needed that would provide what Katz, Earl, and Jaafar describe as "groups of schools working together in intentional ways to enhance the quality of professional learning and to strengthen capacity for continuous improvement, in the service of enhanced student learning" (p. 9). After doing a thorough investigation into the research, district leaders were convinced that continuous improvement and movement toward achieving the vision could be realized through the opportunity for teachers' collaborative inquiry. To help support staff's collaborative inquiry, the district created a teacher leadership role for each school called the Coordinator of Inquiry (COI). The COI teacher leader became a pivotal role in the achievement of the vision, described in greater detail in chapter 5.

Another highly influential resource that inspired the movement from vision to action was Helen Timperley's book *Realizing the Power of Professional Learning* (2011). Timperley's book provided a framework to help unify the shared networks that were being established across the district. She emphasizes the power of professional learning in making a difference in professional practice and she also makes a very clear distinction between professional development and professional learning. She asserts that while professional development is more of an external presentation where individuals participate in acquiring information, professional learning suggests an internal process whereby individuals create new knowledge through actively engaging with others in a collaborative process. Timperley stresses the key purpose of professional learning should be improvement in student learning. Furthermore, it is essential that all participants in the educational setting need to see themselves as learners. Perhaps most importantly, and most influential for the school district, is that systemic inquiry is at the root of effective professional learning leading to improved results for students. "If teacher inquiry is going to make a substantive difference to student outcomes, teachers need to be operating within new frameworks and accessing different kinds of knowledge that will push their thinking and challenge their practice" (p. 10).

Timperley's work helped the district leadership team determine the next critical steps that would be taken to move the district toward achieving Vision 2020. Several themes were percolating at the same time: *a common vision; the need for networked professional collaboration; and a common framework that would allow for the flexibility to meet the needs of each individual school site.* As a result of this new learning, inquiry work in Delta began with Helen Timperley's model of an inquiry cycle, as depicted in figure 1.8 (Timperley, 2011, p. 11).

In Michael Fullan and Joanne Quinn's book *Coherence* (2016), another highly influential resource for the Delta School District, the authors refer to the need for a directional vision. Fullan and Quinn state, "Leaders need to set the directional vision, allow experimentation connected to the vision, put in mechanisms for learning from the work, and then establish ways to share the promising approaches across the organization" (p. 30). There is no question that the creation of Delta's vision had a significant impact on district improvement. According to one school principal, "Since the district vision was established, we have had a common language around what it is we are

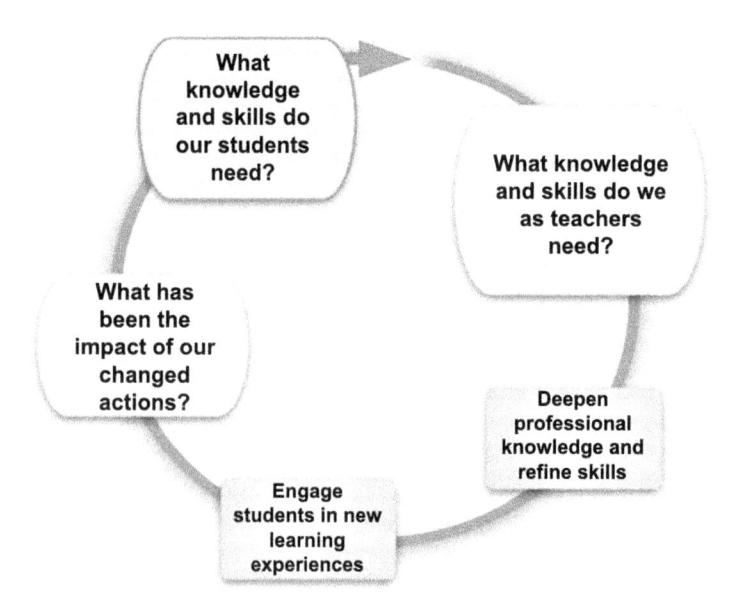

Figure 1.8. Realizing the Power of Professional Learning, Timperley, 2011. *Timperley, 2011*

aiming to achieve for our students. We have common goals and a shared vision because we were part of the process in establishing that vision." Since 2011, the Delta School District has been steadfast and tenacious in aspiring to its vision. Specific steps taken by the district to work toward achieving the vision will be described in greater detail in the remaining chapters of this book.

LESSONS LEARNED

- *Always start with "WHY?"* If you want to engage in whole system improvement, creating "buy-in" throughout all levels in the system matters. Clearly defining WHY you want to move in a particular direction is critical and will increase the likelihood of an initiative being successful.
- *Everyone needs to feel heard and valued.* When a district vision is created from the bottom up, stakeholders feel ownership and pride. Creating a district vision based on the individual visions of every school and every workplace in Delta allowed participants to feel that their input was heard, valued, and included. Participants were able to see their words and phrases expressed in the cocreated district vision.
- *A clear district-wide focus is essential for progress.* Providing a clear focus for a school district is not unlike providing students with clear learning targets. When staff know what is valued and desired, they are able to strive to meet the goal.
- *A simple, clearly articulated shared vision will provide a lens for decision making at all levels in the district.* When the shared vision is complete and owned by all stakeholders in the district, decision making becomes highly focused. Educational and budget decisions are filtered through the vision and an alignment with it must be well understood before being given consideration for resourcing or implementation.
- *All the work in the district needs to be aligned.* Schools and districts are busy places. Therefore, all the work from learning environments to schools to the district level must align well. If educators are unable to make sense of the connections between initiatives, progress and improvement will be limited.

CONNECTING YOUR LEARNING

1. Does your education system currently have a vision? If so, how was that vision created? What are/might be the benefits of a cocreated vision for your organization?

2. How might your district ensure that there is broad awareness of the vision? What deliberate steps would be taken to ensure that students, educators, school leaders, and the community are aware of the vision?
3. Was there an opportunity for all the stakeholders to participate in the visioning process? Is the vision widely shared? If so, how is it shared? If not, what actions might you take to build awareness?
4. What structures currently exist in your context for dialogue and communication with all stakeholders as to the purpose of education (i.e., students, parents, educators, school and district leaders, support staff)?
5. If you have not developed a vision, what has your organization used to help inspire or create system-wide improvement?
6. If no vision currently exists, what steps might you take to ensure that a guiding vision is created?

Chapter 2

Focus on District Support for the Vision

Once the Bold Vision was unveiled, it became apparent that to achieve the vision and the goals that emanated from the vision, it was essential that resources be available in order to realize those goals. Two key steps were undertaken by trustees and district leaders to help ensure the newly created vision did not end up becoming just a piece of paper on shelves in schools.

First, a line item was created in the district budget with resources set aside for costs associated with achieving the district vision. The budget included resource allocations such as inquiry grants for teams of teachers to work together, funds for educator and formal leaders' professional learning, and among other things, funding for reviewing and evaluating the progress being made toward achieving the vision. Second, the district's Policy and Procedures Manual, which was quite outdated and well overdue for renewal, was rewritten to develop and delineate policies, which are defined as the work of the board of trustees, from administrative procedures, which are defined as the work of district staff. Most importantly, at the beginning of the entire policy document, the District Vision became Policy Number One (see appendix A), ensuring that the vision itself would become highly visible and directional for the work of trustees.

Another influential resource used by the district to help achieve the vision came from the extensive research by a well-known and respected Canadian educational researcher, Dr. Ken Leithwood. Leithwood's *Strong Districts* research, conducted in Ontario and other jurisdictions across the globe, has served as a useful framework and template for checking in on the work being done in Delta, and has been used as a guide and reference for what else the Delta School District might need to work on during the journey to become a strong district. Dr. Leithwood engaged with senior leaders at the district level to help advance their thinking about specific district strategies and ongoing work toward school district improvement, while examining various structures and processes that would help make districts stronger.

Throughout part 1 of this book, Dr. Leithwood's *Strong Districts* research serves both as an example of how the Delta School District uses leading educational research in its work, and how that research can contribute to the continuous professional learning of educators.

Leithwood (2013) states that evidence used to define strong districts indicates there is significant alignment of processes and structures in those districts which support the district's mission, vision, and goals. According to Leithwood's description of strong districts, there is a systematic and ongoing process to align preliminary budgets with the goals for improving the outcomes for student learning and well-being. Additionally, he says there are procedures that ensure continuous attention is given to the alignment of personnel policies and procedures with the goals for improving student learning. Leithwood further states that in support of those goals for students there are systematic processes that align organizational structures with staff's instructional improvement work, and there are adequate resources allocated for the professional learning of staff, including leaders, through budget processes (p. 17).

According to the Ontario *Strong Districts* research study conducted by Leithwood, resource allocation in those districts was specifically aligned with the district's focus on improving instruction and student achievement. "Strong districts use the alignment of resources to help close the achievement gaps by ensuring that those students struggling the most have disproportionate access not only to financial supports, but also high-quality teachers and successful peer models, all of which make a demonstrable contribution to student achievement" (Leithwood, 2013, p. 18). Each year, very specific, vision-aligned budget allocations in the Delta School District are reviewed to ensure the students and schools who need the most support are funded in an equitable fashion. In addition, funds are allocated to put programs in place that address the unique needs of individual schools. For example, professional literacy communities are supported in the schools with the greatest need to lift achievement results in literacy for primary students. Additionally, a variety of initiatives were created to help support students of Indigenous heritage with their reading skills. Using authentic Indigenous resources, district staff worked closely with Indigenous students to develop their skills and help them graduate. Further, the Tsawwassen First Nations (TFN) created a school program in their Community Youth Centre to support students at all age levels. Delta teachers were hired to provide individualized learning opportunities for the TFN students. Program development in Delta is aligned with the identified needs of students and options are deliberately designed to be responsive, continuously revised as students' needs evolve.

Since the inception of the Delta School District vision, mission, and goals, the annual budget has contained an allocation of resources specifically categorized as "Vision Achievement." Resource alignment toward achieving the vision and goals of the district has become a clear focus during the annual preliminary budget development process. When the vision was adopted by the board in 2011, the secretary treasurer and the director of finance became deeply engaged in the leadership learning processes aligned with the vision and goals of the district. They often attended professional learning sessions offered to educators and formal leaders so they were able to understand, stay abreast of, and support current educational research and practice. As a result, when the district conducts the annual budget process, they engage staff and stakeholders in the process by asking very focused questions at the budget table. The budget-focus questions relate to how a particular budget item will impact the achievement of not only the district vision, but its strategic goals and the resulting student-learning outcomes. According to Campbell, Fullan, and Glaze (2006), district alignment demands that the work of all members of the senior leadership team, including those responsible for finance, personnel, operations, and academic programs, must all be coordinated and aligned with the district vision. This is especially true in the Delta School District where the secretary-treasurer utilizes the *Spiral of Inquiry* as a tool for goal setting within the Finance Department. To demonstrate this commitment, a message sent from the secretary-treasurer to Dr. Judy Halbert and Dr. Linda Kaser, who developed the *Spiral of Inquiry* currently in use in the school district, stated:

> The *Spiral of Inquiry* booklet is sitting on my desk as my management services team and I are embarking on an exercise to reinvent ourselves and improve our services after a period of much turnover and the resulting disruption. I have a very passionate and committed team and I have a great feeling of where we and the spiral (with a bit of instruction from our amazing educators) can go together.
>
> Nicola Christ, secretary-treasurer

This message from the secretary-treasurer exemplifies the close working relationship that exists between the Finance Department and educators across the district.

Once the annual preliminary budget has been developed in a given school year, trustees in Delta engage in community consultations, deliberations, and final decision making. Questions and queries asked by trustees and by the school district community members are focused through the lens of how a particular budget topic will help to achieve the district vision and goals. It is not unusual to hear a trustee ask staff to explain how a particular budget recommendation will impact the achievement of the vision, goals, and strategic plan and how it will align with improvement in student learning and well-being. Purposeful dialogue, taking place at the budget table, provides clarity and coherence for the impact the district's annual budget will have on achieving the district goals and improving student learning outcomes.

It is evident there is a strong alignment of budgets, structures, policies, and procedures with the vision, mission, values, and goals within the Delta School District. While various parts of the district plan evolve and change over time in response to collective learning and input from numerous sources, the main goal of achieving the vision and aligning the resources to help achieve it is evident and has not wavered.

As an example of this strong alignment, when the decision was made to introduce the collaborative-inquiry process as a way of taking action toward achieving the vision, the position of Coordinator of Inquiry (COI) was created, which will be explained in detail in chapter 5. Included within that initiative was a budget to provide release time for teachers and give them an opportunity to engage in a collaborative inquiry process related to one of the three supporting themes of the district vision. The budget can also provide resources to contract external experts to help lead the inquiry process, for Inquiry and Innovation Grants to support the work, and for the purchase of additional resource materials. In addition, a highly specialized position of District Principal of Inquiry and Innovation was designed to help lead the entire inquiry initiative across the district and it was included in the budget. This position was in alignment with the inquiry process the district created to help achieve Vision 2020. The budget for creating that intentional and focused approach to becoming a district with an inquiry-mindset required a systemic and consistent, ongoing funding commitment. In order to have the type of impact that would result in the desired effect, it required the commitment for that budget line item to be sustained over several years. Beginning in the first year of vision implementation, the board of education continued making the commitment to achieve the goals of the vision by ensuring it was a key foundation within their policy manual. In addition, through the annual budget process, the Delta Board of Education has assured alignment with the goals of the vision. An additional, significant, budgetary commitment was made by the Delta Board of Education when they added specialized music education for students. In addition to providing outstanding music education for elementary school students, the inclusion of that dedicated time for music instruction allowed for additional release time so that elementary teachers would have time during the school day to engage in collaborative inquiry. This remains an ongoing resource allocation that is in alignment with the goals of the vision as it provides teachers with the opportunity for collaborative inquiry and professional learning. This has had a positive influence on teaching practices, and subsequently student learning outcomes, and has resulted in many innovative teacher practices across the district.

An example of one such innovative teaching practice was initiated by a group of four teachers at South Delta secondary school, who created a grade 10 student cohort group. This program, called *Strive,* was designed to bring four curricular areas together and included a commitment for students to spend a minimum of 25% of their instructional time outdoors in the community. The program was designed for students who were interested in approaching their studies on a unique path, and who were capable of working with others within the school and beyond the classroom walls. Teachers work together as an inquiry team to make thematic connections between their subject areas. This grade 10 cohort is designed to improve student understanding and wellness in school by reconnecting them to their natural communities. Working in an English, math, physical education, and science cohort, students explore the physical environments of the Delta community. Cross-curricular connections in the *Strive* program are emphasized through engagement and experiential activities. The program allows for frequent opportunities to explore ideas and curriculum in local surroundings and classes are scheduled in a manner that allows for flexibility during off-campus days. Students provide their own transportation to and from off-campus activities. To emphasize how closely the teachers in the program work together, assessment practices are highly collaborative with students completing assignments for credit across multiple subjects. For example, an essay might be assessed for credit in both English and science.

A second example of an innovative practice at the elementary level was in a school that introduced a modified timetable model at the grade 6 and grade 7 levels. The model allowed students to receive instruction from teachers who had expertise in specific subject areas. It also allowed students to begin to experience a feel for the high school timetable model before they transitioned to secondary school, thus easing the transition from grade 7 to 8. The feedback from students and parents was positive, and teachers enjoyed the opportunity to focus in greater depth on fewer subject areas.

Another area of teacher innovative practice was seen through various applications of technology in teaching. Access to current technology is essential for teachers as many of the learning resources for their use, and for their students' use, can only be accessed online and through district-developed software and programs. Once again, district leaders and the board of education made ongoing commitments to fund technology and ensure that such decisions align with the goals stemming from the vision process. Technology grants were introduced as a method for teachers to learn how to use technology in their teaching practice and ground it in pedagogical approaches. The grants were awarded generously to teams of teachers who were exploring an inquiry related to technology in their curricular area and pedagogical approaches. Significant funds were necessary initially to implement the goals emanating from Vision 2020. Eventually it was acknowledged that if the district was to be innovative for learner success, ongoing, sustained funding for technology would need to be available. Teachers have also cocreated a variety of excellent resources for one another. A website for sharing called Delta Learns (www.deltalearns.ca), has been developed by the school district specifically to assist in the storage of, and access to, those valuable shared resources for teachers. As a result of the increased technology needs required in teaching practice, the district hired specialized staff to support the use of technology and assist teachers with implementing pedagogical approaches that ultimately enhance student learning. One major advancement in the use of technology in the district was the adoption of Google Applications for Education (GAFE). Permission to use the Google platform required permission from the Provincial Privacy Commissioner, but it was clear that having the permission to use this tool would significantly change the way students and educators collaborate and learn. This is an example of how district staff worked to remove barriers so that teachers could take risks and improve their instructional practice. These types of purposeful decisions, made by senior staff, demonstrate the importance of aligning resources and decision making with the district vision during the budget processes.

Finally, as a result of creating a district-wide culture of permission and inquiry, several key papers and books have been published by Delta educators, including *The Decision Playbook: Making Thoughtful Choices in a Complex World* (Failing et al., 2019), which provides youth with a model to assist in making thoughtful decisions related to complex choices. Most recently, *Sorting It Out: Supporting Teenage Decision Making*, a guide for parents, teachers, and anyone who works with teenagers is another publication coauthored by a Delta educator (Gregory & Moore, 2024). In addition, *The Spiral Notebook for Student Changemakers (*Macintosh, 2023), a practical guide for engaging students in social issues, is another publication that came about as a result of creating a district culture of inquiry based on the *Spiral of Inquiry*. According to Joanna Macintosh, a district leader, "the support for risk taking that I felt from senior staff back when I was teaching paved the way for this work." Both these publications exemplify the innovative outcomes of creating a district-wide culture of inquiry.

Since the beginning of the journey to achieve the vision in the district, educators have been engaged in inquiry processes and have developed many inquiry questions related to their own practice and to student learning. They have created resources to share with others and have become deeply engaged in professional learning. The district has supported this enhanced professional learning by increasing the professional learning budget and by introducing structures to support professional learning. Senior district leaders have designed a *Leading for Learning* program that supports the school and district leaders through structures such as a dinner series, coaching, mentoring, professional readings, and a *Toolkit Series* for those beginning a formal leadership role. The *Leading for Learning* program will be described in greater detail in chapter 8.

Throughout the book, connections are drawn to show the alignment between budgetary decisions to implement the various initiatives and the policies and procedures that support the district vision and directions emanating from those governance decisions.

LESSONS LEARNED

- *Allocating limited resources in the most effective manner matters.* A clear, shared vision provides a filter for decision making. This can create efficiencies in the system that allow additional funds to be available for resource allocation. Budget priorities of the district are guided by the vision and are made with clarity and purpose because they are focused on the most important student learning needs that relate to achieving the vision.
- *A clear, unwavering vision helps to ensure that monies allocated are moving the school district forward* in a focused manner. Unspent funds from prior years can be captured and be used in subsequent years to support district decisions that are aimed at helping the school district achieve its vision.
- *A shared vision acts as a "third point"* and can provide a common, shared reference point for decision making through the budget process. It helps to focus budget team debates around a common purpose and unite departments that might otherwise be in competition for funds.
- *Innovative ideas should be encouraged, supported, and resourced.* Don't be too quick to say "no" to a new idea if it is grounded in improving results for students. Focus on the WHY and think of possibilities rather than barriers.
- *Don't believe that you have to do things the way they have always been done.* Being willing to let initiatives go that aren't taking you in the direction needed is a critical skill. Funding is limited in school districts. It is important to let go of past practices that are no longer meeting the needs of learners and replace them with more effective initiatives.

CONNECTING YOUR LEARNING

1. How might your district ensure that funding is allocated to support the initiatives that arise from a cocreated, shared vision? How does your organization ensure resource allocation is done equitably and is effectively aligned with your school and district goals? How are budgetary decisions made in order to ensure the vision is a priority?
2. Does the human resources department in your jurisdiction leverage the vision both with hiring practices and with the creation of leadership positions? If so, how?
3. What would your plan be to ensure that there is widespread support for the vision in your district?
4. What area of your system is, or could be, most impacted by a shared vision? What departments in your district are most in need of the support of a shared vision? How might they be impacted by a cocreated, shared vision?
5. In your system, who is responsible to ensure that all areas of the organization are guided by the district's vision?
6. Are there current initiatives/programs that exist that are no longer meeting the needs of learners? How might a reallocation of resources better address student learning needs? What should stay and what should you let go of?

Chapter 3

Focus on Effective Governance

> Governing well is no easy task. It takes knowledge, skills and experience. It takes courage and character. And it takes teamwork, in the sense of everyone bringing their unique talents and backgrounds to work together for the best interests of the people the board serves. (Brown, 2006)

Continual attention was required by the board of education to remain focused on Delta's vision of being "a leading district for innovative teaching and learner success." Staff believed that if Delta were going to realize gains in achievement, every staff member and the board would need to be focused on common, shared goals. Once again, we paid attention to the research and sought ways to bring it to action. According to Ken Leithwood, another defining characteristic of strong districts relates to the work of elected boards, specifically their contribution toward achieving successful outcomes of student achievement and well-being. He states that these outcomes are "encouraged when elected boards of trustees focus most of their attention on board policy and concern themselves with ensuring the district mission and vision drive the district's improvement efforts" (Leithwood, 2013, p. 20).

The Delta District found the following 12 points from Leithwood's *Strong Districts* research to be very helpful and insightful in describing effective board governance:

- participates with its senior staff in assessing community values and interests and incorporates them into the school system's mission and vision for students;
- helps create a climate which engages teachers, vice-principals, principals, parents, and the wider community in developing and supporting the vision;
- helps create a climate of excellence that makes achieving the vision possible;

- uses the district's beliefs and vision for student learning and well-being as the foundation for strategic planning and ongoing evaluation;
- focuses most policy making on the improvement of student learning and well-being consistent with the system's mission and vision;
- develops policies and supports staff decisions aimed at providing rich curricula and engaging forms of instruction for all students and eliminating those that do not;
- contributes to the development of productive relationships with and among senior staff, school staff, community stakeholders, and provincial education officials;
- provides systematic orientation opportunities for new members and ongoing training for existing members;
- develops and sustains productive working relationships among members of the elected board;
- respects the role of the director (superintendent) and senior staff in their responsibilities for school system administration;
- holds the director (superintendent) accountable for improving teaching and student learning in the school system; and
- holds its individual members accountable for supporting decisions of the board, as a whole, once those decisions are made (Leithwood, 2013, pp. 19–20).

In addition to the research of Dr. Ken Leithwood, Delta senior leaders and trustees were also influenced by the work of Chuck Dervarics and Eileen O'Brien (2019), who conducted research on Effective School Boards for the Center for Public Education. They suggest there are eight characteristics that effective boards share:

1. Effective school boards commit to a vision of high expectations for student achievement and quality instruction and define clear goals toward that vision.
2. Effective school boards have strong shared beliefs and values about what is possible for students and their ability to learn, and of the system and its ability to teach all children at high levels.
3. Effective school boards are accountability driven, spending less time on operational issues and more time focused on policies to improve student achievement.
4. Effective school boards have a collaborative relationship with staff and the community and establish a strong communications structure to inform and engage both internal and external stakeholders in setting and achieving district goals.

5. Effective school boards are data savvy: they embrace and monitor data, even when the information is negative, and use it to drive continuous improvement.
6. Effective school boards align and sustain resources, such as professional development, to meet district goals.
7. Effective school boards lead as a united team with the superintendent, each from their respective roles, with strong collaboration and mutual trust.
8. Effective school boards take part in team development and training, sometimes with their superintendents, to build shared knowledge, values, and commitments for their improvement efforts.

Dervarics and O'Brien state that the existing research on school boards is clear: boards in highly successful school districts exhibit characteristics that are markedly different from boards in lower-achieving districts. There is significant alignment of the eight characteristics with the 12 points of an effective board that Leithwood (2013) presents from the *Strong Districts* research. The research of Leithwood and Dervarics and O'Brien has helped inform the actions of the Delta School District and has been integrated into the structures and professional learning of the board of education. In the school district, leadership learning for trustees has a strong focus on effective governance and has become a prominent part of the induction process for trustees when a board is newly elected. When trustees learn more about their roles, they become familiar with the goals of the district and they learn to focus on the evidence that demonstrates whether or not progress is being made with respect to a specific goal area.

School boards are responsible for setting the overall direction for the school system. This is done through a multiyear vision and a strategic plan, reviewed regularly, keeping the vision and strategic plan as a focus to help set priorities and goals. The board also sets direction through its policies as well as the processes to review and develop policies. A policy-oriented board of trustees is defined as one that focuses on strategic planning and ensures the district mission and vision for student achievement and well-being drives the district's improvement efforts and holds the district superintendent accountable for improving teaching and learning. Additionally, the board creates relationships through an engaging and supportive climate that encourages excellence, respecting the decisions reached by the board as a whole. The following quote exemplifies the strong, unified governance that exists in Delta. Without question, having a strong, shared vision has helped to unify the trustees and provide direction for their work as a board.

Stated as simply as possible, the role of a trustee is to improve student outcomes while demonstrating accountability to the taxpayer. In practice, maintaining public confidence requires a board of education to be able to articulate its goals and to broadly engage all stakeholders, transparently account for its decisions, reflect local priorities for their district and to allocate funds in a way that evidence shows will improve student outcomes. Delta's vision not only articulated the goals of the board of education but it also helped to reign in an all too common governance issue for trustees which is the tendency to drift into operational matters and stray from system-wide improvement. As a board chair, working with the superintendent to develop the agenda and reports with the vision in mind, it became easier to maintain the focus of the board and to guide the deliberations and decision making towards fulfilling the vision.

Laura Dixon, Delta Board of Education trustee

District leaders in strong districts support and encourage trustees to focus on district policy and the achievement of the district's goals and priorities, and they encourage the participation of the elected board in setting broad goals that will support their work of policy-setting and policy-monitoring responsibilities. To effectively do their work, the board requires senior staff to provide regular progress reports that will assist them with their decision making in order to achieve key goals. The superintendent's role is to keep trustees abreast of the rationale for the student learning goals and to share data related to improving outcomes in these areas. The *Spirals of Inquiry* is a useful framework for trustees to refer to in understanding how student learning goals are arrived at, why funds must be set aside for professional learning, and how data is used to determine whether district goals have been met. The *Spiral of Inquiry* can also be a useful tool for district superintendents to refer to in identifying the most important learning need for trustees. By engaging in the inquiry process outlined in the *Spiral of Inquiry*, the learning needs of trustees can not only be identified, but through new learning, taking action and checking the needs of the board can be met.

Trustees in the Delta School District were actively engaged in the visioning process from the beginning and were deeply engaged with the community during the process. They were integral in helping create the climate, engaging teachers, vice-principals, principals, parents, students, and the wider community in the development of the vision. Once the vision process was completed, the Delta Board of Education used the Bold Vision as the foundation for policy, district goals, planning, and budget decisions.

As was mentioned earlier, almost immediately following the visioning process in the Spring of 2011, an identified learning need of the Delta Board of Education was to engage in a revision and renewal of all the policies and administrative procedures for the district. It was acknowledged by the board that the policies and procedures had, over time, become significantly outdated and were overlapping, thus leading to confusion about the work of the board versus the roles and responsibilities of senior staff. Brown (2006) states that "the secret to board effectiveness is understanding the different roles within an organization and how those roles relate." He further states, "the secret formula is not an organization chart; it is a map to clarify the roles and relationships within an effective organization" (p. 35). Delta School District enlisted the assistance of an expert in the field of governance and policy development to help modernize and bring coherence to the policies and administrative procedures that were seen as foundational to good governance. The governance consultant and his team worked with the Delta Board of Education for several months to engage the board in seeking clarity of roles and responsibilities and to align policies with the newly developed district vision. The outcome of that process resulted in a complex revision of policies and administrative procedures, which can be found on the district website (www.deltasd.bc.ca). Strategically placed at the beginning of the new district policy document, the vision, mission, and values have become foundational and directional for all other policy and administrative procedure development. Each of the other district policies flow from that first foundational policy and they are aligned to reflect the vision, the work of the board, and the resulting goal development and attainment going forward in the district. Statements of roles and responsibilities are embedded within the policies and role clarity with respect to policies and administrative procedures is well defined. This organizational model outlines the governance relationship between the board of trustees and the senior leadership of the district. Ken Leithwood (2013) states that effective school board governance requires a board to have clarity with respect to its role and scope of responsibilities and how it will govern. Understanding the way it governs will have a significant impact on the effectiveness of decision making, policy development, and business practices of the board. Trustees in Delta are very clear on their roles and responsibilities, as are staff, which in turn paves the way for effective governance and coherence of accountability for all the roles.

It is important for the review of policy and procedures to be a regular process, as priorities and goals can shift over time. Most recent policy development in the district has focused on the improvement of student learning and well-being, and the curricula development and engaging instruction that would help attain the vision of being a leading district for innovative teaching and learner success. Further policy revision occurred after Delta's Vision 2030 was created in 2022 when it was decided that the district policies and procedures should once again be reviewed. The review was conducted by Jo Chrona, an Indigenous educator, leader, and author, who has extensive experience in both the K–12 and postsecondary systems in British Columbia and she has expertise as a policy analyst. Over the 10 years of Vision 2020, Truth and Reconciliation became a priority and Indigenous Education emerged as an important focus for both the Ministry of Education and the Delta School District. The review conducted by Jo Chrona helped to ensure that the language used in the district by trustees and staff aligned with the United Nations Declaration on the Rights of Indigenous Peoples (UNDRIP) and the principles of antiracism. These two key priorities emerged after the creation of Vision 2030 and the decision was made to place a high priority on them as they needed to be addressed.

Another important outcome of the policy review work that emerged in the *checking* phase of the *Spiral of Inquiry*, was the improved working relationships the board had with one another and with staff and community members. This points to the importance of orientation opportunities for the board, including developing and sustaining strong working relationships among members of the board. Saatcioglu et al. (2011) suggest there is evidence that the internal "bonding" of board members contributes much more to a district's student achievement than efforts by the board to develop relationships with external agencies and groups outside the board. Trustees in the Delta Board of Education are highly effective in their work on behalf of learners in the school district and have developed excellent professional working relationships based on trust and mutual respect.

Policy work in the Delta School District clearly demonstrates that Leithwood's *Strong Districts*' characteristic of "advocating and supporting a policy-governance approach to board of trustee practice" (p. 19) is being implemented in the school district, and has become a guiding focus for trustees.

LESSONS LEARNED

- *The vision aligns board members around a common purpose* and provides an anchor when new trustees are elected, every 4 years. A clear, shared vision reduces system noise and confusion, and helps build coherence in the governance of a school district.
- *Clarity of roles and responsibilities leads to improved governance and builds on the effectiveness of the board.* Clearly defined policies and procedures make it easier for trustees and senior staff to function. The delineation of policies being the work of the board and procedures being the work of district staff clearly defines responsibilities.
- *Effective board governance results in improved opportunities for student success and coherence within the role* of the board, as they

begin to understand the role staff play in realizing progress in the key goal areas.
- ***Role clarity reduces system noise*** and allows all parties the opportunity to complete their work in an efficient manner, by not wavering on the goals outlined in the vision and by remaining true to the responsibilities of their roles.

CONNECTING YOUR LEARNING

1. What is the current model of governance in your context? How is that similar or dissimilar to that of the Delta School District?
2. In your context, who is responsible for providing professional learning and training for the governing body? How do you know what the learning needs are for the governing body?
3. What steps are being taken to ensure that the board of education is aware of the vision, mission, and beliefs? How does your jurisdiction ensure that governing bodies are aware of their roles as they pertain to the vision, mission, and values?
4. Describe ways in which the work of the board of education in your district aligns with the district directions or goals.

Chapter 4

Focus on Learning and Continuous Improvement for All

Another compelling practice of strong districts, according to Leithwood, is the "creation of learning-oriented organizational improvement practices" (2013). In his research findings Leithwood stresses the importance of strategic planning. The Delta School District made a clear distinction between strategic planning and long-term planning. The challenge with a traditional strategic plan is that often such plans remain fixed over time despite the fact that student, school, and district needs may evolve or emerge during that time period. For example, a few years into Vision 2020, the superintendent noticed an alarming trend in the district data. Students who had been identified as having a severe behavior designation had significantly reduced graduation rates. Although this data was not a part of the original goals from Vision 2020, the superintendent was concerned that this student designation was creating an expectation of limited outcomes for these students. To begin addressing this alarming trend, the superintendent elected to leverage the data by sharing it with all schools, and have it looked at through all three goals of Vision 2020. As a result of the sharing, greater attention was taken by staff to ensure that all possible educational support had been exhausted before a student was assigned a behavioral designation. Greater connections were built with the students who would benefit most from improved relationships, and over time the graduation rates for these students improved. This exemplifies the importance of having a responsive district improvement plan that is agile and takes into consideration the changing needs over time.

Vision 2020 in Delta ensured that a desired future was envisioned with the input of all stakeholders. Thus, a shared future for education in the district existed. The vision helped to guarantee that the current needs of the entire system had been examined, and based on data the remaining gaps had been identified. District planning goals emerged from the visioning process. For the district improvement plan to remain responsive to the needs of the system, the *Spiral of Inquiry* (2013) was chosen as the process to help clarify and define the steps required to help achieve the vision. Leveraging the *Spiral of Inquiry* ensured that improvement was viewed as a continuous, responsive process rather than a lock-step strategic plan. A detailed discussion of how the *Spiral of Inquiry* was leveraged will be presented in the following chapters.

Using the *Spiral of Inquiry*, school and district staff continually scan the needs at all levels of the system and use evidence to inform the *hunches* about what the next steps should be for classrooms, schools, and the district. The *new learning* that is required to move from *hunches* to actions is central, and, as a result, continuous attention is paid to the professional learning for the work in Delta to progress successfully. New learning is focused and directed specifically to help meet the evidence-based goals for improvement. Once new professional learning takes place, action is then taken to address the student learning need(s). In the next phase, the spiral evidence is gathered to determine whether or not a positive difference was realized through the deliberate actions taken. It is this integration of the *Spiral of Inquiry* that distinguishes Leithwood's notion of strategic planning from that of the Delta School District. In Delta, strategic planning follows development of the vision and then works backward to bridge the gap from the current reality to the desired outcome.

Leithwood states, "strong districts have a coherent approach to improvement which usually includes a small number of key improvement goals consistently pursued over sustained periods of time" (2013, p. 15). This recommendation connects well to the work related to the British Columbia Ministry of Education provincial's school and district Framework for Enhancing Student Learning (FESL), which is described in detail in chapter 5. As a result of the process used to establish Delta's FESL, four clear goals were established in the district which were closely related to the goals identified in the process the schools undertook. By limiting the number of district goals to four, the district is in alignment with Leithwood's recommendation "to not overload schools with excessive numbers of initiatives" (p. 15) and to "set a manageable number of precise targets for district school improvements" (p. 25). In addition, because the process for determining distinct goals involves consideration of the learning needs across every school, the total number of district initiatives is limited and there is a sense of alignment between school and district goals. This reduces initiative overload and allows educators to focus professional learning toward a narrow range of improvement targets.

As a result of school goals being created by using the *Spiral of Inquiry* as the template, the Delta School District helped ensure "improvement processes would be evidence-informed" (Leithwood, 2013, p. 25). In creating school goals, staff were asked to engage in the scanning process of the *Spiral of Inquiry* which asks, "what is going on for our learners and how do we know?" The *scanning process* of the *Spiral of Inquiry* necessitates the use of data or evidence. Therefore, moving from the *scanning phase* to *developing a focus* cannot be achieved without first collecting evidence that informs the selection of a specific focus. In addition, once the focus is established and action has been taken, it is essential to gather evidence using the same measures that were initially used in the scanning phase. It is essential to use repeated measures to know whether enough of a positive difference has been realized for students. This cycle of assessing, setting goals, engaging in new learning, taking action, and assessing once again to check for improvement has been foundational to the work in Delta.

From the evidence gathered by schools during the improvement process, Delta School District leaders work to develop the subsections of the district's FESL. Leaders from the Learning Services Department, which oversees curriculum, instruction, and assessment, ensure that Delta "develops and implements board and school improvement plans interactively and collaboratively with school leaders" (Leithwood, 2013, p. 25). Once district leaders compiled data related to each of the goals, the data was shared with school leaders and a plan to provide support to schools was developed.

Finally, the district restructured its principal and vice-principal meetings to make better use of the time and to allow for "the ongoing monitoring and refining of school improvement processes" (Leithwood, 2013). Fichtman Dana et al. (2011) state "Giving school-based leaders the gift of time for structured conversations and collegial support to investigate real-life dilemmas not only reinforces the notion that leaders must be learners but also sets the conditions so that principals see inquiry as part of their daily work" (p. 29). The principal and vice-principals' meetings in Delta were altered, not only as per Leithwood's findings, but also in order to implement Jerald's (2012) recommendations for improving principal and vice-principal meetings:

- refocusing principal meetings on effective instruction instead of operational concerns;
- deepening principals' knowledge about curriculum and effective instructional practices;
- providing principals with opportunities for active participation during meetings, often based on authentic "problems of practice";
- using the meetings to model good professional development practices; and
- structuring meetings to better meet principals' different learning needs (p. 31).

Each principal and vice-principal meeting begins with a presentation from the superintendent related to the most important learning needs of the system. For example, when the superintendent shared concerning data related to the fact that students who were identified as having severe behavioral needs had only about a 30% chance of graduating, school leaders took this information back to their sites and there was a significant shift in how educators considered students with severe behavioral needs. After the superintendent shares information at the principal and vice-principal meeting, school leaders are then given a significant amount of time for collaborative learning in groups focusing on the goals of their schools, engaging in professional learning, or working in their professional learning communities. In addition, time has been allocated for vice-principals and principals to have collaborative time to focus on the district's learning goals and provide input. This ensures that the needs of learners in schools drive decisions at the district level and "school-level leaders are included in decisions about district-wide improvement decisions" (Leithwood, 2013, p. 25). Feedback from school vice-principals and principals, through surveys, suggested the restructuring of the meeting time was beneficial for principals and vice-principals, and is in alignment with Leithwood's evidence that states "approaches to district and school improvement which encourage communication between and among districts and their schools and which provide generous opportunities for networking are a powerful source of job-embedded, strategically directed professional learning" (p. 15).

Throughout all the improvement efforts that have occurred in Delta, it has been acknowledged that schools are all unique, and that learner needs vary from site to site. "School-level variation in school improvement efforts" (Leithwood, 2013, p. 25) has been embraced as a construct since the *Spiral of Inquiry* was adopted as a means of achieving Delta School District's Vision 2020. Just as educators need to differentiate for the learning needs of students, the district also created differentiation for the learning needs of staff and schools. Delta School District embraces diversity at all levels of learning and has adopted the motto "we are all learners; we are all teachers; and we are all leaders" to capture the culture of systemic continuous learning and improvement that exists both horizontally and vertically within the district. When everyone within the system is moving forward with their learning, system-wide improvement will be realized.

The following quotes from Delta teachers capture the essence of the shift toward continuous improvement that has emerged in the district:

> For transformational shifts to occur we seem to need a few things. First is time—time to learn, discuss and explore new ideas. As teachers become more knowledgeable, they begin to try ideas in their classrooms. Also, having a

leader/facilitator is important. It seems to help to have someone modeling the new learning. Enthusiasm is infectious, so if a colleague shares their success, more teachers are inspired and willing to try the practice in their own classrooms. Finally, as teachers share their experiences, staff are learning how their students are becoming engaged. The amount of student learning happening inspires others to transform their teaching.

Delta teacher

All schools have noticed that there have been positive transformational shifts in classroom practice. Very little is measurable but everyone has noticed better student engagement, subtle changes and not so subtle changes in student behavior, a willingness by staff to look at new practices, more collaboration among staff members, more risk-taking by teachers.

Delta teacher

If a school district is to truly transform and improve outcomes, a culture must be established where *every* individual within the system engages in continuous learning. The goal needs to be one of improving practices, and ultimately outcomes, for all—students and educators alike. This requires everyone within the system to understand who their learners are and to know them on an individual basis, remembering that relationships and connectedness are critical components of the improvement process.

LESSONS LEARNED

- *Change is difficult for some people*, and sometimes there is a strong attachment to the way things were done in the past. With a sustained *focus on the learners and their needs*, educators become more open to change and their practice becomes more purposeful and meaningful.
- *Collaborative inquiry contributes to collective efficacy and creates a sense of momentum with professional learning.* Learning is social. When colleagues come together and strive toward a common purpose, synergy is created and the power of the group increases exponentially.
- *Working together around common goals contributes to the positive culture* of the school/district and leads to systemic learning and improvement. It creates a culture of "we are all in this together."
- *Connectedness and alignment help to make sense of complex work* and increases the opportunity for vital networking that leads to system-wide improvement.

- ***Keep the most important thing the most important thing.*** Continuous, honest conversations around student and staff learning with school leaders provides opportunities for in-depth and timely professional learning.
- ***Communication is critical and it requires continuous attention and effort.*** The power of an effective flow of information across the system and within schools cannot be stressed enough. Regular communication within the system helps to avoid system confusion, ensures alignment across the system, and contributes to a healthy climate and culture.

CONNECTING YOUR LEARNING

1. How does your context ensure that everyone within the system is focused on continual improvement (for students, staff, and leaders)? How do you prevent "initiative overload" and ensure that deep professional learning is related to the goals of the system?
2. Do educators at every level in your educational context view themselves as a learner (i.e., teachers, vice-principals and principals, and senior-level staff)?
3. Is everyone in your system aware of who their learners are (i.e., teachers, school leaders, district leaders, department managers). Do they believe that they can make a difference in the learning of others? How are learners at every level being supported?

Chapter 5

Focus on Instructional Coherence

Another important characteristic of strong districts is what Leithwood describes as "a coherent instructional guidance system" (2013). This has been an intense area of focus for the Delta School District. Prior to the development of the vision, it had been noted that the district seemed to lack coherence in the area of professional learning opportunities offered for staff. Workshops for teachers in the past consisted of many one-off sessions. When multiple different types of sessions were offered without follow-up, there was no means of ensuring that there was transfer of the learning to classroom instruction. Teachers who participated in that type of professional learning developed the mindset of "we've done that," which unfortunately resulted in little or no change in classroom practice or support for professional learning. An example of this would be the Assessment for Learning one-off sessions that had been previously offered in the district. Although a number of sessions were offered before the district vision existed, there was very little change in assessment practices occurring in classrooms. However, over the past 10 years with a more focused and sustained inquiry-based approach to professional learning, there has been a significant shift in teacher practice.

Following the creation of the vision, a renewed focus on the Learning Services Department allowed a different approach to continuous improvement. Due to budget cuts over several years, the Learning Services Department had been significantly reduced to the point where the department could offer very little support to schools. The creation of the vision paved the way for additional district-wide support and resources to be introduced in the district, specifically targeting key areas of the vision. One of the first staffing positions that the district created to help support achieving the vision was a district principal of innovation and inquiry. Vision 2020 clearly stated that Delta was to become "a leading district for innovative teaching and learner success." As a result, it was important to the board and senior staff that the school district community saw a clear commitment from the district toward achieving this ambitious vision. The creation of a district principalship of innovation and inquiry was a signal to the system that the achievement of the vision was important and was central to everyone's work. Another clear message was delivered at the unveiling of the Bold Vision in April of 2011 when a teacher in the crowd asked the superintendent, "Are you saying that we can take risks and try new things?" The response was an emphatic "Yes!" Finding the innovation would definitely require risks to be taken. This set the tone for a new approach in Delta that aligns with Leithwood's practice of encouraging "staff to be innovative within the boundaries created by the district's instructional guidance system" (2013, p. 24).

As collaborative teacher inquiry was going to be the process that would help achieve the vision, support was needed to help create an inquiry mindset across the district. Leithwood stresses that strong districts should "adopt a service orientation towards schools" (2013, p. 24). Through continuously scanning as outlined in the *Spiral of Inquiry* (Halbert & Kaser, 2013), district leaders asked, "What does the district need to do next in order to move the vision forward in Delta?" It was clear, from listening to school leaders, that support within schools was needed to help create inquiry-mindedness. As a result of that expression of the need for support in each school, a new teacher leadership coordinator role, the coordinator of inquiry (COI), was created and a portion of district-based coordinator staffing was allocated to each school in the district. This is an example of how the repurposing of budget funds can lead to the improvements needed to move the system forward. The purpose of establishing this teacher leadership position was to help schools begin the process of developing inquiry questions, or an inquiry focus, in each school and worksite. Still in existence today, the coordinators participate in ongoing, regularly scheduled, professional learning sessions designed to grow inquiry mindedness and teacher leadership capacity in schools. Scheduling of each school's COI time occurred on a Tuesday afternoon to ensure teachers could be released from their schools to attend professional learning meetings together at that time. An important, unanticipated outcome of the creation of the COI position was the profound impact it has had on building teacher and leadership capacity and collective efficacy across the district. As a result of the COI initiative, Delta has a strong group of future school leaders ready to formalize their leadership roles. Over the past few years, the district has hired several of these highly capable coordinators as school leaders who are grounded in the importance of deep collaboration and inquiry-mindedness. It should be noted that over time, the role of the COI position has evolved to meet the ever-changing needs of the system.

> My personal journey, from teacher to administrator, is a direct result of being part of the Vision 2020 process. When the vision process started, I had been teaching for a while, and I was starting to look for other opportunities. I was so

thoroughly impressed by the process that I knew I wanted to be part of future district initiatives.

Niels Nielsen, elementary school principal

It is noteworthy that around the time the Delta School District's vision was created in 2011, the Ministry of Education was entering into a process of redesigning the entire K–12 curriculum. When the provincial curriculum revision was completed in 2016, effort was made to inform Delta educators about the pending changes and to relate Vision 2020 to the innovative teaching practices required to truly implement the new provincial curriculum. Learning opportunities related to the curricular changes were offered and by the time the revised curriculum was released, educators were anticipating its release and they were excited by the changes. Although this was a daunting amount of change for the province of British Columbia, it created an opportunity for Delta to focus intently on the new curriculum, instructional pedagogy, and assessment practices through the lens of Vision 2020 using a collaborative inquiry methodology. While scanning the system in Delta, district leaders felt that the one thing that would help to move the curriculum forward in the district would be to develop greater internal instructional capacity in schools. In order to help increase that support for instructional capacity building, Curriculum, Instruction, and Assessment (CIA) learning teams were created in each school site in the district. The CIA school team leaders received training on the key elements of the redesigned provincial curriculum; namely a focus on big ideas, inquiry-based learning, development of core competencies, and assessment for learning practices.

According to Leithwood's research findings, strong districts "align curricular goals, assessment instruments, instructional practices and teaching resources" (2013, p. 24). A major goal of the CIA teams was to provide an in-school resource for the redesigned curriculum in order to explore its implications for effective instruction and support for the school goals. In addition, team members were trained in effective assessment practices so that they could assist other teachers with the implementation of sound Assessment for Learning strategies. Assessment for Learning became part of a continuous conversation among teachers in schools, and, as a result, there have been significant shifts in both the assessment and reporting practices across the district.

Another key Ministry of Education change that occurred during Delta's focus on its vision was a shift from district and school growth plans to a model where district and school plans are aligned and based on continuous improvement. No longer were there hard and fast numeric targets that were either "met" or "not met." Rather, the goal was changed to be focused on continuously improving student learning outcomes over time. The new Ministry of Education's Framework for Enhancing Student Learning (FESL) aligned closely to the *Spiral of Inquiry* with the focus being on the continuous assessment of: *Where are we at?*; *How do we know?*; and *Where to next?* Delta used the *Spiral of Inquiry* model as the template for developing school and district goals, which contributes to the coherent instructional guidance system that Leithwood claims is foundational to strong districts. The ministry's approach to school and district improvement connects to Leithwood's recommended practice of expecting schools "to focus on needs of individuals as well as groups of students" (2013, p. 24). According to the FESL, schools and districts must have "a focus on each student, as well as particular populations of students" (BC Ministry of Education, https://www2.gov.bc.ca/gov). Within the new framework approach, goal areas must focus on intellectual, human and social, and career development. In addition, "plans will be expected to reflect local efforts to support each student and specific groups of students, including Aboriginal students, children in care, and students with special needs" (BC Ministry of Education, https://www2.gov.bc.ca/gov). This revised approach to school and district plans clearly supports Leithwood's described practice of establishing coherent instructional guidance.

Another critical component of ensuring there is instructional coherence in schools and across the district came from the new teacher-mentoring program introduced in Delta, which will be described in greater depth in chapter 7. This program supports teachers who are new to the career, but also supports teachers who may be new to the district. The program has evolved over time in response to the needs of the teachers. To organize and support the teacher mentoring program a half-time teacher position was created. Having a teacher codesign the program based on the learning needs described by professionals helped to create a safe and supportive environment for participants without the fear of supervision. A key component of the mentoring program has been to help the teachers unpack the goals of the district vision, to understand the critical role that inquiry plays in teacher practice, and to deeply understand the importance of the coherence between curriculum, instruction, and assessment. As the needs of teachers evolve, the design of the program will continue to adapt to those needs.

Leithwood's research suggests that strong districts "advocate for attention to the best available evidence to inform instructional improvement decisions" (2013, p. 24). Although a focus on data continues to be a necessary, ongoing goal for the district, using the *Spiral of Inquiry* has helped to ensure evidence drives decision making with regard to school and district goals. Within the *Spiral of Inquiry*, evidence must be considered in the selection of a focus, or in other words, the question "What is the evidence that tells us we are selecting the right focus?" needs to be answered. While in the *checking* phase of the *Spiral of Inquiry* we ask, "Does the evidence tell us that we have made enough of a difference?" Establishing the *Spiral of Inquiry* as a district-wide approach to learning across the whole district has helped ensure that evidence is a key foundational consideration of the work being done across the district. Using pivotal questions posed by Halbert and Kaser, *"What's going on for our learners?," "How do we know?,"* and *"Why does this matter?"* helps to ensure that evidence is a continuous consideration in the work that occurs at all levels within the district.

The *Spiral of Inquiry* has provided strong foundational guidance and coherence to Delta's instructional improvement process. Fullan and Quinn, in their book *Coherence* (2016), state "schools and districts that make sustained improvements in learning for *all* students develop explicit frameworks or models to guide the learning process." Bryk, Bender Sebring, Allensworth, Luppescu, and Easton (2010) state that this *instructional guidance system is* crucial because it represents the "black box" of implementation (Fullan & Quinn, 2016, p. 88). According to Fullan and Quinn, at least four components need to be developed for an instructional guidance system to be in place:

- **Build a common language and knowledge base**
  - *This has been a continual goal of the leaders in the Delta School District and is reflected in the Delta Learns online resource site for teachers* (www.deltalearns.ca), *which has been grounded in current research in best practice.*
- **Identify proven pedagogical practices**
  - *Delta's focus on identifying and sharing successful practices across classrooms, schools, districts, and internationally is evidence of this component. The focus on collaboration, networking, and sharing results serves to strengthen pedagogy.*
- **Build capacity**
  - *This is evidenced by the opportunities for continuous professional learning that exist across the school district for all educators and leaders.*
- **Provide clear causal links to impact**
  - *This is a continuous goal of the school district. Used correctly, the Spiral of Inquiry increases the likelihood that a causal link between pedagogy and outcomes is identifiable.*

Throughout the journey to achieve Vision 2020, the Delta School District made instructional coherence a priority. In order to foster innovative teaching practices, risk-taking was encouraged. Professional learning opportunities, instead of being broad and shallow, were in-depth and targeted on the identified needs of the system. For example, assessment for learning (AFL) became a multiyear focus, engaging educators in face-to-face workshops, online support (https://deltalearns.ca/afl/), and social media. Professional learning opportunities were designed with an element of fun in mind. An example of creating fun in professional learning took place when the AFL sessions were focused on setting clear learning targets. Every school received a special cake, decorated with a red bullseye target on it, to remind educators of the district goal at that time. This creative approach served to engage staff members in conversations related to setting clear learning intentions in schools.

Reading instruction is another example of how the district focuses on instructional coherence. Teachers in Delta have access to a host of support materials for elementary (https://deltalearns.ca//elementaryliteracy) and secondary grades (https://deltalearns.ca//secondaryliteracy), which is based on disciplinary literacy and collaborative teacher teams.

It is important to remember that educational resources created by district support staff in Delta are identified by using the *Spiral of Inquiry*. Once a learner need is identified, a hunch is developed and a focus is determined. Professional learning opportunities are created to address the identified need. Specific actions are taken, either by the district support staff creating the resource or the classroom teachers instructing students, and then the intervention is assessed to see if enough of a difference was realized. If enough progress was achieved, then the next most important learning need is addressed. If not, then the goal is revised or refined and the spiral begins anew. This is the process by which continuous school and district improvement in Delta School District is realized.

By making instructional coherence a district-wide priority, powerful practices are shared across educators in the district and discussed collaboratively by the practitioners. This results in increased skill and efficacy for educators and improved outcomes for students.

LESSONS LEARNED

- *Educators need support, especially during the first few years of practice.* Inducting new teachers successfully into the profession is critical. By supporting teachers early in their career, instructional coherence can be built across a system.
- *Don't try to go solo—working in teams is far more effective!* When engaging in professional inquiry, engaging with a partner or group of other curious practitioners is not only more energizing, but it helps to

hold individuals accountable and thus moves innovative, cohesive practices forward.
- **Educators need time to talk with each other about their practice.** Teacher inquiry has led to an increased appetite for teacher learning and collaboration. Creativity and problem-solving skills are enhanced when educators work together. There is no question that educators are stronger together.
- **Time for collaboration needs to be embedded in the timetable.** Embedded time for collaboration that is not an "add-on" allows teachers to work together and co-teach. This has led to significant shifts in the learning conversations that take place. There is power and strength that comes from the group which, in turn, changes the group.
- **Trust must exist between schools and the district so that goals that are unique to individual sites are understood and accepted by the district,** and that goals that are necessary on a broad scale across a district are embraced by school sites. Successful school districts maintain a balance between initiatives that are "top-down" and those that are "bottom-up." Alignment between the goals is critical.
- *Using the "Spiral of Inquiry" helps to sustain the focus* through a process to get to the heart of the inquiry. The spiral provides direction to continuous improvement.
- *School district leaders should expect schools to engage in the inquiry cycle in order to identify the learning needs of their students.* Once identified, school goals should be honored and supported.
- *Inquiry is complex and requires deliberateness.* It requires patience and time. Effective inquiry engages people in processes to seek answers to focused questions.
- *Ensure that the system understands the connectedness of the work through instructional guidance support.* It's helpful to have a balance between collaborative teacher inquiry and proven targeted instructional strategies. New teaching practices and educational innovations result when teachers engage in collaborative inquiry; however, certain instructional strategies have been proven over time and should not be discarded.
- *Building teacher capacity empowers teachers* and reduces the tendency to transfer the blame for lack of student progress to the children and their families.

CONNECTING YOUR LEARNING

1. How are educators in your context supported with regard to their professional learning, particularly related to curriculum, instruction, and assessment?
2. How are educators in your context encouraged and supported to take risks with their practice?
3. How well do the educational practices in your setting align with the vision?
4. What process is used to determine the school goals in your district? Is the selection of school and district goals based on evidence of students' learning needs?
5. What opportunities exist for teacher leadership development within your school and the district?

Chapter 6

Focus on Evidence-Informed Decision Making

For the past several years, the importance of seeking and using multiple sources of evidence to inform practice has garnered the attention of the school district and has impacted decision making. For a variety of reasons, before the creation of the Bold Vision, the Delta School District's use of evidence was not being maximized to inform decisions and directions. Student participation rates in the provincial Foundation Skills Assessment (FSA)[1] had declined to the point that district results were no longer valid or useful to inform practice. With no district-wide assessments to replace the FSA, the district was reliant on sources of data such as attendance records, report card letter grades, surveys (ministry and locally developed), and high school exam marks as ways of tracking student learning. Upon reflection, the use of data in the district was limited by the quality of data available. Rather than seeking data to confirm identified learner needs were accurate, district goals were determined based on the data that was available at the time. Now, using the *Spiral of Inquiry* allows the district to shift the focus to scanning the evidence of student learning to accurately identify the learning needs. This may even involve gathering additional sources of data to ensure the identified focus is accurate. This helps to ensure that the hunches developed by educators are accurate so that the actions taken will ultimately improve student learning.

As was previously mentioned in chapter 5, following the inception of the Delta School District 2020 Vision, the Ministry of Education introduced a new Framework for Enhancing Student Learning (FESL). In the Delta School District this framework is used both in schools and at the district level. It is important to realize that the framework for developing school and district goals is very different from the previous Ministry of Education's accountability model which was focused on SMART (Specific, Measurable, Achievable, Realistic, and Timely) goals and was based on a 3-year accountability cycle. The goals under the old model tended to be long-term, fixed in nature, and at the discretion of the teachers, principals, and parents. In Delta, under the new FESL model, goals are developed using the *Spiral of Inquiry* and are based on specific evidence to determine the learning needs of the students. Consequently, the FESL is continuous, flexible, and responsive to the needs of learners, and therefore correlates well with Simon Breakspear's research on Agile Leadership. Breakspear states:

> Rather than engaging in efforts to create perfect, detailed plans and milestones and then implementing the strategy with fidelity, agile approaches embrace the inherent complexity and ambiguity of change processes in complex-relational environments. As complex challenges do not have a simple, neat plan that can be seen from the beginning, agile leaders must work with the knowledge they have, and remain open to the reality that new information and insights may lead them back to re-evaluate an earlier part of their work, including the very definition of the goals themselves. (Breakspear, 2016a, p. 5)

In recent years there has been increased focus by the BC Ministry of Education on the acquisition and sharing of student and district data. Concern has been expressed by educators in Delta that this should not come at the expense of district and school goals that are developed through a *Spiral of Inquiry* lens as learning needs (at every level) should be evidence-informed, but also flexible enough to evolve to meet the ever-changing needs of students, teachers, leaders, and the system.

A significant factor that is key to the success of the district's work with respect to the FESL is the relationship between school frameworks and the district framework, which has allowed for the alignment of evidence across levels in the system. As stated previously, school goals in Delta were created through the use of the *Spiral of Inquiry*, which identified goals for learners by collecting evidence in the *scanning* phase.

School plans were created based on learner needs identified at each school site. Plans from all schools were then collected by the district and scanned to identify common themes. The school district honored and embraced the goals identified in schools, which provided a solid foundation for, and were incorporated into, the district plan. At the same time, the *scanning phase* of the *Spiral of Inquiry* was utilized to identify the most significant learner needs from *across* the district, thus recognizing that larger data sample sizes may reveal additional and important information that could otherwise be missed. This process ensured that evidence gathered within schools aligned with evidence gathered across the district. From this process four key, actionable goals were identified for the district:

1. **Student Connectedness:** All students will have at least two adults in their school who believe that they will be a success in life and be able to answer "yes" to the question: "Are there two adults in your school who believe that you will be a success in life" (Halbert & Kaser, 2013)?
2. **Reading:** Students in the Delta School District will achieve grade-level literacy by grade 3.
3. **Assessment for Learning:** The district procedure on Assessment for Learning will be understood and implemented. All students will demonstrate an understanding of themselves as learners by being able to answer the "Big Three" questions:
   a. What am I learning?
   b. How is my learning going?
   c. Where to next (Halbert & Kaser, 2013)?
4. **Graduation:** All students will graduate with dignity, purpose, passion, and options (Halbert & Kaser, 2013).

These goals allow for the collection of data at the district level to "provide schools with relevant and accessible evidence about their performance in a timely manner" (Leithwood, 2013, p. 14). Because the goals of the Delta School District were based on the goals that were determined by schools, the district data aligns with and supports the work that is happening in schools. Further, because district staff have been closely involved throughout the process, they are able to "assist schools in using evidence to improve their performance" (Leithwood, 2013, p. 14). It should be noted that the ministry's requirement that districts focus on vulnerable learners (Indigenous students, children in care, and students with special needs) becomes a high priority within the context of each of the district goals. Particular attention is paid to how vulnerable learners are progressing within the goals of connectedness, reading, assessment (i.e., feedback for learning), and graduation, and evidence of improvement is examined for these subgroups. In fact, school staff are expected to know the individual names and stories of each of their vulnerable learners and to plan accordingly for their individual needs.

To maximize progress toward school and district goals, district structures have been designed to create greater internal accountability and support networking within and across schools. Most notably, time for leaders to collaborate has been set aside in principal and vice-principal meetings to allow for planning, sharing, and networking around the school and district goals. Data collected at the district level is reviewed collectively on a regular, ongoing basis during principal and vice-principal collaboration time so that progress can be monitored across schools and the district. This collaborative approach of regularly reviewing data aligns with Leithwood's *Strong*

Districts' characteristic of focusing on the importance of creating "collaborative structures and opportunities for the interpretation and use of evidence in schools" (p. 14).

The Delta School District has consistently worked toward newer and improved methods to gather and monitor the data related to the district's goals. The Information Services Department has the ability to capture student data from schools and produce timely reports, enabling the district to activate Leithwood's recommendation to "implement computerized information management systems" (p. 14). In addition, the Ministry of Education has developed digital portals that contain a wealth of data related to individual school districts. Delta is committed to the use of multiple, aligned sources of evidence to inform decisions across schools and the district. While Delta School District staff were in the early stages of developing the FESL, the likelihood that evidence collected was appropriate and valuable increased because using the *Spiral of Inquiry* ensured that the initial learner needs identified were evidence based.

A key takeaway in the Delta District has been that data sources need to be carefully considered, and, if needed, further explored to ensure that simply because data is available it does not automatically drive school and district goals. Sometimes additional data needs to be gathered in the *scanning phase* to ensure that the identified student-learning needs are truly accurate.

LESSONS LEARNED

- *"Data" and "evidence" are sometimes loaded words for people, so proceed with sensitivity and caution.* It is important to develop assessments that will not only provide information about how well students are progressing on identified learning needs, but will also provide formative information that will guide instruction for further improvement. Unfortunately, in British Columbia, high-stakes testing has been misused by external research organizations as a system measurement tool to rank and compare school districts. Naturally, this has made educators cautious toward system-wide assessments.
- *Support your leaders on how best to use data.* Educators are in the best position to know their students. They have the ability to seek and analyze data that will inform their practice and lead to gains in student achievement.
- *Schools and district leaders need strategies to make data available to teachers and to gather their input on how best to take action on the evidence the data presents.* Bruce Wellman and Laura Lipton's

Data-Driven Dialogue (2004) remains a valuable tool for teachers to use for data analysis and subsequent action.
- ***Keep the focus on student learning and achievement.*** The core work of school leaders and teachers is student learning and achievement. Therefore, when collecting and assessing data, the focus must be on school-wide goals and whether progress is evident toward achieving the learning goal. Data collection should be regular and ongoing. This helps to make data collection a normal part of the teaching process. In addition, waiting too long between reviewing data points eliminates the opportunity to make interventions when results are not improving.
- ***Alignment between schools and the district is key.*** In order to avoid distraction and to ensure maximum progress within the system, there must be alignment between school and district goals. In the Delta School District, school goals were created using the *Spiral of Inquiry*. These goals were used to create the district themes. After the district scanned the entire system an additional goal was added. This resulted in four district-wide goals. Because the school goals were reflected in the district's goals, alignment was achieved and the goals were supported by educators across the system.

CONNECTING YOUR LEARNING

1. Do educators in your context believe that *all* students can learn and that student learning is their shared responsibility?
2. In your context, how well do school goals align with district goals? Is everyone moving in the same direction?
3. What evidence of student learning is used in your jurisdiction to determine school and district goals? Do these data sets provide clear evidence of progress toward school and district goals? Why or why not? Is evidence of students learning based on a variety of measures (i.e., local district/government/ministerial assessments as well as locally developed surveys/questionnaires)?
4. *"If we continue to do the same thing, we will continue to get the same results."* How are the learning needs of staff determined and once determined, what opportunities for professional learning exist? Do these opportunities reflect one-time offerings or ongoing, continuous learning?

NOTE

1. An annual province-wide assessment of all BC students' academic skills in grades 4 and 7. It provides parents, teachers, schools, school districts, and the ministry with information on how well students are progressing in the foundation skills of literacy and numeracy.

Chapter 7

Focus on Continuous Professional Learning

Leithwood describes another significant characteristic of strong districts when he says they "provide job-embedded professional development" (Leithwood, 2013, p. 16). Early on, when Vision 2020 was newly developed and actions were taking place to achieve the vision, Delta School District staff realized how important it would be for the district to provide opportunities for professional learning in support of district transformation. As a result, a focus on professional learning became imperative for the district. Once it was established, that collaborative professional inquiry was the framework that would be used to help achieve the vision, and all professional learning opportunities offered across the district became focused on the needs of learners at all levels, thereby helping to align school and district goals. The Learning Services Department aims to continually demonstrate how the district's professional learning topics align and are interconnected. It is worth noting that with the creation of the district vision, it was decided that there would be a shift in the terminology used to describe the learning of staff in the district. References to "professional development" were replaced with "professional learning," which became the term of choice when describing ongoing, continuous staff improvement. The term "development" no longer seemed to resonate, as by definition it is the process of developing or being developed, which implies an external influence rather than personal ownership of growth. Staff in the district wanted to emphasize the notion of continual, intentional improvement through *learning*. There was a need to emphasize that learning is not something "done to us," but rather it is an integral process within the profession of education that involves deliberate, continual engagement in order to realize improvement.

Once professional learning opportunities began to be offered in the district, related to achieving Vision 2020, there was a need to provide a complete overview of them all. Not surprisingly, given the variety of topics being addressed through professional learning in Delta, school principals and vice-principals asked that the district provide some form of graphic organizer to help all educators understand the interrelationships and interconnectedness between the vast array of professional learning topics being offered in the district. As seen in figure 7.1, a graphic was created not only to help build better understandings across the district, but to also demonstrate the complexity and the interrelationship between the various professional learning opportunities being undertaken.

First, although dense in text, the School Connectedness graphic organizer document helped to demonstrate the complex array of work taking place within the district, the interconnections between topics, and its relationship to the broader perspective of the district vision and goals. Learning at all levels across the system is complex; however, all of the work falls under the umbrella of the district goal of school connectedness. A report by Healthy Schools BC,[1] published in 2014, contained research related to the impact of school connectedness for both students and staff. Among other positive outcomes, students who feel connected to school staff have a much higher likelihood of graduating. A sense of connectedness is a powerful predictor of whether students stay in school. A goal of the Delta School District is to have every student feel that there are at least two adults in their school who believe they will be a success in life (Kaser & Halbert, 2017). It is vital that students feel there are many reasons for them to attend school and to engage in their learning and that there are people who believe in them, thus creating a stronger sense of belonging.

Paralleling student connectedness, staff who work closely with other educators through effective collaboration have reported higher levels of collective efficacy, which is one of the most powerful predictors of student achievement and teacher job satisfaction (Hattie, 2016). Educators should know that there are at least two colleagues who believe they are/will be successful in their practice. Teacher colleagues often feel more comfortable talking to each other about the successes and the challenges of their practice rather than with their supervisors. Learning new and innovative teaching practices involves taking risks and practice might not be perfected immediately. Occasionally mistakes are made. We need to normalize this fact with both students, educators, and especially school leaders who must ensure that a culture exists where teachers feel inspired to try out innovative practices.

Next, the School Connectedness graphic organizer provided a depiction of how professional learning is related to what we refer to as "the learning equation": Growth Mindset + Innovative Teaching = Learner Success. The equation reflected the essence of the Delta School District's Bold Vision. After working with the vision for some time, the need to have a shared understanding of the terms introduced in the vision statement, mission, and values

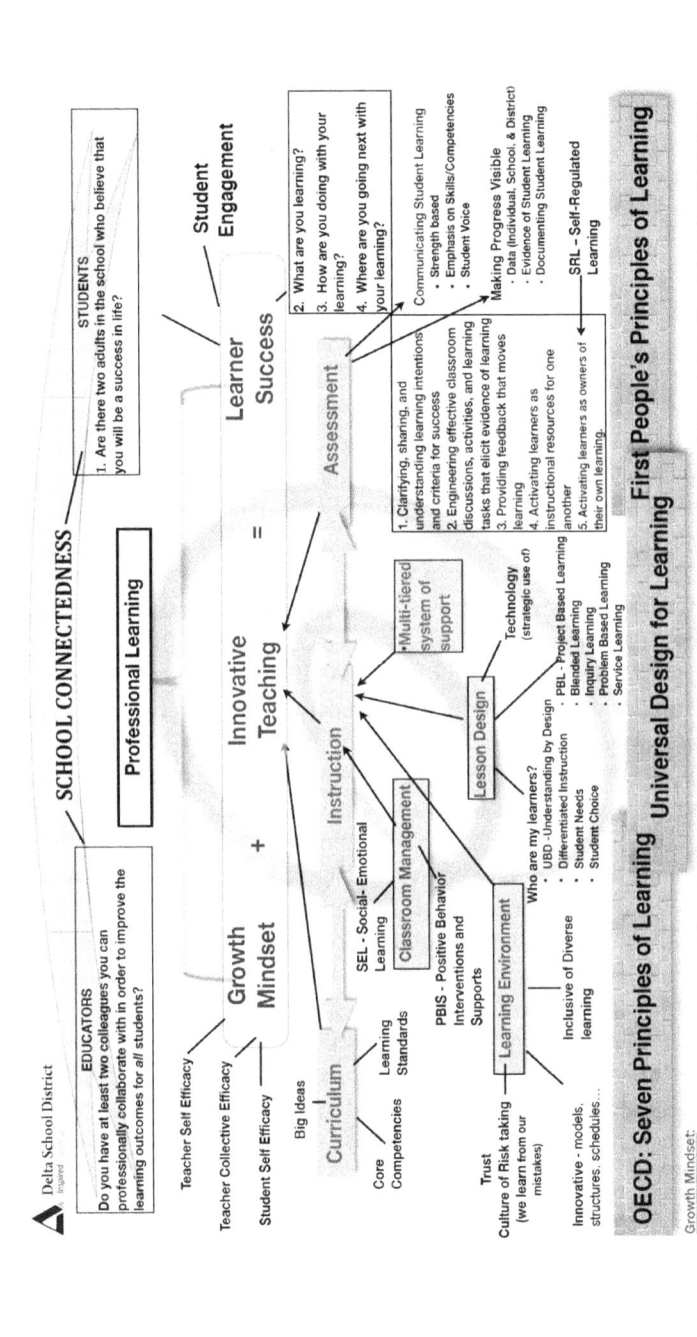

Figure 7.1. Graphic Organizer. *Author*

became quite apparent. A collective process was undertaken with school principals and their staffs to further define and bring clarity to the terms "innovative teaching" and "learner success." Definitions for these terms, along with "growth mindset," are located at the bottom of the graphic. Innovative teaching relates to the work educators do in the areas of curriculum, instruction, and assessment (a focus of the CIA Learning Teams that were outlined previously in chapter 5). From there, all areas of professional learning in the district were inserted into the graphic to help articulate the interconnectedness of the professional learning opportunities that existed within the district.

Finally, shown in figures 7.2 through 7.4, much of the professional learning work in the Delta School District has been based on three key foundational bodies of research: the OECD's Principles of Learning; Universal Design for Learning; and the First People's Principles of Learning. Staff in Delta were given these graphics referencing the three foundational pieces of research which became an organizer for them to use throughout their learning journey.

Each of these three key graphic organizers have been valuable tools and have proven useful for educators, especially in discussions and conversations related to the establishment of school goals for the school's Framework for Enhancing Student Learning. It has been helpful for educators to gain a visual perspective of where the current focus for their school is and how it connects to the bigger picture. For example, a school that was initially focused on Positive Behavior Interventions and Supports (PBIS) came to realize that they were really focusing on classroom management, which in turn connected to instruction and innovative teaching. This broader perspective enabled the school to start to discuss student behavior through the lens of Universal Design for Learning (UDL) and innovative teaching, and, as a result, the focus of the school shifted to teachers feeling empowered to make a difference in the learning outcomes and environments in their class by focusing on student intellectual engagement. The conclusion was that students who are intellectually engaged in their learning demonstrate fewer behavioral concerns. That, coupled with students feeling valued and connected to their educators, served to reduce the number of inappropriate student behaviors.

It is important to note that the original graphic organizer (figure 7.1) was a working document, intentionally designed to evolve over time. It emerged through work with the *Spiral of Inquiry* when it became apparent the learners (in this case formal school leaders) were expressing a need for greater coherence, clarity, and understanding with respect to the variety of professional learning needs among staff.

Although there has been an abundance of professional learning opportunities for educators in the Delta School District, all of them are filtered through the scanning stage of the *Spiral of Inquiry* with a constant focus on the learning needs of educators in relation to the goals of the district vision.

In addition, the learning opportunities are no longer designed to be one-off events. Sessions are planned as a part of a series to ensure that educators engage in new learning, commit to trying something new in their classroom or school, and then reconvene to collaborate and network about the experience and what they noticed and learned. Further, professional learning opportunities are often offered in schools with teachers being given release

The 7 Principles of Learning

This project has explored the nature of learning through the perspectives of cognition, emotion, and biology, and provided analyses of the implications for different types of application in learning environments. The research was synthesized to create seven transversal "principles" to guide the development of learning environments for the 21st century.

1. Learners at the centre

The learning environment recognises the learners as its core participants, encourages their active engagement, and develops in them an understanding of their own activity as learners.

- Learners are *the* central players in the environment and therefore activities centre on their cognition and growth.
- Learning activities allow students to construct their learning through engagement and active exploration.
- This calls for a mix of pedagogies, which include guided and action approaches, as well as co-operative, inquiry-based, and service learning.
- The environment aims to develop "self-regulated learners", who:
  - develop meta-cognitive skills
  - monitor, evaluate and optimise the acquisition and use of knowledge
  - regulate their emotions and motivations during the learning process
  - manage study time well
  - set higher specific and personal goals, and are able to monitor them.

2. The social nature of learning

The learning environment is founded on the social nature of learning and actively encourages well-organised co-operative learning.

- Neuroscience confirms that we learn through social interaction – the organisation of learning should be highly social.
- Co-operative group work, appropriately organised and structured, has demonstrated very clear benefits for achievement as well as for behavioural and affective outcomes. Co-operative methods work for all types of students because, done well, they push learners of all abilities.
- Personal research and self-study are naturally also important, and the opportunities for autonomous learning should grow as students mature.

3. Emotions are integral to learning

The learning professionals within the learning environment are highly attuned to the learners' motivations and the key role of emotions in achievement.

- Learning results from the dynamic interplay of emotion, motivation and cognition, and these are inextricably intertwined.
- Positive beliefs about oneself as a learner in general and in a particular subject represent a core component for deep understanding and "adaptive competence".
- Emotions still tend to be regarded as "soft" and so their importance, though accorded in theory, are much more difficult to be recognised in practice.
- Attention to motivations by all those involved, including the students, is about making the learning first and foremost more effective, not more enjoyable (though better still if it is both).

4. Recognising individual differences

The learning environment is acutely sensitive to the individual differences among the learners in it, including their prior knowledge.

- Students differ in many ways fundamental to learning: prior knowledge, ability, conceptions of learning, learning styles and strategies, interest, motivation, self-efficacy beliefs and emotion; they differ also in socio-environmental terms such as linguistic, cultural and social backgrounds.
- Prior knowledge – on which students vary substantially – is highly influential for how well each individual learns.
- Learning environments need the adaptability to reflect these individual and patterned differences in ways that are sustainable both for the individual learners and for the work of the group as a whole. Moving away from "one size fits all" may well be a challenge.

5. Stretching all students

The learning environment devises programmes that demand hard work and challenge from all but without excessive overload.

- Being sensitive to individual differences and needs also means being challenging enough to reach above their existing level and capacity; at the same time, no one should be allowed to coast for any significant amount of time.
- High-achieving students can help lower-achieving students, which helps stretch all learners.
- This underscores the need to avoid overload and de-motivating regimes based on grind, fear and excessive pressure—not just for humanistic reasons but because these are not consistent with the cognitive and motivational evidence on effective learning.

6. Assessment for learning

The learning environment operates with clarity of expectations using assessment strategies consistent with these expectations; there is a strong emphasis on formative feedback to support learning.

- The learning environment needs to be very clear about what is expected, what learners are doing, and *why*. Otherwise, motivation decreases, students are less able to fit discrete activities into larger knowledge frameworks, and they are less likely to become self-regulated learners.
- Formative assessment should be substantial, regular and provide meaningful feedback; as well as feeding back to individual learners, this knowledge should be used constantly to shape direction and practice in the learning environment.

7. Building horizontal connections

The learning environment strongly promotes "horizontal connectedness" across areas of knowledge and subjects as well as to the community and the wider world.

- A key feature of learning is that complex knowledge structures are built up by organising more basic pieces of knowledge in a hierarchical way. If well-constructed, such structures provide understanding that can transfer to new situations—a critical competency in the 21st century.
- The ability for learners to see connections and "horizontal connectedness" is also important between the formal learning environment and the wider environment and society. The "authentic learning" this promotes also fosters deeper understanding.

Figure 7.2. OECD's Principles of Learning. *OECD (2010)*

time to observe lessons in other classrooms. Educators co-plan, teach, and then debrief their lessons to ensure continuous, collaborative learning. This professional learning model supports Leithwood's premise that strong districts "provide extensive PD opportunities for both teacher and school-level

FIRST PEOPLES PRINCIPLES OF LEARNING

Learning ultimately supports the well-being of the self, the family, the community, the land, the spirits, and the ancestors.

Learning is holistic, reflexive, reflective, experiential, and relational (focused on connectedness, on reciprocal relationships, and a sense of place).

Learning involves recognizing the consequences of one's actions.

Learning involves generational roles and responsibilities.

Learning recognizes the role of indigenous knowledge.

Learning is embedded in memory, history, and story.

Learning involves patience and time.

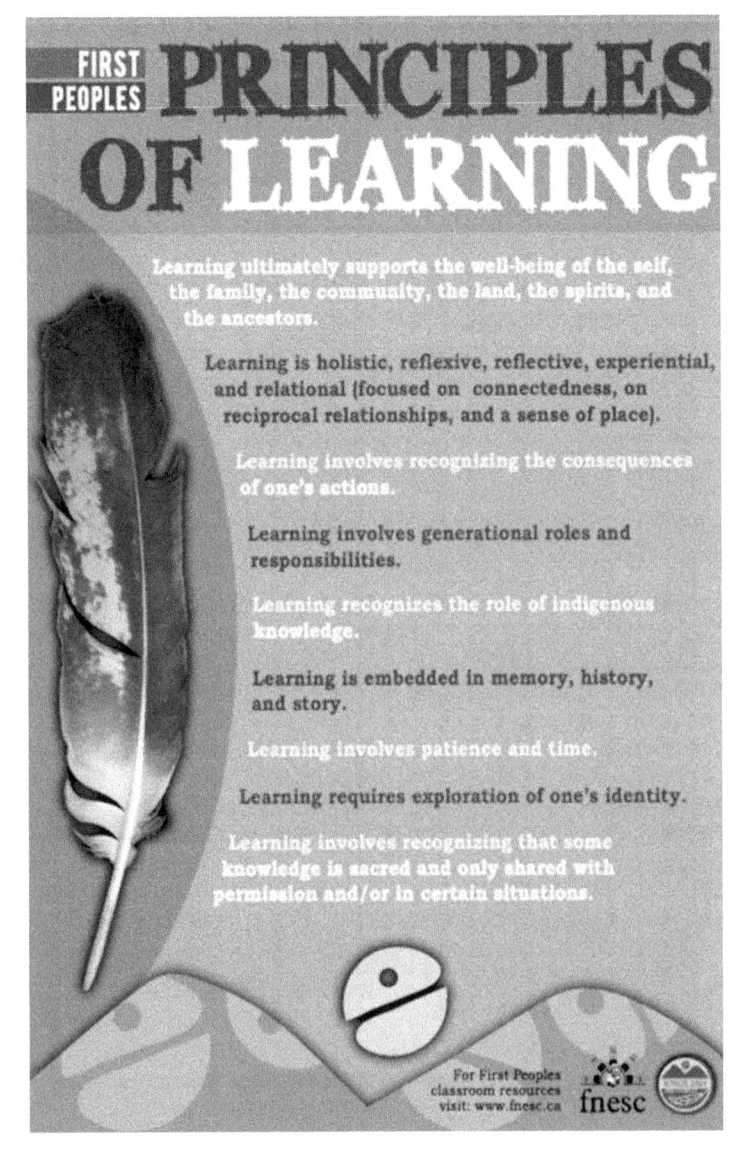

Learning requires exploration of one's identity.

Learning involves recognizing that some knowledge is sacred and only shared with permission and/or in certain situations.

For First Peoples classroom resources visit: www.fnesc.ca fnesc

Figure 7.3. The First Peoples Principles of Learning printed here with permission of the First Nations Education Steering Committee (FNESC, 2006).

leaders, most of it through some form of learning community or on-the-job context" (2013, p. 25).

As mentioned previously, a strong example of professional learning that has helped to establish coherence in Delta is the teacher mentoring program. After Vision 2020 was created, the power of teacher mentoring became a

Chapter 7

The Universal Design for Learning Guidelines — CAST | Until learning has no limits

Provide multiple means of Engagement
Affective Networks — The "WHY" of Learning

Access — Provide options for Recruiting Interest
- Optimize individual choice and autonomy
- Optimize relevance, value, and authenticity
- Minimize threats and distractions

Build — Provide options for Sustaining Effort & Persistence
- Heighten salience of goals and objectives
- Vary demands and resources to optimize challenge
- Foster collaboration and community
- Increase mastery-oriented feedback

Internalize — Provide options for Self Regulation
- Promote expectations and beliefs that optimize motivation
- Facilitate personal coping skills and strategies
- Develop self-assessment and reflection

Goal: Expert learners who are... **Purposeful & Motivated**

Provide multiple means of Representation
Recognition Networks — The "WHAT" of Learning

Access — Provide options for Perception
- Offer ways of customizing the display of information
- Offer alternatives for auditory information
- Offer alternatives for visual information

Build — Provide options for Language & Symbols
- Clarify vocabulary and symbols
- Clarify syntax and structure
- Support decoding of text, mathematical notation, and symbols
- Promote understanding across languages
- Illustrate through multiple media

Internalize — Provide options for Comprehension
- Activate or supply background knowledge
- Highlight patterns, critical features, big ideas, and relationships
- Guide information processing and visualization
- Maximize transfer and generalization

Goal: Expert learners who are... **Resourceful & Knowledgeable**

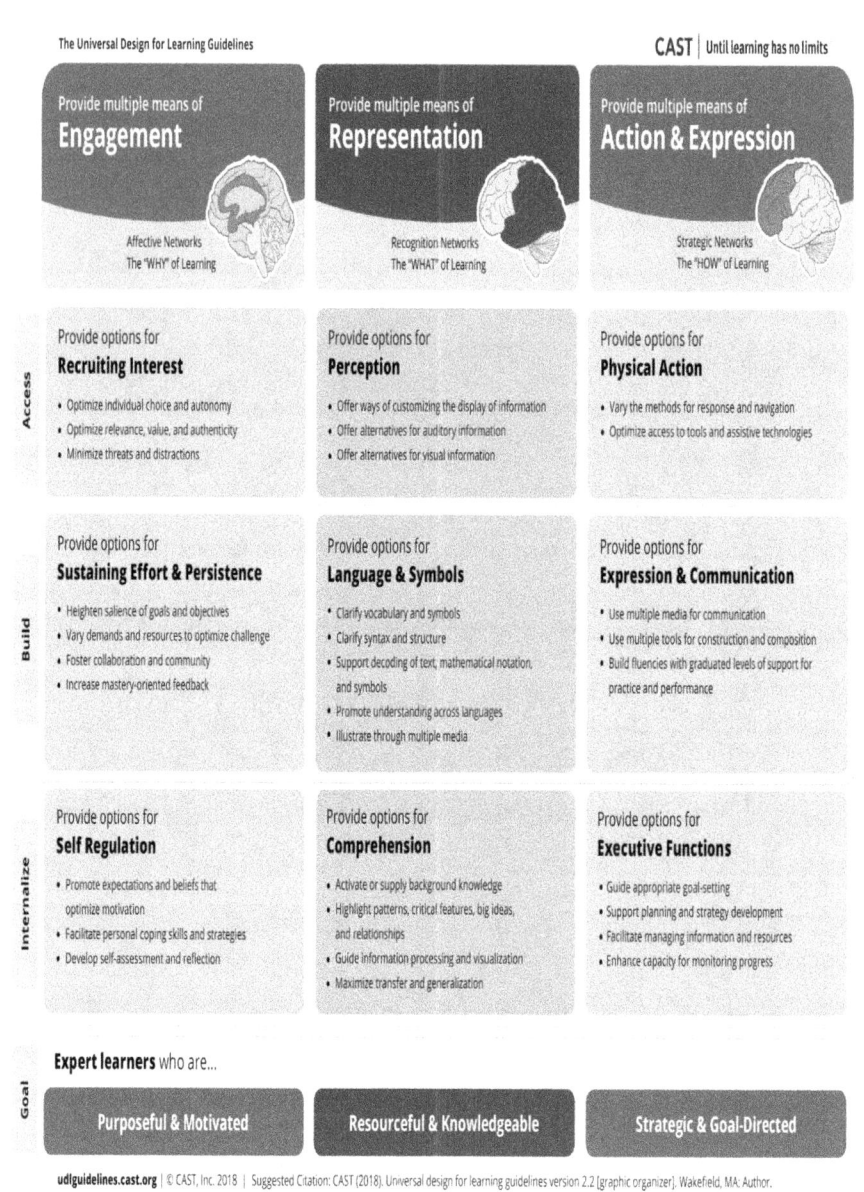

Provide multiple means of Action & Expression
Strategic Networks — The "HOW" of Learning

Access — Provide options for Physical Action
- Vary the methods for response and navigation
- Optimize access to tools and assistive technologies

Build — Provide options for Expression & Communication
- Use multiple media for communication
- Use multiple tools for construction and composition
- Build fluencies with graduated levels of support for practice and performance

Internalize — Provide options for Executive Functions
- Guide appropriate goal-setting
- Support planning and strategy development
- Facilitate managing information and resources
- Enhance capacity for monitoring progress

Goal: Expert learners who are... **Strategic & Goal-Directed**

udlguidelines.cast.org | © CAST, Inc. 2018 | Suggested Citation: CAST (2018). Universal design for learning guidelines version 2.2 [graphic organizer]. Wakefield, MA: Author.

Figure 7.4. Universal Design for Learning, CAST, 2018.

focus of both the Ministry of Education and the British Columbia Teachers Federation (BCTF). Based on a scan of the learning needs for teachers in Delta, a unique support model was created where teams of teacher mentors worked with groups of educators who were within the first 2 years of their career, were new to the district, or were feeling the need for support in specific areas. The success of this model lies in the fact that both experienced and novice teachers learn from each other and improve their practice together. Additionally, if one person in the group retires or leaves the program, the mentoring situation does not fall apart as it is not based on a one-on-one partnership. A district teacher coordinator, who is a member of the teachers' association, developed the Delta mentorship program with input from other educators in the school district. Each year, feedback is gathered on the success of the program as well as how the mentoring program could be improved. The teacher mentoring program is an excellent example of the *Spiral of Inquiry* in action—scanning, focusing, developing hunches, engaging in new learning, trying something new, and checking to see if it made a positive difference are foundational to the mentoring model.

> Although I wasn't actively involved in the creation of Vision 2020 when I started in my role as Coordinator of Mentorship in 2012, the vision was foundational to my work. The Mentorship Program was designed using the core values of Vision 2020 and with the vision of being a "leading district in innovative teaching practices" at the center. Having the Vision 2020 document helped me to connect my work to other initiatives in the district and perhaps just as importantly, to make those connections tangible and visible. My role as Mentorship Coordinator was my first formal role as a teacher-leader and the Vision 2020 document helped me to situate myself in the system and see how my work was connected to improving the learning of all Delta students.
>
> Tashi Kirincic, district coordinator

A variety of networking systems have been established to help spread and support professional learning across the district. Social media platforms have been created to highlight professional learning across the district including a website called Delta Learns (https://deltalearns.ca), which contains a wealth of resources for educators. In addition, a blog called 180 Days of Learning (https://deltalearns.ca/180daysoflearning) was developed where each day educators shared their stories of shifting practice. The Delta Learns website is an open source available to educators everywhere, and, while the 180 Days of Learning blog is no longer active, it successfully served the role of rallying educators around Vision 2020 for several years by highlighting and celebrating the innovative practices that were unfolding across Delta.

Using the *Spiral of Inquiry* as a framework for learning in the district has helped to ensure that "the content of professional development aligns with capacities needed for district and school improvement" (Leithwood, 2013, p. 25). It has also led to significant change in teacher practice, has deepened professional learning, and has strengthened professional collaboration.

Overall, I get a sense that due to the district's vision/inquiry model, staff at the various schools are much more in-tune with inquiry in general. There is an overall sense that staff are open to new ideas and open to changing or revising aspects of their practice to suit the needs of students. I think more teachers are increasingly comfortable taking risks, and that they are using their resources/energy/time to collaborate and implement ways to support one another. This would not be possible without the guidance and resources from the district and principals.

Delta teacher

The creation of the school and district Frameworks for Enhancing Student Learning (FESL) has ensured that there is, and will continue to be, alignment between what learners need and the professional learning opportunities offered to support staff. As stated earlier, the school FESLs were based on the student learning needs identified in each school, and all school frameworks were collected and collated to determine the focus and goals for the district. This "requires individual staff growth plans to be aligned with district and school improvement priorities" (Leithwood, 2013, p. 25). As school and district plans are based on the *Spiral of Inquiry*, gathering evidence is a key component of these plans and the continual monitoring of progress is central to the process. In Delta, there has been a shift from performance evaluations for leaders to continuous professional growth plans which are reviewed annually with the assistant superintendent. The growth plans are founded on the *Spiral of Inquiry* and it is encouraged that the leadership goals relate to the skills needed to achieve the school goals.

The *Spiral of Inquiry* resulted in the identification of another key learner need. The strong focus on teacher professional learning and leadership development showed that the district would also need to focus on the professional learning of school and district leaders. In scanning the needs of the district, it became clear that a focus on the professional learning of formal school leaders (principals and vice-principals) was emerging. Principals asked, "What is the district looking for in its principals?" Their important question suggested that for some, the expectations for the role of formal school leaders were not entirely clear and that the district would need to provide support for the diverse learning needs of this group of leaders. The result of this scanning inquiry led to the development of the *Leading for Learning* series, which will be discussed in detail in the next chapter.

LESSONS LEARNED

- *School district improvement is dependent on every employee in the learning organization realizing that continuous improvement is the goal of everyone at every level.* Continuous professional learning is an integral part of being a professional. The learning must be ongoing and relevant to every employee's role within the district and based on an area of identified need (rather than personal interest).
- *Keep the professional learning focus narrow enough to ensure that the new learning actually addresses the goal identified* through the *Spiral of Inquiry*. It is easy to "spiral out of control" and take on new learning that may not actually result in progress toward the identified goal. Focus matters!
- *Ensure the learners understand the interconnectedness of various professional learning opportunities.* Too many initiatives will result in the system becoming overwhelmed. For example, rather than having a goal around the impact of using visible learning targets in the classroom and another goal related to how to provide effective feedback for learning, it might be more manageable to link the two goal areas and examine the impact of providing specific feedback on the learning targets selected.
- *Improvement in student learning is more likely to be realized when professional learning is centered on samples of student work.* When educator dialogue is related to samples of students' work, the focus will generally be on instructional practices that are within the control of the teacher.
- *It takes time to develop a habit of mind, and continual practice to develop inquiry-mindedness is required.* Inquiry is hard, messy work; however, once the inquiry stance is established the outcomes will be focused, intentional, and results-focused.
- *Professional learning for adults must be scaffolded and supported* (just like learning for students). Similar to the classroom, educators are diverse in their learning needs and as a result, professional learning must be designed to meet the range of experience and ability of the adults engaged in the learning. The professional learning model utilized must be designed to meet the needs of the learners and based on the principles of the three learning frameworks.
- *It is important to get everyone on the same page.* When staff are collectively striving toward a common goal, the likelihood that the target will be realized expands exponentially.

CONNECTING YOUR LEARNING

1. Is professional learning in your context focused on continuous improvement over time? Do the professional learning sessions offered build on prior knowledge or are they a one-time offering?
2. How does your jurisdiction ensure alignment between the goals of the district and the professional learning opportunities offered so as to avoid "initiative overload"?
3. When planning professional learning, can you see value in using the OECD's seven Principles of Learning, the First Peoples Principles of Learning, and Universal Design for Learning? Why or why not?
4. How does your district determine what the professional learning needs are for educators? What evidence is used to check that new professional learning is making a difference to student learning?
5. How are teachers new to the profession or to the district supported? What opportunities exist for teacher mentorship to learn from one another? How does your jurisdiction ensure that teachers feel supported so that they remain in the profession? How does your teacher mentoring ensure there is instructional coherence across your district?
6. What are you currently reading, learning, or studying and how is it impacting your practice?

NOTE

1. Healthy Schools BC involves a partnership between the ministries of Health and Education, health authorities, education partners, and other key stakeholders in order to create schools where students have many opportunities to foster their physical, mental, social, and intellectual development.

Chapter 8

Focus on Leadership Learning

Leithwood's findings in his *Strong Districts* research related to leadership development have also been a central focus in the Delta School District. Despite knowing that within current research, school leadership is found to be second only to teaching among school-related factors that positively impact student learning (Leithwood et al., 2004), Delta had not developed a comprehensive, continuous approach to leadership development. Over the years, a multitude of one-off leadership programs had been offered, however, these tended to be a "one-size fits all" approach, with the programs being offered through a somewhat siloed approach. Further, in the planning of most of these sessions, input from the leaders in the field had been limited, other than their own conferences planned by the Delta Principal and Vice Principal Association. Over the past few years, a more focused, connected approach to leadership development has been taken by the district, with significant school leader input informing and helping to develop the program and topics.

Using the *Spiral of Inquiry scanning* phase to help identify the leaders' learning needs, it was determined that a stronger focus on developing a comprehensive approach to leadership development was required. The fact that some principals were questioning what qualities the district was looking for in its principals and vice-principals was a good indication that senior staff needed to be clearer with the learning intentions for principals and vice-principals. Although the district had done some work in the past on leadership development, the *checking* phase of the *Spiral of Inquiry* suggested that the district had not yet made enough of a difference in the area of capacity building for leaders.

Initially, Delta began a focus on leadership learning by offering a series of sessions led by Dr. Judy Halbert and Dr. Linda Kaser. The purpose of this series was to introduce vice-principals, principals, and teacher leaders to the use of inquiry as a framework for professional learning and to provide an overview of current research related to educational leadership at the international level. This series was well received by participants, but because participation was voluntary only some of the district's leaders benefitted from the program. Survey results indicated that those who participated spoke highly of the opportunity, and many teacher leaders who took part have gone on to become school-based leaders. They suggested that the introduction to leadership learning offered in those sessions had a strong impact on their professional decision making and learning.

After this series ended, school-based leaders were surveyed regarding their professional learning needs. Citing Sinek's Golden Circle (2009), principals articulated very clearly that they understood the *WHY* of educational transformation. They also felt that they understood *WHAT* things needed to be done to contribute to that transformation. What principals were still asking for however, was assistance with *HOW* to help make continuous school improvement a reality. Many of their needs appeared to be related to communication skills, conflict resolution, and how to reach consensus with a group. In order to provide the new learning that district leaders were seeking, a private consultant was contracted to share her knowledge regarding the structure and skills required for productive workplace conversations. This six-part series, which included all school and district leaders, provided them with common language and knowledge around how to engage in difficult conversations. Although the feedback from this series was extremely positive, the evidence collected from the surveys helped the district to identify yet another learner need and more work would be required to address it. Such is the continuous and iterative nature of inquiry.

Based on the evidence provided, it became clear that to meet the diverse learning needs of vice-principals and principals, there was a need to differentiate the professional learning opportunities available. After providing 2 years of common foundational learning, it was now time to embrace the complexity of leadership development and focus on what Leithwood calls "a comprehensive performance management system for school and district leadership development" (2013, p. 18). The practices that Leithwood uses as examples include:

I. Using the best available evidence about successful leadership . . . as a key source of criteria used for recruiting, selecting, developing, and appraising school and district leaders;
II. Matching the capacities of leaders with the needs of schools;
III. Providing prospective and existing leaders with extended opportunities to further develop their leadership capacities;
IV. Developing realistic plans for leadership succession; and
V. Promoting coordinated forms of leadership distribution in schools.

When considering these five indicators, it became clear that there were areas where the Delta School District was strong and areas that would require further attention. Although the district has a formal administrative procedure related to effective administrative practice, it became evident that many of these practices would benefit from being reviewed and revised. It is important that the newly revised practices be shared and referred to on an ongoing basis, particularly when vice-principals and principals are establishing and reviewing their own professional growth plans.

The district has historically worked hard to assign school leaders to specific schools, matching the skills of its leaders to the needs of schools. A few years into Vision 2020 a system was introduced that allowed vice-principals and principals to provide their own input into school administrative transfers and placements, which contributes to the decision making around administrative transfers among school leaders. Leadership succession is a constant consideration for the district's senior administrative team and hiring decisions are undertaken with succession planning in mind.

Since the inception of the district's vision, there has been a much stronger focus on developing leaders at all levels in the system. The creation of Curriculum, Instruction, and Assessment Learning Teams and Coordinators of Inquiry school-based positions are just two examples where leadership opportunities have been created for teachers. The area where the Delta School District still required greater focus was in providing diverse, in-depth leadership learning opportunities for aspiring and current leaders to further develop their leadership capacities. The work of educational researcher and professor Dr. Meredith Honig has become central in the Delta School District's approach to leadership development:

> [D]istricts generally do not see district-wide improvements in teaching and learning without substantial engagement by their central offices in helping schools build their capacity for improvement. Central offices and the people who work in them are not simply part of the background noise in school improvement. Rather, *school district central office administrators exercise essential leadership, in partnership with school leaders, to build capacity* throughout public educational systems for teaching and learning improvements. (Honig, 2007)

The Learning Services Department and senior district staff are dedicated to working alongside teachers, vice-principals, and principals to partner with and build leadership capacity. This strategy was very useful when district staff worked closely with schools to assist them with the development of their school Framework for Enhancing Student Learning. Once the goals for each school were established, schools were clustered and networked according to their goal areas. District staff then served as facilitators to support the work that was happening in schools and assist them in achieving their goals.

Assistant superintendents in Delta developed a shared and collaborative approach to senior leadership by modeling shared decision making and joint planning. They developed a collaborative, continuous learning partnership and adopted a coordinated approach to their formal school visits with codeveloped questions that focus on student, teacher, and leader learning. This collaborative approach has resulted in vice-principals and principals talking about how the role of the school administrator has shifted (see table 8.1).

Honig (2007) cites three areas that districts need to focus on in order to realize district improvement:

- *School Leadership investigation:* The reconfiguration and exercise of leadership within elementary, middle, and high schools to enable more focused support for learning improvement
- *Resource Investment investigation:* The investment of staffing and other resources at multiple levels of the system, in alignment with learning improvement goals, to enhance equity and leadership capacity
- *Central Office Transformation investigation:* The reinvention of central office work practices and relationships with the schools to better support district-wide improvement of teaching and learning (Honig, 2007)

All three of these areas have been a focus as the Delta School District moves ahead with a comprehensive, evidence-based, multiyear plan for leadership improvement. At the end of the 2016–2017 school year, school, and district leaders were surveyed regarding their professional learning needs. This survey was conducted in partnership with the Delta Principals and Vice Principals Association (DPVPA). The results of the survey indicated:

- a high level of interest (90%+) in a variety of leadership development activities/a willingness to put in significant time and energy;
- a desire for opportunities to connect their professional growth to their school improvement goals;
- a desire for structures that allow for collaborative learning in teams/networks;
- a very high level of interest in mentorship and coaching opportunities (small group and individual); and
- experienced principals and vice-principals want opportunities to share their knowledge, experience, and learning.

Table 8.1. Shift in School Leadership

From...	Toward...
Building manager	Lead learner
Supervisor	Capacity builder/Leader of teacher learning and development
Change manager	Improvement leader
Culture keeper	Culture developer
Focus on fairness	Focus on equity

The evidence gathered from this survey led to the development of a professional leadership learning program titled *Leading for Learning*. This program, designed for principals, vice-principals, and exempt staff leaders, was created to address the learning needs of a highly diverse group. As such, it offered multiple strands and areas of focus. Extensive research (Leithwood, 2013; Honig, 2007; Jerald, 2012) identified one of the key characteristics of high-performing school districts as having a sustained, comprehensive leadership-development program for school and district leaders. The *Leading for Learning* program meets the diverse needs of both experienced and novice principals and vice-principals with full or partial participation across all of the strands. Leaders participate in the strands that are best suited to their current professional learning needs. To promote leadership at all levels in the system, components of the program are co-planned by members of the DPVPA, assistant superintendents, and district directors.

Table 8.2 identifies the strands of the *Leading the Learning* program along with the targeted participants and a brief description of the leadership component.

This comprehensive, multipronged approach to leadership development is specifically designed to meet the needs of the diverse pool of vice-principals and principals and aspiring leaders. In addition to this six-strand approach to leadership development, the district has allocated a minimum of one hour at the beginning of each bimonthly principals' meeting for professional learning. Learning needs are determined by using the scanning phase of the *Spirals of Inquiry* and considering "what are the needs of our learners?" and "how do we know?" A planning committee provided the senior team with input regarding what should be included as topics on the bimonthly meeting agendas and to ensure that the learning needs of school leaders are being met. Creation of the *Leading for Learning* program is based on the OECD's *Principles of Learning* (OECD, 2010), the First Peoples Principles of Learning (First Nations Education Steering Committee, 2006), and Universal Design for Learning (CAST, 2018). These principles are foundational to all levels of learning including students in the classroom, educators in a school, and leaders in a district. Using these principles as the foundation for *Leading for Learning* helped to model them for the learning at all levels in the district. The seven principles include:

Table 8.2. Leading the Learning Program Components (Bauman & Gordon, 2018)

STRAND	PARTICIPANTS	DESCRIPTION
Learning Alliance Research and Practice Series	Interested principals and vice-principals	Journal/research articles distributed each week for one month related to a theme, followed by a social event to discuss the topic and commit to an action.
New Principal and Vice-Principal **Toolbox Series**	For vice-principals and principals in their first 2 years of service	A series of workshops related to school administration with a focus on topics such as school organization, SAFE schools, school finances, professional growth plans, communication with parents, staff and students, human resources, leading inclusion, and instructional leadership to name just a few.
Mentoring Series	Open to all principals and vice-principals	A networked model of mentorship (two mentors working with four to six mentees). Series developed in conjunction with participants. Approximately five formal sessions per year. Groups have a budget of $1,000 to use for interim meetings including resources and food.
Leading the Learning **Dinner Series** with key thought leaders in education	Open to all principals and vice-principals	Organized by the assistant superintendents in partnership with Learning Services.
Teacher Leaders Series	Teacher leaders, department heads, district and school coordinators.	District staff, principals, vice-principals, and teacher leaders.
Leadership **Coaching**	Open to principals and vice-principals	Experienced principals and vice-principals trained as district coaches by an external facilitator. They engage in short-term coaching with those who have an identified learning need.

1. **Learners at the center:** The learning environment recognizes the learners as its core participants, encourages their active engagement, and develops in them an understanding of their own activity as learners.
2. **The social nature of learning:** The learning environment is founded on the social nature of learning and actively encourages well-organized cooperative learning.

3. **Emotions are integral to learning:** The learning professionals within the learning environment are highly attuned to the learners' motivations and the key role of emotions in achievement.
4. **Recognizing individual differences:** The learning environment is acutely sensitive to the individual differences among the learners in it, including their prior knowledge.
5. **Stretching all students:** The learning environment devises programs that demand hard work and challenge from all but without excessive overload.
6. **Assessment for Learning:** The learning environment operates with clarity of expectations using assessment strategies consistent with these expectations; there is a strong emphasis on formative feedback to support learning.
7. **Building horizontal connections:** The learning environment strongly promotes "horizontal connectedness" across areas of knowledge and subjects as well as to the community and the wider world (Istance et al., OECD, 2010, p. 325).

Leading for Learning was designed to incorporate each of these foundational key principles and it clearly demonstrates a comprehensive approach to leadership development as cited by Leithwood (2013) in the *Strong Districts* research.

It is important to note that the school district has invested heavily in the professional learning of its vice-principals and principals. Since 2015, the Delta School District has had more than 30 (approximately one-half) of its leaders participate in the Transformative Education Leadership Program (TELP)[1] offered through the University of British Columbia. Program developers and instructors of the TELP program are Dr. Judy Halbert and Dr. Linda Kaser, who introduced the *Spiral of Inquiry* to educational jurisdictions around the world, including Delta. The superintendent and two assistant superintendents in Delta have participated in TELP, which served to model the importance of continuous learning for everyone within the school system and allowed them to engage in an inquiry project related to their own leadership work. It was because of an inquiry project in TELP that the *Leading the Learning* program was created in Delta. Finally, because TELP is highly focused on system change, leading through simplicity and complexity, creating cultures of deep learning and innovative practice, and leading professional learning for adaptive expertise, it has created increased system capacity thus resulting in a pool of skilled leaders who are ready and prepared for succession into leadership roles beyond the school level.

In addition to the leadership program and participation in TELP, Delta School District has also supported its leaders' participation in workshops and

78   Chapter 8

professional learning related to Compassionate Systems Leadership, influenced by Peter Senge. It is important to note the relationship between Senge's work and the model of *Schools as Learning Organizations* (SLO). Currently the SLO framework, which will be discussed in greater detail in part 2, consists of seven dimensions and four transversals: Time, Trust, Technology, and Thinking Together. Due to the learning that resulted from experiencing the global pandemic, which the Delta School District participated in, Louise Stoll and Claire Sinnema (2021) have added a fifth transversal related to compassion, seen in figure 8.1.

As all leaders in Delta are trained in Compassionate Systems Leadership; they are well prepared to work with the SLO framework in as complete and effective a manner as possible. In the Delta School District, the characteristics of Leithwood's findings related to leadership development and leadership learning have been a central focus. Attention to developing effective leaders at all levels will continue to be a high priority in the district for the years to

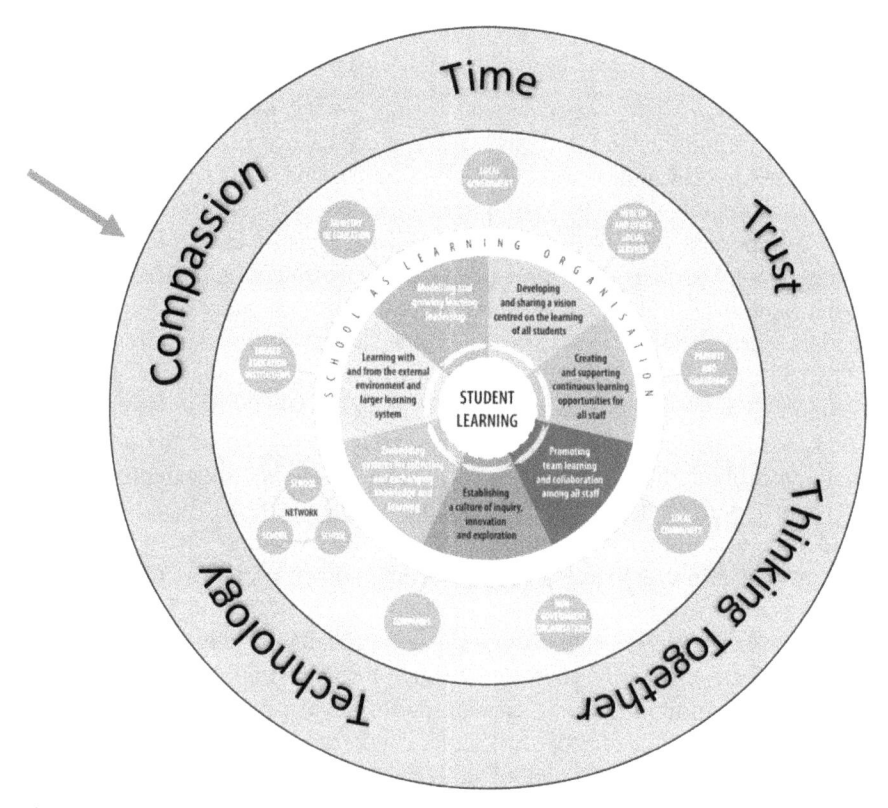

Figure 8.1. The SLO Framework with the fifth transversal of compassion. The figure is based on Stoll and Sinnema (2021), updated from Kools and Stoll (2016) and OECD (2016). *Stoll & Sinnema, 2021*

come, and adaptations will be made in response to any changing needs leaders across the district identify.

LESSONS LEARNED

- *When developing professional learning for leadership in a school district, consider using the stance of Helen Timperley's work "Who is my class?"* This will help to ensure that every educator and leader sees themself as a teacher, with a responsibility for continuous improvement at every level.
- *Central office staff must become the lead learners in the district.* They need to be purposeful in modeling their own learning, thereby actively demonstrating their own learning to the field. It is critical that senior staff engage in, and model, networked collaborative inquiry.
- *School leadership learning is a high-leverage strategy.* When districts develop a culture where continuous improvement is the norm for leaders, there is an impact up, down, and across the district that impacts all educators.
- *Hiring practices must reflect the goals of your vision.* Interview questions should align with what the district values. For example, if it is important that candidates understand inquiry and engage in continuous professional learning, there should be questions asked that reflect these district values. If the district values continual professional learning, expecting candidates to be able to speak to what they have been reading, participating in, and learning is not unreasonable.

CONNECTING YOUR LEARNING

1. Does your district/jurisdiction have a professional learning program to support the needs of school and district leaders? How do you determine what the learning needs are for your leaders? How do you differentiate for their learning needs? Are program decisions evidence-based? Is there an opportunity for leaders to provide input into their learning needs?
2. Should professional learning for leaders be linked to the goals of the schools/district? How might a district vision impact professional learning for leaders?
3. When thinking about your current role, who are your learners and how do you determine what their learning needs are?

NOTES

1. The Transformative Educational Leadership Program (TELP), offered through the University of British Columbia (UBC) is a course for individuals in a Canadian or international K–12 system and other connected sectors, who are interested in system transformation.

Chapter 9

Focus on Strong, Collaborative Working Relationships

According to Leithwood's *Strong Districts* research, the relationships that matter most are described as the relationships within the district's central office and between the central office and its schools, parents, local community groups, and the Ministry of Education (Leithwood, 2013). Evidence suggests that in a successful school district, central office roles are interconnected and work is undertaken in a collaborative and service-oriented way. Leithwood's research also suggests that in strong districts communication is frequent and cordial and school staff often participate in system decision making, have significant input into processes, and are in frequent contact with central office staff for support and assistance (Togneri & Anderson, 2003).

Communication plays a vital role within the education system and is particularly important within schools. Leithwood's extensive research further suggests that communication is nurtured by structures which encourage collaborative work, that schools are responsible for productive working relationships with parents, and that it is imperative the school system is in regular two-way communication with the Ministry of Education (Leithwood, 2013).

Mirroring this research, relationships within the Delta School District seem to develop most effectively when staff in the district office work collaboratively, when the work is purposefully interconnected, and when they are focused on shared responsibility and purpose. Decision making and the work of the Delta School District is highly collaborative. An example of providing structures that support highly collaborative interactions among staff took place in recent years between two departments at the district level. Based on the importance of collaboration and networking, there has been a complete realignment and reconfiguration of the physical working spaces within the Learning Services Department to eliminate what was perceived as siloed and segregated working units. This change encouraged stronger collaborative teams. Additionally, at the school level, there has been a greater emphasis on involving school staff in school and system decisions. Networks and professional learning connections across the system have become a way of building professional capacity and efficacy, and there has been a distinct focus on using collaborative inquiry to solve problems and develop goals.

In *Change Leadership* (2011) Michael Fullan cites the work of Gittell (2009), whose research findings clearly describe that successful organizations have developed cultures of relational coordination with shared goals, shared knowledge, and mutual respect, and they have transparent communication. Gittell goes on to say that those cultures continually clarify and reinforce the focused efforts of the organization. He suggests that because the core ideas in those organizations are pursued collectively and collaboratively, they tend to generate deeper, consistent practices across the organization. As would be expected, there is a greater shared depth of understanding and corresponding skills (Gittell, 2009).

There is no doubt that improvement in schools and school districts is impacted by the quality of conversations among individuals and groups. Working collaboratively through vision development, implementation of new curriculum, and inquiry around goals have all provided purposeful and meaningful opportunities for educators to engage in collaborative inquiry in the Delta School District. They have worked through challenges and differences that have enabled the problem solving and decision making that has led to improvement, and, in turn, that has improved relationships and trust among staff. The discourse that takes place during collaborative inquiry in the Delta School District has had a significant impact on the development of trust-based relationships, which in turn has had a strong influence on system-wide improvement.

"Where there is growing trust, the quality of discourse increases, again helping stimulate greater engagement and real collaboration . . . Trust-based relationships are essential if schools and districts are to fundamentally disrupt the extreme isolation of educators and help build a profession of teaching" (Wagner & Kegan, 2006, p. 150). Bryk and Schneider (2002) uncovered important ways in which trust contributes to relationship building in an educational organization, particularly in terms of the four distinct elements that must be present for trust to exist: respect, integrity, competency, and personal regard. They conclude that the development of trust is foundational to the development of relationships in educational settings. Evidence from interviews and surveys in the Delta School District suggests that there has been an important change across the system toward a growth mindset that has come about as a result of staff engaging in collaborative inquiry. The collective efficacy that has resulted among professionals has generated a deeper understanding of how to support learners. District leaders in Delta created structures and strategies that encourage relationships and relational trust to develop between themselves and staff in schools through purposefully aligning their work in a more focused manner. Leaders in schools have similarly developed ways of providing opportunities for teachers to engage in collaborative inquiry, which has resulted in the development of a professional culture where there is shared responsibility for student learning and goal attainment. Leana (2011) states, "When relationships among teachers and leaders in a school are characterized by high trust and frequent interaction—that is, when social capital is strong—student achievement scores improve. In other words, teacher social capital was a significant predictor of student achievement gains above and beyond teacher experience or ability in the classroom" (p. 19).

Kouzes and Posner (1998) identify seven essential actions that contribute to developing strong relationships: setting clear standards, expecting the best, paying attention, personalizing recognition, telling the story, celebrating together, and setting the example. The working relationships that have developed in schools and across the Delta School District have been supported by paying close attention to these seven essentials, particularly while engaging in collaborative inquiry processes. When surveyed following various professional learning activities, staff in Delta frequently report that they truly enjoy their work and feel engaged as professionals. Their comments often attributed this to the working relationships they have with one another, describing that there are greater levels of social and professional capital among educators than there was prior to the creation of the vision, and the resulting professional learning and opportunities for collaborative inquiry. They also express greater pride and a stronger sense of positive morale from working within a professional learning culture, which has enhanced their sense of professionalism.

Feedback from the district vision reflection process that took place in 2016, at the halfway mark of Vision 2020, indicated that collaborative inquiry and flexibility in structures within school schedules have allowed educators to focus on student learning and on strategies for improvement. Opportunities for continuous professional learning that focus on developing instructional practice and collaborative inquiry have allowed real-time professional practice to change and improve. Over the decade following the 2011 visioning process, staff identified that a strong culture of professional learning emerged. Ken Leithwood suggests that "continuous learning in the interests of improving the success of all students becomes a foundational premise of the organization's culture" (Leithwood, 2013, p. 21).

District leaders in Delta have intentionally worked to facilitate opportunities for schools to network together, to share their learning, to create shared pedagogical innovations, and to build a collaborative culture among teachers, school leaders, parents, and students. Additionally, they have worked together to identify constraints that might prevent them from being able to improve their work and the learning outcomes for students. Once that was determined, staff worked together to make suggestions and devised solutions to the constraints. They have made their exemplary practice visible across the system through various tools for sharing their learning, which will be discussed in greater detail in chapter 10, and was referred to previously in chapter 7. District teachers and leaders have also had the privilege of sharing their own learning through various presentations at conferences and some of the tools for sharing have been highlighted in articles published in educational journals.

Teachers and leaders in Delta have taken on the responsibility of developing quality curriculum resources together and have engaged in professional learning that has impacted their instructional practice in the classroom. Through all of this work, staff have made huge investments of professional and social capital with one another. The culture that has evolved in the school district is a much stronger culture of learning and the relationships between the educators have been strengthened through this collaborative work. Powerful stories of shared learning have been told by staff across the district, illuminating their professionalism and pride. Leadership among staff and students is developing and emerging in every school, while district leaders continue to support the great work that is happening in each school across the district. One example of how inquiry learning and improvement is celebrated is the Inquiry celebration, which is held annually at the end of the school year. Each school highlights their focus of inquiry for the school year. This has been done in a variety of forms, including a district open house where attendees are able to observe story boards describing a school's inquiry journey, and on one occasion a movie theater was rented and participants watched short video clips describing the inquiries that took place across the district's schools. These networking sessions and the storytelling that took place contributed to the creation of a culture of innovative practices through networking and storytelling.

> One of the biggest changes in Delta that I have seen has been toward a more hands-on-learning approach to teaching and students being more engaged—where teachers are the facilitators of learning. For the first time in my career in Delta many teachers are leading the way with innovative teaching practices. The district has supported teachers to engage in inquiry regarding their teaching practice, and become more innovative and cutting edge. We used to be the little district that followed the lead of other districts. But now Delta has become the little district that is leading the way in innovative teaching and inquiry

mindedness. Teachers are adapting to 21st-century teaching and changing to meet the needs of their students.

Todd Clarke, secondary school teacher

Survey feedback from Delta's parent community has shown that they too have embraced the importance of the collaborative inquiry work that teachers are engaged in and they have expressed appreciation for the opportunity to hear about the important professional learning taking place across the district and in schools. When parents are aware of what staff are learning and why they are engaged in that learning, and if they see a positive impact on student learning, mutual support develops. Staff frequently share the vision and goals at parent meetings, in schools, and at the District Parent Advisory Committee (DPAC), asking for input to inquiry questions. Engaging parents in the process of vision development, vision reflection, and goal development has been an integral part of the work since the beginning of the vision process in 2011, and the contributions made by parents continues to help drive some inquiries that lead to improved outcomes for learners.

LESSONS LEARNED

- *Positive and supportive relationships are critical to the work done in school districts.* These relationships include within schools, between schools, between the district and schools, as well as with parents, the local community, and the Ministry of Education. Relationships and connectedness at all levels in a system are important and as such, they need to be nurtured and attended to.
- *A key foundational element of all relationships is trust* and this is built through getting to know others, responding to needs in a timely manner, being curious, and listening carefully.
- *Providing time for collaboration* (at all levels in the system) *is a key foundation of creating good communication and strong relationships.* Trust is developed through quality discourse that occurs while engaged in collaborative inquiry. Discussions related to student learning should not, however, be deferred until trust is built. Rather, trust is built through conversations related to improved outcomes for learners.
- *"Find your person" and become a champion for the learning of others.* Finding another person to be your learning companion can make a huge difference to your professional learning. Supporting the learning journey of others serves as a catalyst to development. Create professional and social capital through collaborative inquiry and engagement.

- ***Learning cultures emerge from relationships between educators as they engage in professional learning***, inquiry, and doing complex work together.
- ***Learning Conversations matter!*** Listen to the dialogue in your school and district and comment when you notice conversations are changing for the better and becoming learner focused.

CONNECTING YOUR LEARNING

1. Conversations build trust. In your context, what opportunities exist for conversations related to student and adult learning?
2. How are teachers and leaders in your school/district supported in ensuring learning conversations with their staff take place?
3. What formal opportunities are offered to ensure co-planning and collaboration are the norm?
4. Who is/are your learning companion(s)? Who do you feel safe with engaging in conversations related to student learning?

Chapter 10

Focus on Sharing the Learning across Schools and Districts

While working toward achieving the vision, we were able to identify a 10th characteristic that is paramount for the realization of district-wide transformation and of becoming a strong district. In addition to the nine characteristics of strong districts described in Ken Leithwood's research, we believe it is essential that professionals find ways to *share their learning* in order to achieve networked horizontal connectedness. It is critical for schools and school districts to share stories of successes (and failures) to help increase shared knowledge and to strengthen collective efficacy among educators.

In the book *Rethinking Educational Leadership: From Improvement to Transformation* (2009), John West-Burnham cites storytelling as the number one strategy that is relevant in the context of transformation. "Because much of the work of a transformational leader involves storytelling and the conscious use of metaphors, those who would lead transformation must seek experiences that get them outside the world of education" (Schlechty, 2009, p. 267). According to Michael Fullan (2002), "creating and sharing knowledge is central to effective leadership. Information, of which we have a glut, only becomes knowledge through a *social* process" (p. 18).

The Delta School District has embraced the philosophy of storytelling and knowledge sharing. Once the district vision was created in 2011, a variety of structures were created to allow sharing and networking to occur across the district. Initially, a website called 180 Days of Learning was created (https://deltalearns.ca/180daysoflearning/). For the first 5 years of Vision 2020, teachers, students, and district leaders shared one story of learning on social media for each day of the school year. In the first few years of sharing what they had been learning, several powerful stories were highlighted each week. This website for sharing served to encourage risk-taking and networking across schools, districts, and countries. Recently, there has also been an increased reliance on Twitter (now known as X) as another social medium for

Delta teachers, vice-principals, and principals to share professional learning across Delta schools and beyond. Once the 180 Days of Learning site was a part of the culture in the district, a second sharing site was created. Delta Learns (https://deltalearns.ca) is an open-source, "one-stop shop" that was created for Delta educators but it is available to anyone. Here, educators are able to access blogs, create groups, and share resources. Perhaps most importantly, there is a toolkit for innovative teaching and learner success where educators can find a wealth of resources related to:

- Powerful Practices
- Powerful Learning
- Communicating Student Learning
- Assessment for Learning
- Teacher Mentoring
- Technology for Teaching and Learning
- Indigenous Education
- Antiracism
- Decision-Making Skills
- Outdoor Learning
- Staff Health and Wellness
- Career Education
- Kindergarten Resources
- Physical Literacy
- Numeracy
- Inclusive Learning
- Literacy

In addition to these valuable sites for sharing, there is an online learning site for assessment for learning (https://deltalearns.ca/afl/) called *Just One Thing*, consisting of learning modules where educators can learn more about Formative Assessment knowledge, skills, and strategies. This site offers an interactive platform that supports a district-wide focus on assessment designed to deepen educators' knowledge and practice in assessment.

Fullan states "a norm of sharing one's knowledge with others is the key to continual growth for all" (2002, p. 18). One way the Delta School District supports Fullan's findings is by participating in the Network of Inquiry and Indigenous Education (NOIIE). "NOIIE is a voluntary network of inquiry-based schools and school districts in British Columbia, with partner networks around the world. Using an inquiry-oriented, evidence-based approach to learning and teaching through the *Spiral of Inquiry*, teams work toward improving outcomes for all learners in their settings and submit case studies to share their progress in a spirit of generosity, curiosity, and growth" (http://noii.ca).

NOIIE was the inspiration of Dr. Judy Halbert and Dr. Linda Kaser, two prominent educators from British Columbia, who have served as consultants and longtime critical friends to the Delta School District. Over the years they have presented many professional learning sessions within the district. Research has shown that having external input is essential to system growth and development (Costa & Kallick,1993; Gurr & Huerta, 2013). There is a fine balance between relying on the expertise within the system and introducing new thinking based on external knowledge. Without new thoughts and ideas, a system runs the risk of stagnating. Dr. Halbert and Dr. Kaser have served to elevate the thinking in the district by introducing international research and knowledge to the professional learning taking place across the Delta School District, and by encouraging the district to participate in international research projects.

Another example of how the Delta School District encourages learning across schools is by arranging visits to other schools for school leaders. Arranged by the superintendent's office, each month, principals, vice-principals, and district leaders receive a formal invitation to visit a colleague's school. Leaders are given permission to leave their site for a half day and attend another school. Often, they are given specific questions to address during their visits that are related to themes such as promoting the district vision, school and district goals, or the themes of the *Schools as Learning Organizations* framework. The school visits are extremely popular with staff. To encourage the joy of learning at the next principal and vice-principal meeting, a draw for a prize is held for those who participated in the school visits during that month. This is a fun, low cost, and highly effective way of promoting networking and sharing across schools. It also serves to reduce competition between schools and enhance positive relationships and networking between leaders who might not otherwise know one another. Knowing more about each other's schools also makes leadership transfers between schools a smoother transition.

A third key action that has provided networking opportunities across school districts in British Columbia, and across countries, has been the willingness of the Delta School District to do presentations while their work was still in the process of being developed, rather than waiting until the work was fully completed. The *Spiral of Inquiry* makes it abundantly clear that the work in schools and districts is never fully completed. Continuously scanning, focusing, taking action, and checking ensure that schools and districts are constantly engaged in continuous improvement. Delta School District staff have done presentations at multiple conferences, with the intent of sharing the learning and demonstrating the value of beginning with a shared vision and engaging in collaborative inquiry as powerful professional learning. They have shared their learning on several occasions at British Columbia School Superintendents Association (BCSSA) conferences and other conferences across Canada and the United States. Also, district work was shared at the 2014 Organization for Economic Co-operation and Development (OECD) in Paris, France, at the ULead Conference in Banff, Alberta, and at the 2016 Learning Forward Annual Conference in Vancouver, BC. Staff from the Delta School District have also done presentations at the International Congress for School Effectiveness and Improvement (ICSEI) in Ottawa, Singapore, Stavanger, and, during the early phase of the pandemic, several ICSEI presentations were made virtually.

In addition to sharing the actions being taken in the district and in schools at conferences, Delta continues to host international contingencies from a wide variety of countries. Because knowledge creation and sharing are critical to educational improvement, sharing the work nationally and internationally and learning from other jurisdictions is a high priority for the district. One of the first visitors hosted in the Delta School District was Dr. Ben Jensen, from Learning First in Australia. His visit to Delta was part of the preparation for Learning First's *Beyond PD: Teacher Professional Learning in High-Performing Systems* (2016), which shows how British Columbia, Hong Kong, Shanghai, and Singapore dramatically improved teaching—and how the rest of the world can learn from them. Since that time, educators from Wales, England, Sweden, Switzerland, Australia, Denmark, the United States, and New Zealand, to name just a few, have visited Delta to discuss the inquiry framework and to learn from the district. These international delegations are welcomed to Delta because the opportunity for two-way learning is viewed as incredibly valuable for everyone involved.

An example of the international influence one school system can have on another occurred in 2017 when a school principal and two teachers from Delta were invited to Australia to share important learning that had taken place in their school. Once they returned from that experience, they shared with teachers and leaders what they had learned while visiting and presenting their work. This is an excellent example of the Delta School District firmly supporting knowledge creation and sharing within and across schools, districts, the province, and internationally. Michael Fullan supports this philosophy of creating and sharing knowledge within the education community:

> Creating and sharing knowledge is central to effective leadership. Information, of which we have a glut, only becomes knowledge through a *social* process. For this reason, relationships and professional learning communities are essential. Organizations must foster knowledge giving as well as knowledge seeking. We

endorse continual learning when we say that individuals should constantly add to their knowledge base—but there will be little to add if people are not sharing. A norm of sharing one's knowledge with others is the key to continual growth for all. (Fullan, 2002)

An example of the connections and impact that the school district has made internationally is evident within Delta's International Student Program where Vision 2020 was used to promote the district with countries around the world. The values, mission, and vision of the district caught the attention of educators internationally, and sparked conversations globally.

LEVERAGING THE *SPIRAL OF INQUIRY*

During the first 5 years of Vision 2020, by *engaging in new learning* and *taking action*, the district had learned a great deal. The halfway point of Vision 2020 was a natural time to engage in a *checking* process to see if, in fact, a positive difference was being made. The district engaged in a deep examination of how the district was doing with respect to achieving vision 2020. In the Spring of 2016, the district began a formal process to assess progress related to all parts of the vision and the goals that had emanated from the original process.

> The appreciative inquiry method of gathering input to the initial vision helped to establish a very positive culture in the district and created a sense of hope around the vision itself. Five years after the vision was initially conceived it became time to check our progress and ask if we were on the right track. It was good to see that the vision had created a sense of trust that people could be candid about areas where challenges remained and yet the confidence in the vision and the process remained unchanged. Trustees are dependent upon stakeholder input and it is my observation that success isn't just about the result but is dependent upon *how* you go about something (your process).
>
> Laura Dixon, Delta Board of Education trustee

The review process titled *"How Are We Doing? Vision Review 2016"* was launched using various creative feedback mechanisms, including Twitter (now known as X) and other social media platforms, as well as surveys to gather information and data about what was going well and what required further action and attention in the district. The *Spiral of Inquiry* was an essential part of the vision review process. Using the information gathered during this process would help refocus the attention on the areas requiring greater emphasis through the creation of specific, intentional goals and actions. In

92   *Chapter 10*

addition, the same graphic artist who captured Vision 2020 created a visual image from the review process that provided descriptors for both schools and the district as to what achieving Vision 2020 would look like, as shown in figure 10.1.

Of particular interest was the feedback from the vision review process that indicated:

- With respect to the central vision statement—*The Delta School District is a Leading District of Innovative Teaching and Learner Success*—81% of respondents agreed or strongly agreed that the district was working well toward achieving the vision, while 13% replied that they did not know if the district was working well toward the vision (see figure 10.2).
- The feedback on the Delta School District Values: *Caring, Respect, Responsibility, Community and Excellence*, depicted in figure 10.3, showed that most respondents agreed or strongly agreed that these values were being demonstrated across the district.
- Under the vision theme of *Our Schools Nurture Caring Relationships, Connections, and a Sense of Belonging* (see figures 10.4a, 10.4b, and 10.4c), between 86 and 95% of participants agreed or strongly agreed. Students were noticed to be experiencing a strong degree of caring relationships, connections, and a sense of belonging within the three subtheme statements of Vision 2020.
- Within the theme of *Students Are Engaged and Develop a Lifelong Passion for Learning* (see the bottom of figure 10.5) an aggregated total

Figure 10.1.   Vision 2020 Review Graphic 2016. *Delta School District*

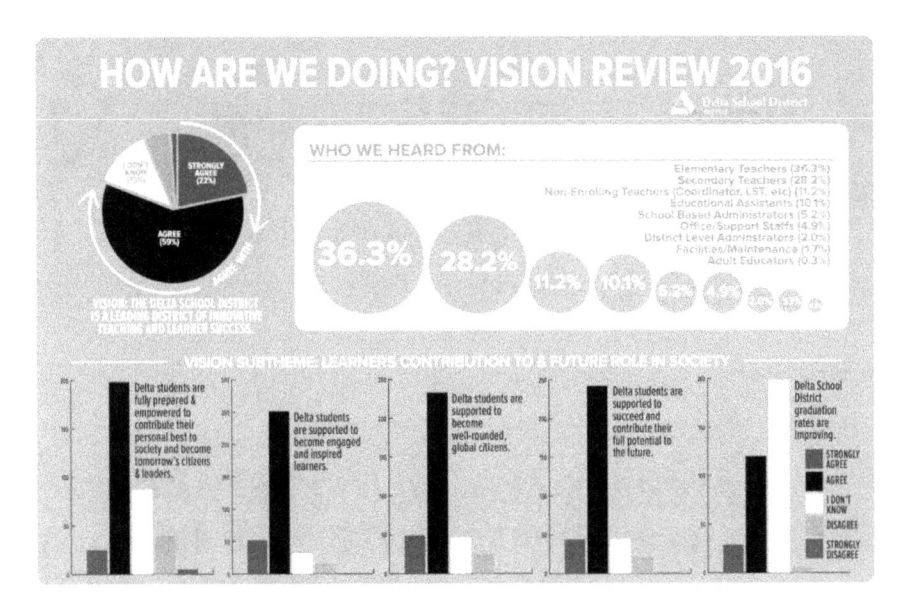

Focus on Sharing the Learning across Schools and Districts 93

Figure 10.2. Vision Review Graphic One 2016. *Delta School District*

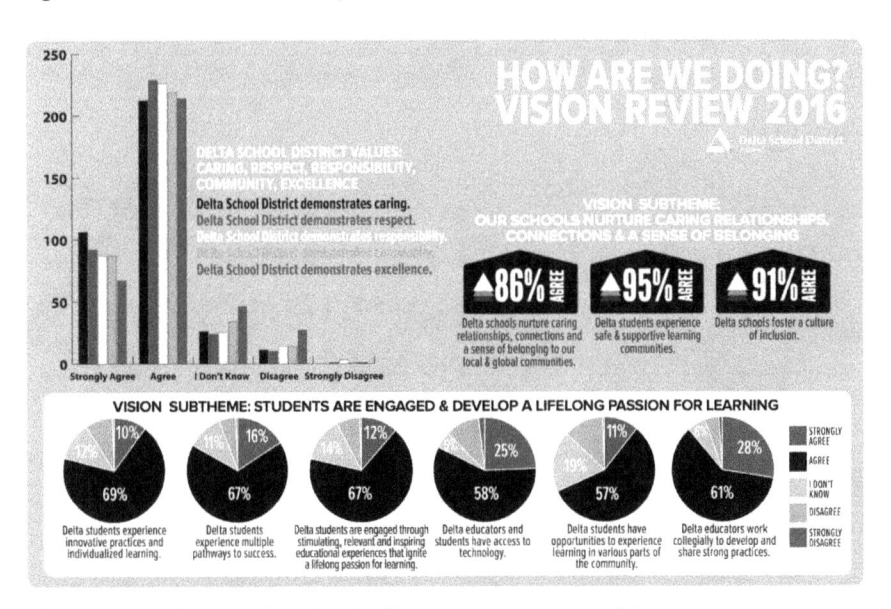

Figure 10.3. Vision Review Graphic Two 2016. *Delta School District*

of roughly 80% of respondents agreed or strongly agreed with five of the six different vision subtheme statements. The subtheme that rated highest was *Delta Educators work collegially to develop and share strong practices* (89%). The subtheme that rated the lowest was *Delta Students*

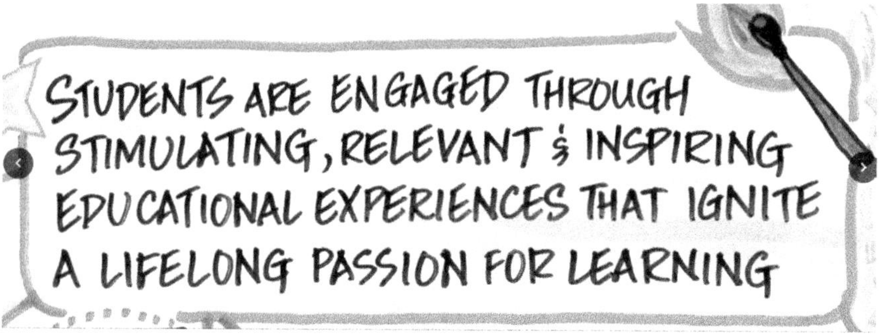

> STUDENTS ARE ENGAGED THROUGH STIMULATING, RELEVANT & INSPIRING EDUCATIONAL EXPERIENCES THAT IGNITE A LIFELONG PASSION FOR LEARNING

Figure 10.4a

> LEARNERS ARE FULLY PREPARED + EMPOWERED TO CONTRIBUTE THEIR PERSONAL BEST TO SOCIETY & BECOME TOMORROW'S CITIZENS & LEADERS

Figure 10.4b

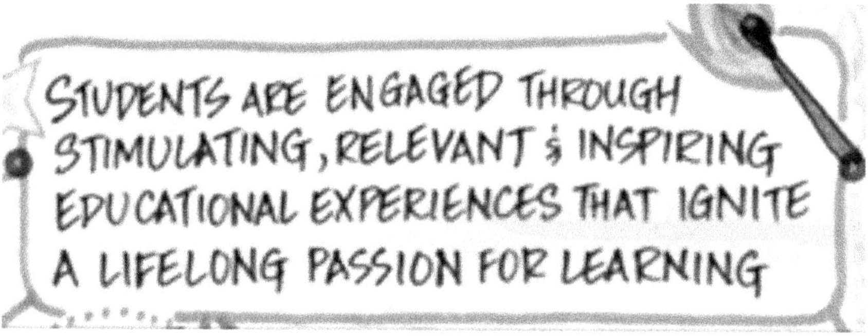

> STUDENTS ARE ENGAGED THROUGH STIMULATING, RELEVANT & INSPIRING EDUCATIONAL EXPERIENCES THAT IGNITE A LIFELONG PASSION FOR LEARNING

Figure 10.4c. Three Themes of Vision 2020. *Delta School District*

have opportunities to experience learning in various parts of the community (68%). Since this finding, educators have worked hard to develop outdoor learning opportunities, including examples where kindergarten classes that spend one day a week learning outside, classes starting with a focused outdoor "walk and talk," and students spending part of their time tending to school gardens.

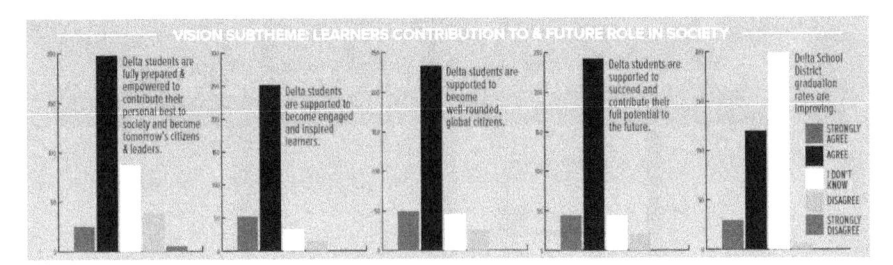

Focus on Sharing the Learning across Schools and Districts   95

Figure 10.5.   Summary of the Vision 2020 Subtheme Midway Check (2016). *Delta School District*

- When examining the results for *Learners Contribution to and Future Role in Society* (see figure 10.5), one subtheme emerged as a concern. Many respondents did not know if the Delta School District graduation rates were improving. This provided much needed feedback on the importance of providing regular communication in the area of student achievement results. Graduation rates were in fact improving in all areas, but people were not aware of that fact.

In addition, staff were asked to post on Twitter (now X) what they believed had been the greatest accomplishments since the initiation of Vision 2020. Figure 10.6 captures the key themes of their responses.

A powerful graphic (see figure 10.7), created by the artist who documented the vision initially, captured a summary of the midway check-in of Vision 2020.

This graphic summary captures the successes along the bottom of the image, as well as the strengths and challenges related to each of the three themes of Vision 2020: *students are engaged, learners are fully prepared and empowered,* and *our schools nurture caring relationships.* It clearly shows that 5 years into Vision 2020, the district had much to celebrate, but it also outlined the many challenges that still existed. Of critical importance is that once this check-in process was complete, the resulting data rallied the district into action to address some of the key areas that still needed attention, such as reporting practices that did not align with current assessment practices, as well as the challenges of meeting the needs of diverse learners (which was also seen as a strength).

Once the data and information were reviewed and shared, there was a renewed commitment to continue focusing on the themes and subthemes already showing success. The data also helped to place an emphasis on putting more resources and more intentional actions toward improving themes and subthemes that would require additional attention to achieve the goals of the vision. For example, a subtheme that was identified as needing greater

96   Chapter 10

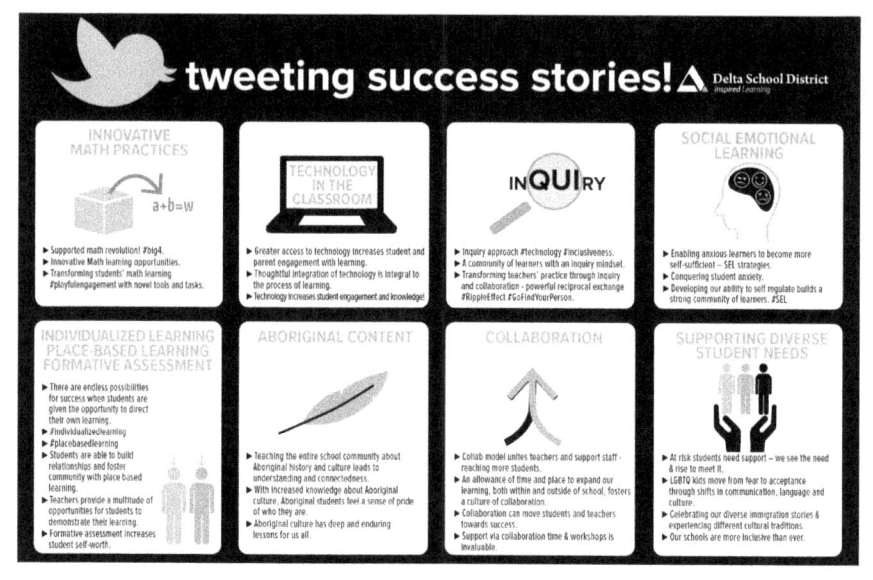

Figure 10.6. **Staff Twitter Posts.** *Delta School District*

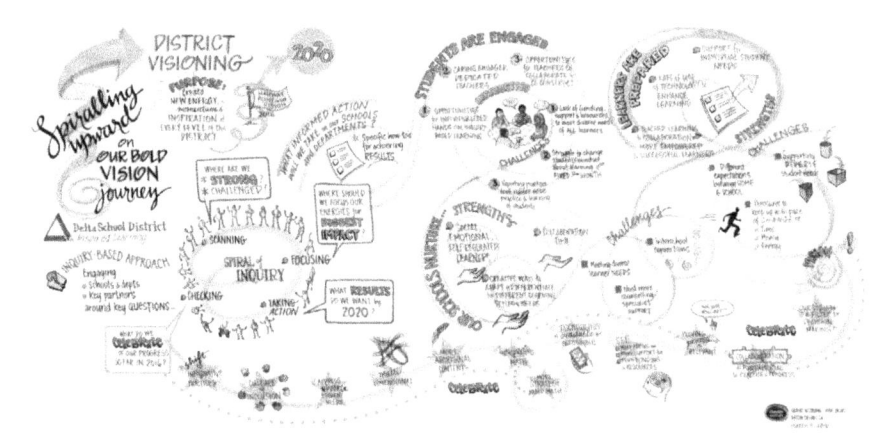

Figure 10.7. **Strengths and Challenges of Vision 2020 (2016).** *Delta School District*

attention was the lack of opportunities for learning to take place beyond the walls of the school. Engaging in this midway *checking* phase was critical as it led the district right back into the *scanning, focusing, developing a hunch,* and *learning* phases that are essential in the *Spiral of Inquiry*. Some of these actions are described in the next sections of the book.

LESSONS LEARNED

- *Sharing what we have learned helps us to engage with our own knowledge in a more meaningful, deeper way*, thus strengthening our understanding of what we have learned.
- *Networking encourages us to be receptive to feedback* while sharing what we have learned helps build collective efficacy across the system.
- *Storytelling has a way of becoming transformational.* Sharing our knowledge and telling stories that demonstrate key takeaways are crucial to continual growth for all, not to mention that storytelling is a key principle of learning for First Peoples.
- Sharing what we have learned, by using the *Spiral of Inquiry* as a framework, helps us understand that *our learning is never complete,* that *it is continuous,* and *is iterative in nature.*
- *Doing a formal check-in part way through* the 10-year cycle, and sharing what has been learned during that time, *helps to refocus the attention on areas that require more support* and intentional resource allocation.
- If improvement is to be actualized, *student achievement data needs to be shared widely and celebrated or*, if needed, *acted upon.*

CONNECTING YOUR LEARNING

1. In your context, how are the stories of school and district improvement told? How is your school/district sharing stories of success with staff, the district, and the public?
2. Is student achievement data widely shared? How do you celebrate improvement? How do you act upon areas of concern?
3. What opportunities exist for educators in your context to network with staff in other schools? If this is not happening, what steps might be taken to develop cross-school (or cross-district) networking?
4. Are indicators of success toward improvement made available beyond your context? If so, how?
5. What structure(s) are you using to share data?

Chapter 11

Connections to Other Research

Although part 1 has focused extensively on the research of Dr. Kenneth Leithwood and the nine characteristics he shares as being essential for strong districts, it is important to note that the learning that has taken place in the Delta School District aligns with, and has been supported by, the work of many other researchers that have not been elaborated on in this book. Included among those researchers are Fullan and Quinn (2016); Hargreaves (2018); Katz, Earl, and Ben Jaaffar (2009); Donohoo and Velasco (2016); Butler, Schnellert, and MacNeil (2015); Campbell et al. (2016); Harris (2011); Breakspear (2016a and 2016b); and McGregor, Halbert, and Kaser (January, 2022) to name just a few. We believe that now, more than ever, the work of national and international researchers is aligning—a phenomenon that is likely due to the advances of social media, virtual meetings, conferences, and podcasts, and the fact that research can be shared around the globe almost instantaneously.

The story of the change process that has taken place in the Delta School District aligns well with the framework necessary for system-wide change presented in Fullan and Quinn's book *Coherence* (2016). According to Fullan and Quinn, four+ components must be present to allow for systemic change. These include:

- **Focusing Direction:** "establish a focused direction that engages everyone with shared moral purpose, a small number of goals, a clear strategy for achieving them and change leadership that mobilizes action" (p. 48).
- **Cultivating Collaborative Cultures:** "Collaborating is not just about creating a place where people feel good but rather about cultivating the expertise of everyone to be focused on a collective purpose" (p. 75).
- **Deepening Learning:** "We must shift to a deeper understanding of the process of learning and how we can influence it. This requires knowledge-building partnerships for everyone engaged" (p. 108).

- **Securing Accountability:** "The most direct way of understanding what is needed for internal accountability is to work diligently on . . . focusing direction, cultivating collaborative cultures and deepening the learning" (p. 124). "The best approach for securing accountability is to develop conditions that maximize 'internal accountability' and reinforce internal accountability with external accountability" (p. 126).
- **"+" Leadership:** "Leaders influence the group, but they also learn from it. Joint learning is what happens in effective change processes" (p. 138). "One of the marks of an effective leader is not only the impact they have on the bottom line of student achievement but also equally how many good leaders they leave behind" (p. 138).

In Delta there are examples of each of the key dimensions described by Fullan and Quinn. The district's Bold Vision is a clear example of how *Focusing Direction* can positively impact transformation. In addition, the work the district has done to align the 31 school Frameworks for Enhancing Student Learning (FESL) with the district's FESL has provided alignment and has allowed for strongly focused energy on goals that were established based on the needs of the learners.

When considering the dimension of *Cultivating Collaborative Cultures*, it is important to note the Delta School District has demonstrated that ensuring collaboration time during the school day for teachers to network and discuss their practice is a critical factor in transformational change. The schools where collaboration time was introduced with a clear, shared understanding of the purpose and a formal, predictable structure was created have demonstrated significant improvement in curricular planning, instructional strategies, and assessment practices. Further, the district has expanded the collaborative cultures to include school and district leaders with time set aside each month at principals' meetings to allow for deeper collaboration and networking to occur among school vice-principals and principals.

The Delta School District has had a long-term focus on Fullan and Quinn's third dimension, *Deepening Learning.* Fullan and Quinn (2016) stress that this involves establishing clear learning goals. From the start of Vision 2020 the district has consistently had a clear intention of developing this element across the district. In fact, following the vision process in 2011 there was a 3-year sustained professional learning focus on assessment for learning, with the 1st of the 3 years concentrating on the importance of setting clear learning targets (in classroom lessons as well as with school and district goals). It is interesting to note that although the district had been focusing on assessment for learning for many years prior to the vision, the one thing that made the biggest difference to teacher practice in Delta was revising the report card template to a communicating student learning (CSL) document that embeds the tenets of the redesigned BC curriculum and the elements of effective assessment. This, more than any other professional learning opportunity on assessment offered to date, served to advance stronger pedagogy in the area of assessment. Fullan cites the importance of precision in pedagogy that aligns with the district's well-established long-term goal of expanding educator knowledge related to curriculum, instruction, and assessment. Delta's work related to communicating student learning aligns with Fullan's notion of precision in pedagogy. Finally, deepening the learning makes reference to shifting practice through building teacher capacity. From the inception of the vision, this has been a goal of the district with positions being developed (such as the coordinators of inquiry; Curriculum, Instruction, and Assessment Learning teams; professional literacy communities; teacher mentoring) to create opportunities for teacher leadership. School vice-principals and principals are talking specifically and in-depth about ways to continuously build teacher capacity as well as how to enhance teacher leadership.

Fullan and Quinn's fourth dimension for coherence is *Securing Accountability*. Specifically, they refer to internal and external accountability. "Internal accountability occurs when individuals and groups willingly take on personal, professional, and collective responsibility for continuous improvement and success for all students (p. 110). Delta School District's use of Halbert and Kaser's *Spiral of Inquiry* has provided a consistent framework that has helped build teacher ownership of student learning needs. Helen Timperley's practice of reflecting on "Who Is My Class?" (Timperley, 2011) expands on the levels of the system and encourages educators to consider who is responsible for the learning of students, teachers, school leaders, and district leaders. Every individual who works within the school system has a set of learners that they are responsible for, and should consider their learners' needs through the lens of the *Spirals of Inquiry*.

> Teachers, leaders and facilitators of professional learning must know 'their class' in all its diversity if they are to be successful in promoting student, teacher and leader learning. Policy officials have classes that are even more complex and diverse than others but nowhere in the system is it more important to know one's class. Without this knowledge, the most likely outcome is for policy officials to be left wondering why the implementation of their carefully developed policies does not resemble what was intended and does not have the desired impact. (Timperley, 2011, p. 174)

Educators in Delta at every level have embraced the notion of continuous professional learning with the goal of improving the educational outcomes of all students. Fullan and Quinn state "External accountability is when system leaders reassure the public through transparency, monitoring, and selective interventions that their system is performing in line with societal expectations and requirements" (2016, p. 111). We fully concur with Fullan and Quinn's assertion that internal accountability must *precede* external accountability. Focusing on internal accountability first is demonstrated throughout Delta's vision and inquiry processes.

Fullan and Quinn's final key dimension of systemic change is *Leadership*. They emphasize "it takes the group to change the group, and it takes many leaders to change the group" (p. 123). The district has embraced this notion and is working hard to develop leadership at all levels throughout the system. This is why the district has created a multifaceted, differentiated approach to leadership development—the *Leading the Learning* series previously described in chapter 8. Anecdotal evidence suggests that the district's efforts are making a difference. Professional conversations have deepened over the past 10 years with teachers, vice-principals, and principals talking about curriculum, instruction, and assessment at a level of understanding not previously seen. Fullan and Quinn (2016) would likely attribute this success to Delta's central office staff focusing on investing in internal accountability and projecting and protecting the system (p. 126). "The more that internal accountability thrives, the greater the responsiveness to external requirements and the less the externals have to do" (p. 126). This has certainly proven to be the case in the Delta School District. Focusing on improvement for all learners, and especially for the most vulnerable, has resulted in improved outcomes with regard to graduation and school completion rates. This focus on internal accountability has allowed external accountability to take on a different approach.

Little improvement can be generated at the system level until a mindset of collective efficacy exists within schools. Donohoo (2017) makes the case that "Collective beliefs about the staff's efficacy to motivate and promote learning affect the types of learning environments created in schools and the teaching behaviours exhibited by staff" (p. 13). It makes sense that when staff members feel confident in their ability to positively impact student learning, they will then have faith in their ability to share their learning across schools and districts. John Hattie states, "When you fundamentally believe you can make the difference, and then you feed it with the evidence you are—then that is dramatically powerful" (2016). The Delta School District has been leveraging the current research related to collective efficacy and Hattie's (2016) finding that collective efficacy has an effect size of 1.57 on student achievement. Donohoo's book *Collective Efficacy* (2017) has been used as a book study in principal and vice-principal meetings, and Jenni Donohoo was the featured speaker for 2 years at the District Principals and Vice-Principals Fall Conference, furthering the dialogue about collective efficacy in Delta.

LESSONS LEARNED

- *Staying abreast of the current research in education is critical.* Too often there is a disconnect between research and practice. Being aware of how research can positively inform practice in schools and districts will ultimately result in improved outcomes for learners.
- *Collective efficacy matters!* Providing opportunities for educators at all levels to work together to make an impact is incredibly powerful. Success breeds success.
- *Ensure learning is occurring at every level of the system!* If continuous improvement is to become the norm, then everyone within the system needs to be a curious questioner who is constantly learning. This includes students, educators, and school and district leaders.

CONNECTING YOUR LEARNING

1. What research are you paying attention to and why? How is research impacting your practice? How are you sharing your learning with others?
2. How does the research that you are reading directly relate to the learning goals for your students?
3. Are you engaged in action research? If so, how are you sharing your findings?
4. Who are you currently learning with? Are you a part of a team of collaborative learners? If not, what steps might you take to create a professional learning team?

Part 1 has focused extensively on the foundational elements that research has shown make a school district strong. Delta's Vision 2020 was launched in 2011 and work began straightaway on achieving it. When Leithwood's paper came out in 2013 it provided a useful framework for the district and served as a valuable tool for helping to focus the steps required for Delta to truly become a strong district. Although the work of many researchers has provided input into helping shape district improvement in Delta, the key contributions that Dr. Leithwood, as well as Drs. Halbert and Kaser, have made to Delta are significant. Part 2 will focus on the impact of yet another key researcher, Dr. Louise Stoll, whose work in the area of schools as learning organizations has helped Delta move toward further improvement by providing a framework for strong schools.

PART 2

Schools as Learning Organizations

Chapter 12

Schools as Learning Organizations

Once the Delta School District ensured that all the elements of a strong school district were in place there was a recognition that, when considering the concept of overall systemness, the next step should be to introduce research related to the elements that would make schools in the district be the best learning environments possible. As is the iterative nature of inquiry, new learning often emerges at critical moments—especially when engaging with the *Spiral of Inquiry* at the *scanning* stage. When individuals are viewing their work from the perspective of inquiry, they are constantly considering "What do our learners (or in this case, the system) need?" While attending the International Congress for School Effectiveness and Improvement (ICSEI) conference in Singapore, an important connection was made that had a significant impact on the direction that the Delta School District was going to take next in achieving the district vision. Educational leaders from Delta attending the ICSEI conference met with Dr. Louise Stoll who, along with Marcus Kools, wrote the article "The School as a Learning Organisation: A Review Revisiting and Extending a Timely Concept" (2017) based on their working paper for the OECD (Kools & Stoll, 2016). Dr. Stoll gave an overview of her research and it piqued the curiosity of Delta's district leaders who then began to reflect on the work of the district through the lens of Kools and Stoll's paper, which formed the basis for the OECD (2016) guide for policy makers, school leaders, and teachers, *What Makes a School a Learning Organisation?*

This paper states:

> The concept of the learning organisation began to gain popularity in the late 1980s. While the literature is disparate, it is generally agreed that the learning organisation is a necessity, is suitable for any organisation and that an organisation's learning capability will be the only sustainable competitive advantage in the future. Most scholars see the learning organisation as a multi-level concept involving individual behaviour, teamwork, and organisation-wide practices and culture. A learning organisation is a place where the beliefs, values and norms of

employees are brought to bear in support of sustained learning; where a "learning atmosphere," "learning culture" or "learning climate" is nurtured; and where "learning to learn" is essential for everyone involved. (p. 1)

The OECD Guide for Policy Makers suggests that an integrated model of the *School as a Learning Organization* is based on seven key dimensions:

- developing and sharing a vision centered on the learning of all students;
- creating and supporting continuous learning opportunities for all staff;
- promoting team learning and collaboration among all staff;
- establishing a culture of inquiry, innovation, and exploration;
- embedding systems for collecting and exchanging knowledge and learning;
- learning with and from the external environment and larger learning system; and
- modeling and growing learning leadership (p. 1).

For each of these seven dimensions, there is a set of elements that further defines the seven dimensions (see figure 12.1. See appendix B for a description of the elements).

After meeting with Dr. Stoll and reading the research of Kools and Stoll, the *Spiral of Inquiry* was used as a framework to consider the most important learning needs of the Delta School District (see figure 12.2). As the school district had just completed multiple inquiries based on Leithwood's characteristics of a strong district, leaders determined, through using the *Spiral of Inquiry* scanning process, that it was now time to deepen the focus, specifically for the schools.

SPIRAL OF INQUIRY

As leaders, our *hunch* was that if the district created a common definition of what constituted a strong school, and if a common language could exist across all the schools in the district, then learning for staff, and thus students, would be improved. The belief was that there would be value in educators and leaders having a common, research-based framework to discuss the strengths and the needs of their schools. For formal school leaders who might be assigned to a particular school, the framework would help provide them with a better understanding of where their new school sites were at, and what they needed to focus on to ensure that the school continued on its journey to becoming a strong learning environment for student learning. Once the decision was made to use the *School as a Learning Organization* (SLO) model in

Schools as Learning Organizations

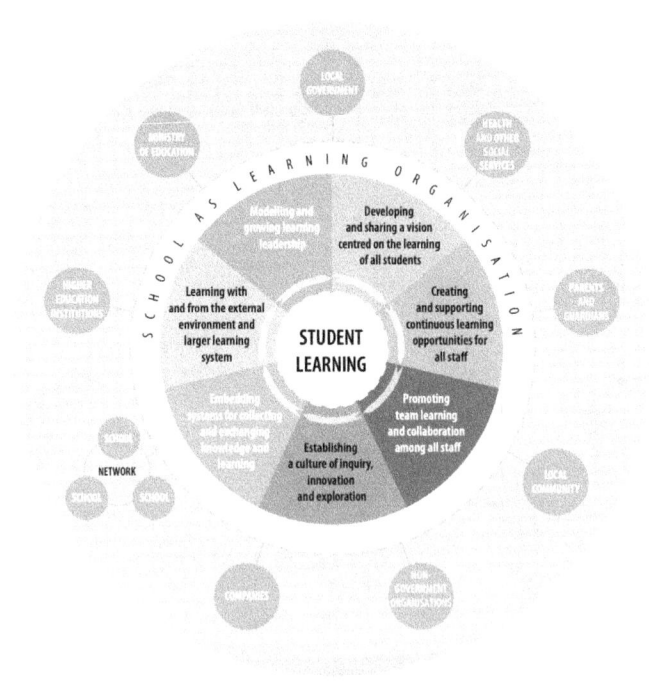

Figure 12.1. Schools as Learning Organizations Graphic (Kools & Stoll, 2016).

the Delta School District, Dr. Stoll was invited to become a critical friend and external advisor to the school district and provide her expertise and guidance on the next phase of the journey to achieve Vision 2020.

In the spring of 2018, district leaders began regular Skype conversations with Dr. Stoll and through those conversations a plan was established to introduce her seven dimensions of a *School as a Learning Organization* to school leaders. In August of 2018, Dr. Louise Stoll began her work with the Delta School District, visiting some schools and introducing her research to school leaders. At that annual August meeting of district and school leaders, Dr. Stoll discussed the background of the *School as a Learning Organization* (SLO) research and introduced the seven dimensions. She deepened the scope of the SLO research by working with the three directors of Delta's Learning Services Department, which comprise Inclusive Learning (often referred to as Special Education); Equity and Success (which includes Indigenous Learning); and Curriculum, Instruction, and Assessment. The goal of meeting with those department leaders was to consider the merits and applicability of the seven SLO dimensions within schools and within entire departments in the district. Over the 1st year of working with Dr Stoll, it became apparent that the seven dimensions of the SLO framework were a good fit to measure

the spiral of inquiry

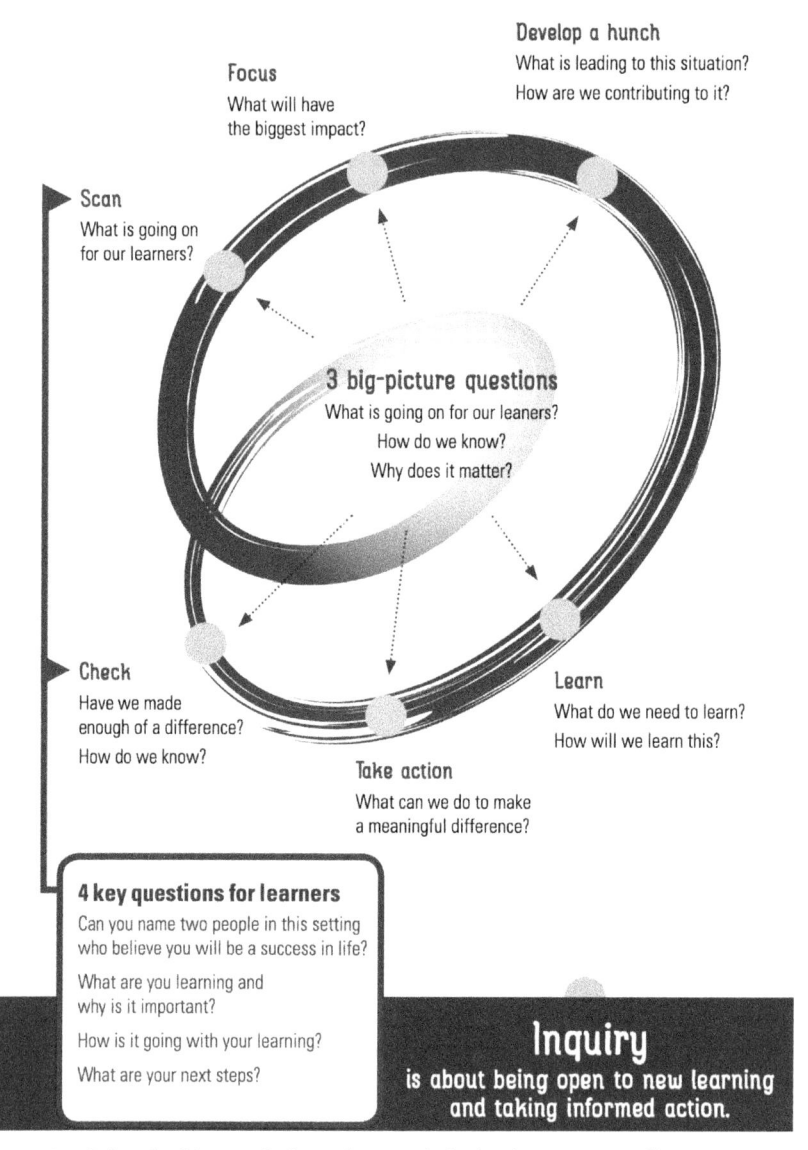

Focus
What will have the biggest impact?

Develop a hunch
What is leading to this situation?
How are we contributing to it?

Scan
What is going on for our learners?

3 big-picture questions
What is going on for our learners?
How do we know?
Why does it matter?

Check
Have we made enough of a difference?
How do we know?

Learn
What do we need to learn?
How will we learn this?

Take action
What can we do to make a meaningful difference?

4 key questions for learners
Can you name two people in this setting who believe you will be a success in life?
What are you learning and why is it important?
How is it going with your learning?
What are your next steps?

Inquiry is about being open to new learning and taking informed action.

Figure 12.2. Printed with permission: *The Spiral Playbook* (**Kaser & Halbert, 2017**).

Schools as Learning Organizations 111

not only schools as learning organizations, but also district departments as learning organizations.

During the 2018–2019 school year, the assistant superintendents devoted a significant portion of the monthly principal and vice-principal meetings to the SLO model. Initially, time was spent reading the Kools and Stoll article and learning what the seven dimensions were and then studying the specific elements of each dimension. Once the seven dimensions were well understood, school leaders were then asked to complete an assessment of their schools using the graphic organizer shown in figure 12.3.

School leaders were asked to consider each dimension and then rate their school as either red, amber, or green (RAG) within each of the dimensions. Green would mean they were proficient and red would indicate that they were beginning work in the area. Amber meant that although some progress had begun, more focus was still needed. Additionally, they were asked to provide supporting evidence for their ratings. School leaders were then asked to contemplate what else they might do as a leader to enhance and provide support for improvement in a particular dimension.

At a follow-up meeting, school leaders were organized into family-of-schools groupings, with the secondary school and each of the surrounding elementary feeder schools meeting together. The seven dimensions, with the descriptors of the elements, were placed on posters around the meeting room and teams of school leaders rotated through each station, carousel-style, to provide feedback on what RAG in a school setting would look like. Using that input, a draft rubric was created with descriptors of RAG for each dimension.

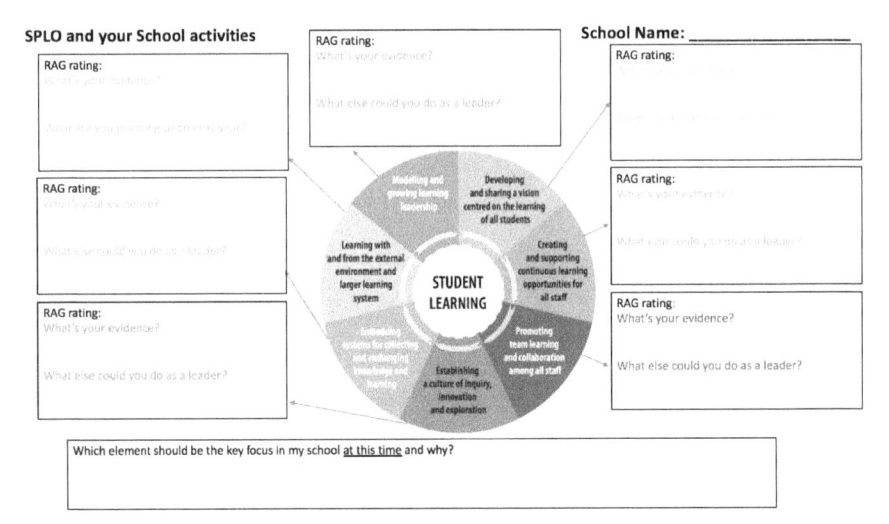

Figure 12.3. School as a Learning Organization Assessment Tool (OECD, 2016). *Kools and Stoll (2016)*

Table 12.1

DEVELOPING A SHARED VISION CENTERED ON THE LEARNING OF ALL STUDENTS

	RED	AMBER	GREEN
• A shared and inclusive vision aims to enhance the learning experiences and outcomes of all students • The vision focuses on a broad range of learning outcomes, encompasses both the present and the future, and is inspiring and motivating • Learning and teaching are oriented toward realizing the vision • Vision is the outcome of a process involving all staff • Student, parents, the external community, and other partners are invited to contribute to the school's vision	• No shared vision • Vision is not central to the decision-making process • Limited range of learning outcomes • Teaching and learning is not connected to the vision • Parents, staff, students not able to say what the vision is • The vision does not involve all students, families, cultures, and languages	• Vision evident but not contributed to by all parties • Not necessarily reviewed regularly • Learning outcomes evident but not tied to all students learning—more focus on high/low—lack of challenge for high achievers • Some teaching and learning is connected to the vision • Some stakeholders able to articulate the vision—but not all. Evidence of vision is available to some but not all • Visioning exercise more about "checking a box" rather than an authentic exercise • Vision developed "Top Down"	• Staff, students, and parents contributed to vision and process in place to continually review and adapt vision • Broad range of learning outcomes and tied to all students' learning • All learning and teaching is connected to the vision • Vision is evident in schools and class and can be reiterated by parents, staff, and students • Anyone in the school can talk freely about the vision and goals of the school and what they are doing to contribute • Including in an authentic way all families, cultures, and languages in the vision and school goals • "Buy-in" by all community members because they were a part of the process • Active revisitation of vision or goals to check for relevancy • Celebrating benchmarks toward the vision • Systems created to reflect, review, and refine

PROMOTING AND SUPPORTING CONTINUOUS PROFESSIONAL LEARNING FOR ALL STAFF

	RED	AMBER	GREEN
• All staff engage in continuous professional learning • New staff receive induction and mentoring support • Professional learning is focused on student learning and school goals • Staff are fully engaged in identifying the aims and priorities for their own professional learning • Professional learning challenges thinking as part of changing practice • Professional learning connects work-based learning and external expertise • Professional learning is based on assessment and feedback • Time and other resources are provided to support professional learning • The school's culture promotes and supports professional learning	• One-off, stand-alone professional development (Pro-D) not taken beyond the day • Lack of reflection on own practice • No in/formal connection to new staff • Working behind closed doors, no sharing of practice • Lack of risk taking in practice—the way we have always done it—unsafe, no trust • No consideration of impact of learning for students • Admin. involvement in collaboration seem as an accountability measure • Do not revisit decisions or initiatives for efficacy or value • Top down Pro-D, mandated by Admin. • Pro-D committee lip service • Lack of Pro-D committee	• Some staff engage in continuous professional learning • If directed/prompted—will reflect/share on own practice • Taking risks within their spaces • New staff need to ask or are not accessing mentorship opportunities (nothing embedded in culture) OR "old staff" are reluctant to mentor • Teachers hesitant to share growth or successes • Professional learning in silos • Limited teachers participating in professional learning committee and planning for continual yearlong learning • Ad hoc	• All staff engage in cohesive, collaborative professional learning • Ongoing—almost every day on their minds (not just Pro-D days) • Admin. provide safe environment for staff to take risks in trying new • Publicly sharing innovative practice—sharing ideas • Multiple ways of accessing professional development • Learning and collaboration continues beyond formal structure (release time) • Collaboration time is scheduled/built in • Professional learning embedded in daily routines • Staff is focused on gathering evidence (as a collective) of student learning • Development of growth plans • Personal, school is a collaborative process, i.e., critical friend

PROMOTING AND SUPPORTING CONTINUOUS PROFESSIONAL LEARNING FOR ALL STAFF	RED	AMBER	GREEN
			- Teachers stepping forward to actively lead Pro-D and share growth
- Abundance of teachers participating in Pro-D committee and planning-bottom up initiatives and learning
- Long-term planning and regular opportunities for everyone to have input
- Admin. having forethought to needs of professional learning and are very tied in to the process and willing to provide all resources requested
- Celebrating (K&G)
- Resources
- Modeling professional development for all teachers teaching to diversity

PROMOTING TEAM LEARNING AND COLLABORATION AMONG ALL STAFF

	RED	AMBER	GREEN
• Staff learn how to work together as a team • Collaborative working and collective learning—face-to-face and through information and communication technology (ICT)—are focused and enhance learning experiences and outcomes of students and/or staff practice • Staff feel comfortable turning to each other for consultation and advice • Trust and mutual respect are core values • Staff reflect together on how to make their own learning more powerful • The school allocates time and other resources for collaborative working and collective learning	• Silos created in community cliques on staff lack of committees • Focus on what is best for staff only—individual ICT • Collaboration time not accessed; limited time offered; time used to organize lessons • Core values not identified or valued • Reflection on own or not at all • Collaboration an "event" • No understanding of what collaboration means • Some colleagues lacking connection or colleagues to collaboration with • Peer policing of collaboration • Staff unaware of collaboration groups	• Some communication with little focus. Small pockets of teamwork led by strong personalities • Pretend/guess what ICT means • Core values not clearly defined or consistently adhered to • Reflect their learning on own or in smaller groups • Collaboration is a part of the weekly schedule but not always focused on student learning • Limited understanding of what collaboration means	• Collaborative structure to flatten hierarchy. Passion to collaborate. All voices are valued. Safe place to share. Embedded in culture • Rubric/exemplars for collaboration • Know what ICT means • Staff feel safe to grow • A conscious focus and effort to share the impact of collaboration of student learning • Trust • Sharing successes and growth of collaboration groups • Extending outside of the collaboration structure • Values live in thoughts and actions • Structures for collaboration time embedded in the schedule—and used for collaboration • Staff collaboratively reflect on their learning and student learning • Collaboration is part of how we exist • Collective understanding of collaboration

ESTABLISHING A CULTURE OF INQUIRY, EXPLORATION, AND INNOVATION	RED	AMBER	GREEN
• Staff want and dare to experiment and innovate in their practice • The school supports and recognizes staff for taking initiative and risks • Staff engage in forms of inquiry to investigate and extend their practice • Inquiry is used to establish and maintain a rhythm of learning, change, and innovation • Staff have open minds toward doing things differently • Problems and mistakes are seen as opportunities for learning • Students are actively engaged in inquiry	• No resiliency • Doing the same thing that has always been done • Culture of fear • Shame and blame • No student voice—students not engaged in the process of inquiry • "Mistakes" stop/stall progress and are seen as bad • Not flexible/fearful • (Reluctant) avoid sharing learning • Closed minded • No Sprints initiated • Lack of trust/confidence in research or initiatives	• Inquiry is happening but it may be individual—not collective • "Mistakes" are acknowledged, but not used as a tool for learning (they stall learning) • Pockets of inquiry—not connected—to goals—to others • Reluctant, but willing to change and try new things • Sharing learning when "asked" • Start "Sprints" but don't follow through or reflect on student needs	• A culture of innovation with supports in place • Student engaged actively • Teacher-led collaboration to improve practice • Teacher presenting/sharing publicly • Built-in collaboration—teachers collaborating and celebrating their collaboration • A safe environment • Being okay with failure/stretches • "Mistakes" are acknowledged, visible, and celebrated as part of the learning process • Inquiry is school-wide, connected—to goals—to others • Open-minded • Sharing learning is part of a regular day/week/month—happens naturally • Interest in seeing what others do • Celebration of successes • Short and long learning Sprints exist

EMBEDDING SYSTEMS FOR COLLECTING AND EXCHANGING KNOWLEDGE AND LEARNING

	RED	AMBER	GREEN
• Systems are in place to examine progress and gaps between current and expected impact • Examples of practice—good and bad—are made available to all staff to analyze • Sources of research evidence are readily available and easily accessed • Structures for regular dialogue and knowledge exchange are in place • Staff have the capacity to analyze and use multiple sources of data for feedback, including through ICT, to inform teaching and allocate resources • The school development plan is evidence-informed, based on learning from self-assessment, and updated regularly • The school regularly evaluates its theories of action, amending and updating them as necessary • The school evaluates the impact of professional learning	• Focus of professional learning Staff specific, rather than student driven • Little or no data collection • Not recognizing value of data collection/interpretation • No data, no timeline, no push/incentive to change • No connection between data and professional learning • No connection between theory and practice • Never in each other's classes to observe teaching • Little to no understanding on how to collect meaningful and authentic data	• Inconsistent collection of data • Data driving the hunch • Data collected and evaluated but it doesn't impact change • Some interest in research and how it impacts practice • Data shared—but no follow-up—not understood • Observe each other teaching—but does not translate into change in class—(without purpose)	• Providing access to "our schools" data • Teachers watching other teachers teach with purpose • Evidence informed/enhanced decision making • Embedded collaboration time, driven by evidence • Concerted move to meaningful data collection and analysis and creating new structures and a time line for change based on data collection • All professional learning is driven by data

LEARNING WITH AND FROM THE EXTERNAL ENVIRONMENT AND LARGER SYSTEM	RED	AMBER	GREEN
• The school scans its external environment to respond quickly to challenges and opportunities • The school is an open system, welcoming approaches from potential external collaborators • Partnerships are based on equality of relationships and opportunities for mutual learning • The school collaborates with parents/guardians and the community as partners in the education process and the organization of the school • Staff collaborate, learn, and exchange knowledge with peers in other schools through networks and/or school-to-school collaborations • The school partners with higher education institutions, businesses, and/or public or nongovernmental organizations in efforts to deepen and extend learning	• Insular as a school • Closed school, lacking connection to community • Classroom doors closed • Groups operating in silos • No collaboration • Not reaching out to district coordinators • Lack of confidence in external supports	• Limited connection to larger system or community • Limited collaboration within department • One-off Pro-D's/speakers/initiatives • Shallow focus of collaboration—instructional strategies • Being open to external supports • Pockets of staff reaching out	• Use of a website to communicate with community • Use of app to communicate • Work experience programs—business • Elementary school connections with secondary • Peer mentors making connections • School-to-school collaboration on joint topics • District programs/learning services connections linking and linking schools • Individual Education Plan (IEP) parent/teacher collaboration • Cross department/school collaboration • Place-based learning • Opportunities for input from stakeholders • Using our partners as resources for learning, i.e., police presentations and Delta Youth Mental Health presence

- ICT is widely used to facilitate communication, knowledge exchange, and collaboration with the external environment

- Bring in community expertise into class or taking classes out to community
- Participation in research projects with postsecondary
- Take advantage of opportunities to connect with external organizations quickly/ effectively
- Bringing in "experts" to share with parents
- Involve parents with the understanding of learning

MODELING AND GROWING LEARNING LEADERSHIP	RED	AMBER	GREEN
• School leaders model learning leadership, distribute leadership and help grow other leaders, including students • School leaders are proactive and creative change agents • School leaders develop the culture, structures, and conditions to facilitate professional dialogue, collaboration, and knowledge exchange • School leaders ensure that the organization's actions are consistent with its vision, goals, and values • School leaders ensure the school is characterized by a "rhythm" of learning, change, and innovation • School leaders promote and participate in strong collaboration with other schools, parents, the community, higher education institutions, and other partners • School leaders ensure an integrated approach to responding to students' learning and other needs	• Principal holds onto "power" • Micro manages • Little to no collaboration • Little to no conversation and development of vision and values with regard to student learning • Vision and goals are not clear • Inherent distrust in district supports or initiatives • No trust • No Pro-D community • Top-down decision making • Closed system • Lack of transparency • Favoritism	• Some consultation with other leaders (dept. heads, COI) only • Asks for input, but makes final decisions • Limited trust • Selective, repeated use of go-to middle leadership staff • Some visions and goals are central to decision making • Pro-D with lack of focus/cohesion "one-offs" • Identifying and building capacity in possible leaders • Formal, surface-level sharing	• Wraparound supports for student needs • Engaged in a spiral of inquiry or rhythm of learning • Multiple school leaders can be identified—"Diversity of Leadership" • Collaborative approach to School-Based Team (SBT) with multiple partners • Vision and goals are central to all decisions made by school • Leaders share their personal growth plans • Active participation by all in Pro-D • Trust among staff • Providing opportunities for teacher leadership • Actively recruiting, promoting, cultivating leaders within schools • Open system • Distributed leadership • Building capacity • Capitalizing on teacher passions

Participation and engagement of the leaders in the development of the rubric was a powerful way for schools to begin using the SLO model. Table 12.1 is an example of a rubric that was created for one of the seven dimensions.

To ensure that the school ratings were as accurate as possible, a subsequent meeting was devoted to rereading the elements of each dimension and reviewing the rubric that had been created for each dimension (see figure 12.4).

Time was provided for school leaders to recalibrate their initial ratings. These ratings were collected by district leaders for analysis and publishing (see figure 12.5).

The findings of the initial ratings were organized into a spreadsheet and totaled to provide a district summary of strengths and weaknesses across schools. The results are summarized in figure 12.6.

What emerged in the baseline data was the need for the district to focus specifically on two dimensions of the seven that comprise the *School as a Learning Organization* framework: *Systems for Collecting and Exchanging Knowledge* and *Learning with and from the External Environment*.

In the Spring of 2019, Dr. Stoll returned to the Delta School District to visit more schools and meet with school leaders and teams of teachers from each school to introduce the *School as a Learning Organization* model to teachers. Feedback provided evidence that the model was well received by staff members and it had sparked an interest with the teacher leaders who were present. That initial meeting, where school leaders were asked to introduce the seven dimensions to staff as a framework for considering the strengths and weaknesses of their schools as learning organizations, set the stage for the 2019–2020 school year. Over the course of the year, school leaders were asked to replicate the same process they had engaged in during principal

Figure 12.4. Rubric Development Process. *Gordon*

Figure 12.5. Completed Copies of Individual School Rating Forms. *Bauman and Gordon*

meetings, this time with their staff, to determine the area of most important focus for each school site.

In February of 2020, Dr. Louise Stoll returned to Delta once again, this time to study the impact of leadership on the implementation of the SLO framework. She reinterviewed leaders whom she had spoken to before to examine the relationship between teaching, learning, and the vision. Once the interviews were complete, Dr. Stoll summarized her findings and presented them to the district leadership team. This was important feedback for the district to work with as it provided data as a part of the *checking* phase of the *Spiral of Inquiry*. It also provided evidence as to what was going well, as well as areas requiring further attention.

Throughout the 2019–2020 school year, schools were encouraged to align their school goals with the area of greatest need they had identified from the *Schools as Learning Organizations* (SLO) ratings. For example, if the school's goal was to improve reading comprehension and the area of greatest need in the SLO model was teacher collaboration, then it made sense to

BASELINE DATA

Summary School Ratings	VISION CENTRED ON THE LEARNING OF ALL STUDENTS	CONTINUOUS LEARNING FOR ALL STAFF	PROMOTING TEAM LEARNING AND COLLABORATION	CULTURE OF INQUIRY, INNOVATION AND EXPLORATION	SYSTEMS FOR COLLECTING AND EXCHANGING KNOWLEDGE AND LEARNING	LEARNING WITH AND FROM THE EXTERNAL ENVIRONMENT	MODELLING AND GROWING LEARNING LEADERSHIP	Totals
Red	5	3	3	7	16	10	1	45
Amber	17	19	19	17	13	17	23	125
Green	10	10	10	8	3	5	8	54

Figure 12.6. District Summary of School Rating Forms. *Bauman and Gordon*

leverage professional collaboration as a means of improving student reading comprehension. Similarly, if the school's goal was to ensure all vulnerable students graduate and the area of need on the SLO framework was a shared vision and mission, developing a shared vision related to the goal of having at-risk students graduate ensured alignment. Placing a school goal at the center of the SLO framework helps educators assess which dimensions need to be a focus in order to maximize progress toward the goal. For example, if a school used the *Spiral of Inquiry* to determine that implementing the curriculum related to Indigenous Knowledge and Perspectives was a goal for the school, the SLO framework could be a useful tool to help focus the learning in the school around this goal so as to maximize improvement (see figure 12.7).

By examining the seven dimensions with the learning goal at the heart, educators in a school can determine whether or not a school-wide vision for the goal exists, if new learning is available to teachers related to the goal, and if staff are collaborating around how to achieve the goal. Similarly, how educators connect to others both internally and externally as well as how they collect and analyze data related to the goal increases the likelihood that the goal will be achieved. We learned that the SLO framework, used in conjunction with the *Spiral of Inquiry*, is highly effective in setting and working toward achieving school goals.

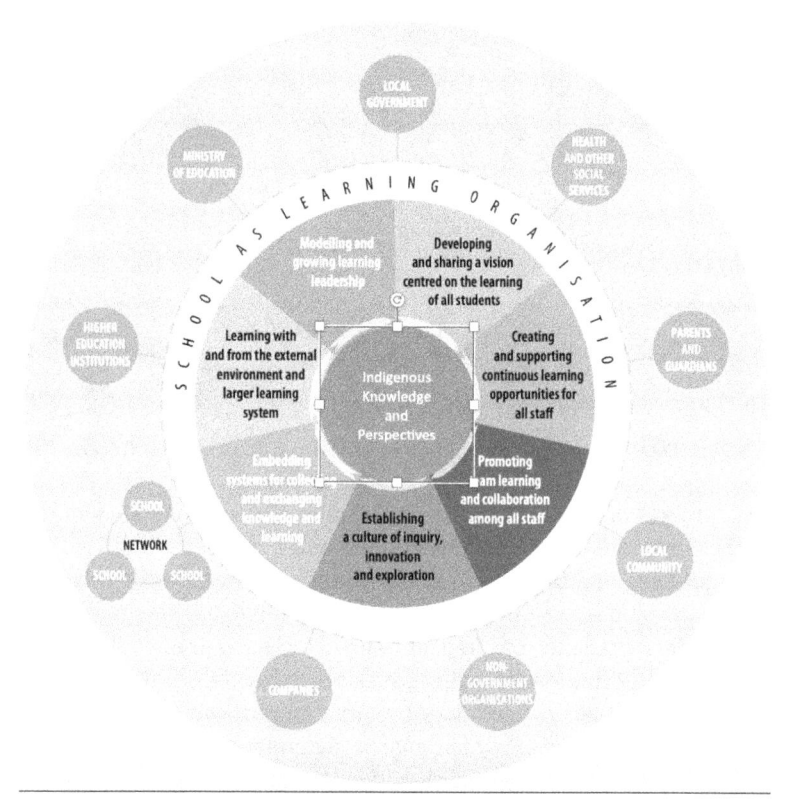

Figure 12.7. Example of Using the School as a Learning Organization Framework to Focus on Indigenous Knowledge and Perspectives (OECD, 2016). *Kools and Stoll (2016)*

LESSONS LEARNED

- ***The* School as a Learning Organization *Framework (SLO) is an essential framework to support learning-oriented organizational improvement processes.*** It is one more example of what Leithwood would refer to as a coherent instructional guidance system—"When a district's curriculum standards and frameworks, instructional practices, professional development emphases and assessment tools are all focused on achieving the district's mission, vision and goals, the district is providing 'coherent instructional guidance' to its schools, an important part of what strong districts do" (2013).
- *Use an appreciative inquiry process when beginning to explore the seven dimensions of the* **School as a Learning Organization** *framework.* Remember to focus on what the school is already doing well. For example, in Delta, the following district attributes provided a strong foundation to build on when examining the SLO dimensions:

- Strong district vision
- Long-standing commitment to ongoing professional learning
- Structures to support professional collaboration
- The *Spiral of Inquiry* as a foundation for improving student learning
- Coordinators of Inquiry
- **The SLO framework is a valuable tool to ensure that the focus for school improvement becomes actioned.** Once the student learning goal has been established through the *Spiral of Inquiry*, staff should consider which dimension(s) of the *School as a Learning Organization* framework needs to be focused on first to ensure the goal is realized.
- **It is critical that leaders at every level of the district clearly see themselves as learners and leaders of learning.** Role clarity is critical and determining that clarity is the role of senior district leaders. Senior district leaders need to be well-versed in the SLO framework in order to be in a position to support their vice-principals and principals as learners.
- **The SLO framework can be used by school leaders as a lens for determining the goals of their individual professional growth plans** with regard to their leadership. Based on the outcome of the RAG rating for their school, principals and vice-principals should consider the leadership qualities they need in order to bring the dimension of greatest need alive in their school.
- **Alignment and coherence between the district vision, the district FESL/Strategic Plan, and school goals are very important** and becomes increasingly more apparent and possible when using the SLO. The dimensions of the SLO framework are indicators of success in realizing improvements at the district and school level.
- **The SLO transversals—time, technology, thinking together, trust, and compassion are critical considerations** if a school (or district) is to truly become a learning organization.

CONNECTING YOUR LEARNING

1. When you study the SLO framework, do you see it as something that would be useful in your context? Why or why not?
2. How might the SLO framework be leveraged to strengthen your schools or district? What steps might you take to build awareness of the framework?
3. Are the five transversals—time, technology, thinking together, trust, and compassion—present in your context? Which of the transversals might require greater attention and why?

126   Chapter 12

Part 2 has focused on work being done in the Delta School District to help create strong schools. The research related to *Schools as Learning Organizations* (SLO) serves as a framework for understanding the key dimensions and elements that make a school a strong place of learning. The SLO model has also served as a highly useful tool for assessing the strengths and the areas requiring greater focus in a school. The guidance of Dr. Louise Stoll has been incredibly valuable as the Delta School District moves toward ensuring that its schools are indeed learning organizations that are focused on maximizing outcomes for learners.

Part 3 will outline the most recent focus in Delta—that of strong learning environments. When considering the elements that contribute to a strong learning environment, we believe that the SLO framework has utility in helping to maximize the power of learning spaces. By placing the concept of a strong learning environment at the center of the SLO framework, it is possible to consider how the seven dimensions can be used to reflect on and ensure that the learning environment is as effective as possible (see figure 12.8).

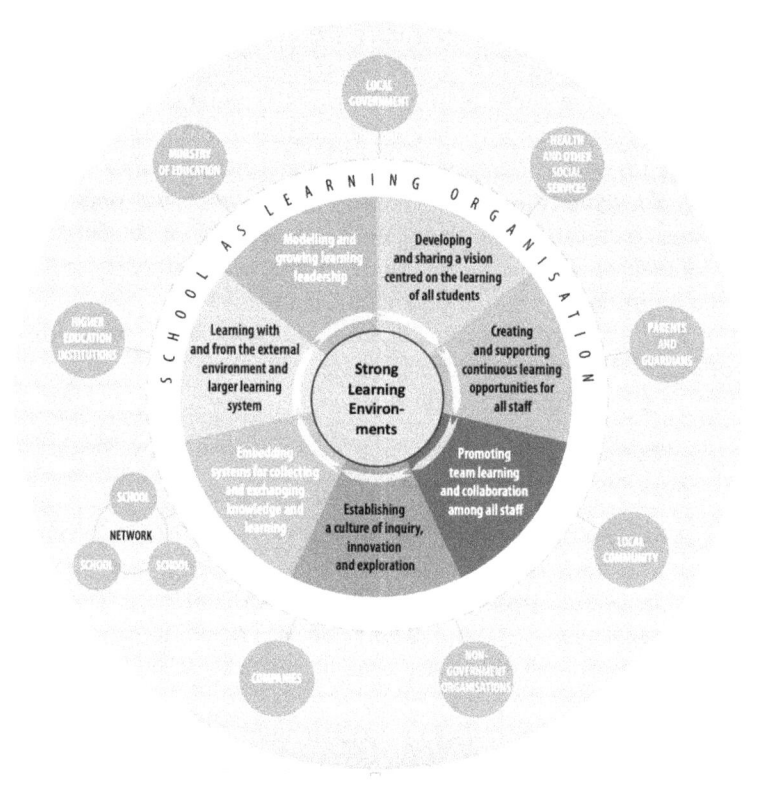

Figure 12.8.   Example of Using the School as a Learning Organization Framework to Focus on Strong Learning Environments (OECD, 2016). *Kools and Stoll (2016)*

When considering each of the dimensions through the lens of a strong learning environment it is possible to strengthen the elements that contribute to an effective learning environment. For example, what is the shared vision within the school for a strong learning environment? How might staff learn more about what constitutes an effective learning space? Is time provided for professional collaboration related to the topic? What might a school-wide collaborative inquiry look like related to effective learning environments? How is the staff gathering data related to the effectiveness of the goal? Are there opportunities to share what is learned and how might staff learn from those beyond the school? Which educators are passionate about the topic and might become teacher leaders in this area? It is exciting to envision how the SLO framework might be used to help achieve a school-wide goal related to powerful learning environments.

PART 3

Strong Learning Environments

Chapter 13

Strong Learning Environments

An area that has been gaining recent focus across the district is the question of what elements contribute to a strong learning environment? When considering the notion of what makes a strong learning environment, we once again turned to the research and discovered that while this is an area of more recent investigation, the work done by the OECD is extremely useful. Since publishing the research related to *Innovative Learning Environments* (2013), the OECD has continued to investigate effective learning environments. OECD's director of education and skills, Andreas Schleicher, states that "The design of the physical learning environment can foster, or hinder, the teaching and learning of 21st century skills" (OECD 2013, p. 3). He states further that

> Recent studies of innovative learning environments indicate there are positive associations between school improvement, spatial redesign and student learning. Evidence suggests that well-designed buildings and facilities with integrated ICT can be the catalyst for innovative pedagogies that impact on student learning. Improved student learning is most likely to be achieved if certain preconditions are met. Well-designed learning spaces maximise the options available for innovative pedagogies through flexibility, adaptability and connectivity. (OECD, 2013, p. 10).

This speaks to the broad definition of what constitutes an effective learning environment, one which goes far beyond sound delivery of the curriculum and proven assessment practices to include design of the physical space, as well as the affective domains of learning such as belonging and connectedness.

A powerful, inclusive learning environment can be discussed at three levels: *effective, innovative instruction; effective relationships;* and *an effective physical space*. However, we believe when there is effectiveness at all three levels, the learning opportunities for students will be maximized, as shown in figure 13.1.

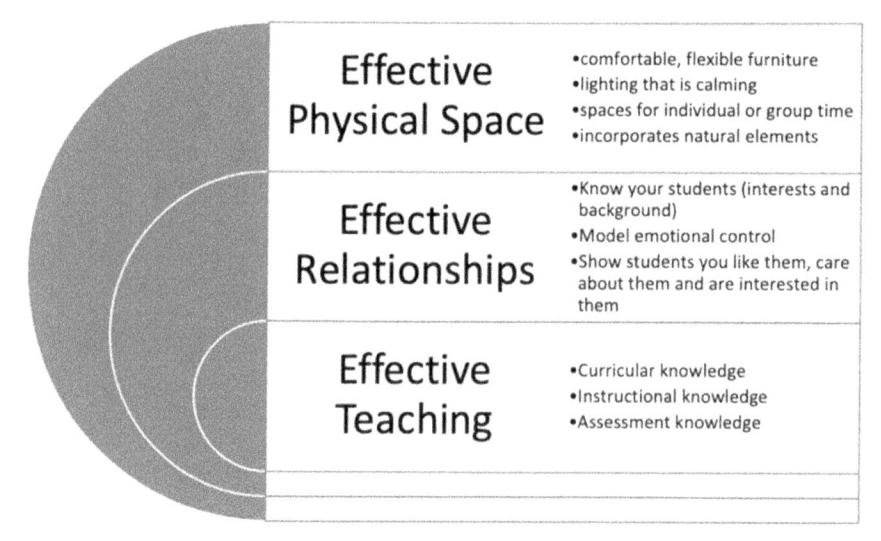

Effective Physical Space	•comfortable, flexible furniture •lighting that is calming •spaces for individual or group time •incorporates natural elements
Effective Relationships	•Know your students (interests and background) •Model emotional control •Show students you like them, care about them and are interested in them
Effective Teaching	•Curricular knowledge •Instructional knowledge •Assessment knowledge

Figure 13.1. Components of a Powerful Inclusive Learning Environment. *Gordon and Turner (2023)*

POWERFUL INCLUSIVE LEARNING ENVIRONMENTS

EFFECTIVE PHYSICAL SPACE

For many years the Delta School District focused on teachers' knowledge of the curriculum, as well as instruction and assessment practices. Since the implementation of Vision 2020, student connectedness and sense of belonging became an important central focus. More recently, Delta teachers from across the district have been exploring physical design elements that make a classroom a comfortable, calm place for learning. This was due to an unintentional yet welcome result of Vision 2020 and the permission that was granted for teachers to be innovative and try new approaches. Based on a teacher's explorations of the Reggio-Emilio approach to learning, one school developed an inquiry question around what would happen to learning if classrooms became more natural and less institutional (depicted in figures 13.2a and 13.2b).

Interest in this school's work spread across the district and it inspired teachers to reassess their classroom environments. Now, more learning spaces across elementary schools in the district are removing the traditional classroom furniture and fluorescent ceiling lights and introducing wooden tables and chairs for gathering, comfortable sofas and beanbags, and warm-lit lamps

Figure 13.2a.

Figure 13.2b. Example of a school inquiry at a Coordinator of Inquiry (COI) year-end celebration. *Delta School District*

and strings of lights. These learning environments contain natural elements such as wood, wicker, and stone. There may be calm music playing during transitions and even aromatherapy diffusers to help reduce stress.

Research has found that learning environments play a crucial role in student success. Several factors can affect learning ability, including seating, light, noise, and even colour. Students who study in a positive learning environment have been shown to be more motivated, engaged, and have a higher overall learning ability. On the other hand, students learning in poor environments—those that are uncomfortable, loud, or full of distractions—will find it far more difficult to absorb information and stay engaged. (Hendrix, 2019)

Accordingly, these elementary school classrooms focus on the elements of comfort, lighting, color, noise, and organization. Students who are calm and comfortable are able to stay focused longer. Studies are beginning to show that not only can the physical environment positively impact mood and help to reduce stress and anxiety, students learning in comfortable spaces with more natural lighting achieve higher grades than those in poorly lit classrooms. Further, traditional fluorescent lighting tends to cause students to feel tired more quickly. Additionally, color has been shown to impact emotion. For example, bright colors such as red can raise stress levels while yellow has been shown to enhance positive feelings. For these reasons, many classrooms in Delta are asking students for input into how to adopt a more natural and calming approach to their environment. This includes ensuring that students have an opportunity to be outside and connect with nature. The following photos (figures 13.3a, 13.3b, and 13.3c) depict a learning environment in Delta that is focusing on design elements.

Not only are teachers noticing positive results for themselves and their learners, but students are reporting that they appreciate the calmer learning spaces and that it helps them to regulate their emotions.

EFFECTIVE RELATIONSHIPS

In exploring the classroom context, the physical environment is just one small component of an effective learning environment. A comfortable, welcoming space alone is not enough to boost student achievement. In addition to the physical space and the instructional practices, the quality of the relationships between teachers and their students is critical. There is abundant research that points to the importance of the relationship between the teacher and the students as being a critical component of an effective learning environment. Coristine et al. (2022) state:

> a student-teacher relationship in the classroom is a positive relationship between the teacher and the student in efforts to gain trust and respect from each other. This relationship may consist of getting to know your students better, providing choice and encouraging the students to become stronger learners everyday. By

Figure 13.3a.   Figure 13.3b.

Figure 13.3c. Learning Environment Focused on Design Elements. *Delta School District*

doing this, teachers are showing respect to their students, valuing their individuality and being polite. Having a positive relationship with your students helps them become more successful in the classroom as well as makes your classroom a safe and welcoming environment for all. (p. 1)

Cleary et al. (2018) state that relationships teachers build with their students have the power to result in success or failure. Academic success cannot be separated from the relationships that teachers build with their students. Valuing respect and welcoming diversity is essential if all students are to feel they belong. Additionally, the social and emotional development of all students needs to be considered and taught like any other subject area. Quality relationships need to be fostered for achievement to be maximized. Finally, classroom management should be consistent, predictable, and fair with consequences focused on learning and not punishment. The benefits of establishing positive student-teacher relationships include:

- decreasing student behavioral concerns and thereby reducing distractions for all learners
- Improving academic performance in the classroom
- teaching social-emotional skills that will enhance outcomes in life
- teaching students that mistakes are a part of learning—academically, behaviorally, and emotionally
- making the learning environment a positive place for everyone

According to John Hattie (2012), teachers who create positive teacher-student relationships are more likely to have above average effects on student achievement. This in itself is a compelling reason for educators to focus on strengthening the professional relationships they have with all of their learners. In addition, according to Hattie, teacher-student interaction has a .72 effect size on student accomplishment. It is important to note that an effect size of .4 and above is highly significant for student achievement. Listening skills, empathy, mutual respect, care, and positive regard for students were found to strengthen connections, according to the research (Hattie, 2016).

Although strategies that help to build positive relationships in the classroom may seem intuitive, the following strategies are beneficial:

- believing that all students can succeed and holding high academic expectations for all of them;
- getting to know your students (interests, strengths, hobbies, sports they play) and their families, and then including this knowledge in conversations with them;

- having a sense of humor and making laughter a part of the classroom;
- allowing students choice in their learning;
- being accepting of all students (including their mistakes);
- valuing all students equally for the strengths they bring to the learning space;
- greeting students at the door and saying hello and good-bye to every student every day;
- listening carefully to your students and having casual conversations with them;
- spending time with your students in nonacademic settings such as clubs and coaching;
- making yourself human by sharing things about yourself with them such as your hobbies, interests, and projects;
- offering individualized support to students that need it during, and if necessary, outside of class time; and
- providing praise and positive encouragement to *all* learners for effort and achievement.

Positive student-teacher relationships are a critical component of a strong, effective learning environment and have been shown repeatedly to positively impact academic achievement.

EFFECTIVE INSTRUCTION

Effective instruction is perhaps one of the most studied aspects of education and the research is abundantly clear—there are specific teaching practices that have been shown to make a significant difference to student learning. However, in a school setting, often little time is spent engaging educators in discussions related to effective classroom instruction. As Hattie (2010) states, "If the classroom is at the heart of students' opportunities to learn, the quality of teachers' instructional practices, are of paramount importance." Quality instructional practices need to be understood and practiced if student achievement is to be maximized. One way to ensure that effective instruction is understood is to engage educators in collaborative conversations related to the research on what works. Experienced teachers have a great deal of knowledge to share in this area, yet teachers who are new to the profession also have current research and practice that can add to the repertoire of seasoned educators. That being said, there is no one recipe for effective teaching. There are, however, strategies that have been proven to make a difference to student learning. Taken from *What Works Best: 2020 Update (*NSW Department of Education, 2020), these include:

- ***Holding high expectations for every student.*** Research evidence consistently finds that teachers' high expectations are linked to their students' performance and achievement, as well as their behavior, motivation, self-esteem, attendance, and secondary school completion.
- ***Explicit teaching.*** "Explicit teaching practices involve teachers clearly explaining to students why they are learning something, how it connects to what they already know, what they are expected to do, how to do it and what it looks like when they have succeeded. Students are given opportunities and time to check their understanding, ask questions and receive clear, effective feedback" (p. 11). Put simply, tell students what they are going to learn, teach them, tell them again what they learned, and then check to see if they have mastered the concept.
- ***Providing effective feedback.*** Feedback impacts students' learning by explaining *how* to improve. Every student should receive quality feedback related to their progress toward the learning goals and objectives.
- ***Using data to inform teaching practice.*** The gathering of student data through formative assessment practices informs the teacher of next steps and should be used regularly. The use of data has been shown to improve student outcomes. When students know what they are learning, how they are doing, and what they need to do to improve, outcomes improve.
- ***High-quality formative and summative assessment practices make a difference.*** Formative assessment is gathered throughout the teaching process to inform both the student and the teacher of progress and next steps. Summative assessment occurs at the end of a unit of study to indicate a student's achievement in comparison to a set of standards. Significant gains in learning, especially for the students who need it the most, have been linked to formative assessment.
- ***Effective classroom management.*** "Effective classroom management is vital for creating an environment that minimises disruptions, maximises instruction time, and encourages students to engage in learning. Evidence shows that improving classroom management practices can help improve students' performance" (p. 29). Behavioral expectations that are cocreated, and agreed upon, with the students and the teacher can be beneficial.
- ***Focusing on well-being.*** Closely linked to the section on effective relationships, a focus on student well-being is critical if outcomes are to be maximized. Student well-being is linked to academic achievement and school completion. Well-being at school is fostered by educators who know their students, foster a sense of belonging, and value student input. Once again, the relationship between the student and the teacher is one of the most important predictors of positive outcomes for students.

- ***Effective collaboration matters.*** Teachers who are able to break down the silos and share what works in education report higher job satisfaction and increased collective efficacy (one of the greatest predictors of improved outcomes for students). Co-planning, co-teaching, observing others practice, and providing peer feedback are all strategies used by professionals to improve effectiveness.
- ***Learning should relate to the real world and involve student choice and voice.*** It is important that educators are able to relate student learning goals to the real world and present new learning in an innovative and engaging manner. Learning should be enjoyable, and purposeful.

A full review of effective teaching is beyond the scope of this book. There is a plethora of research on what defines quality instruction that has scanned decades and has cited debates. We believe that effective instruction needs to be considered as one of three domains that make a positive difference to student learning—*effective teaching and instruction, effective relationships,* and *an effective physical space.* The elements of physical space, quality instruction, and the affective domain all interact and ultimately impact student learning as a whole. No one area of focus is enough to maximize learning—all three are essential. Only when students feel a calm sense of belonging, and are in an environment where they feel welcome and valued, will high-quality teacher pedagogy maximize student achievement. We have highlighted the critical factors that contribute to an effective learning environment to demonstrate how the goals in the Delta School District have evolved since the inception of Vision 2020.

To illustrate how the district goals in Delta have transitioned over the past few years to be more focused on student-teacher relationships and learning environments, we provide an overview of the district goals from the past few years. From 2018 to 2021, the Framework for Enhancing Student Learning (FESL) began to go beyond the curricular goals and include those related to the affective domain. During this time, the district focused on the four goals of Connections, Reading, Assessment, and Graduation, highlighted in the following poster (figure 13.4).

To reiterate, these goals were established by all schools engaging in the stages of the *Spiral of Inquiry* and developing goals that were based on the learning needs of the students in the district's 31 schools. The goals of all schools were collected and three major themes emerged. The district-wide data was then *scanned* and it was determined that reading literacy would need to be an additional goal. Through *focusing*, it was determined that the literacy focus should become more concentrated on reading. A *hunch* was developed that if all children could be reading by the end of grade 3, that school success and retention for intermediate and secondary students would increase and

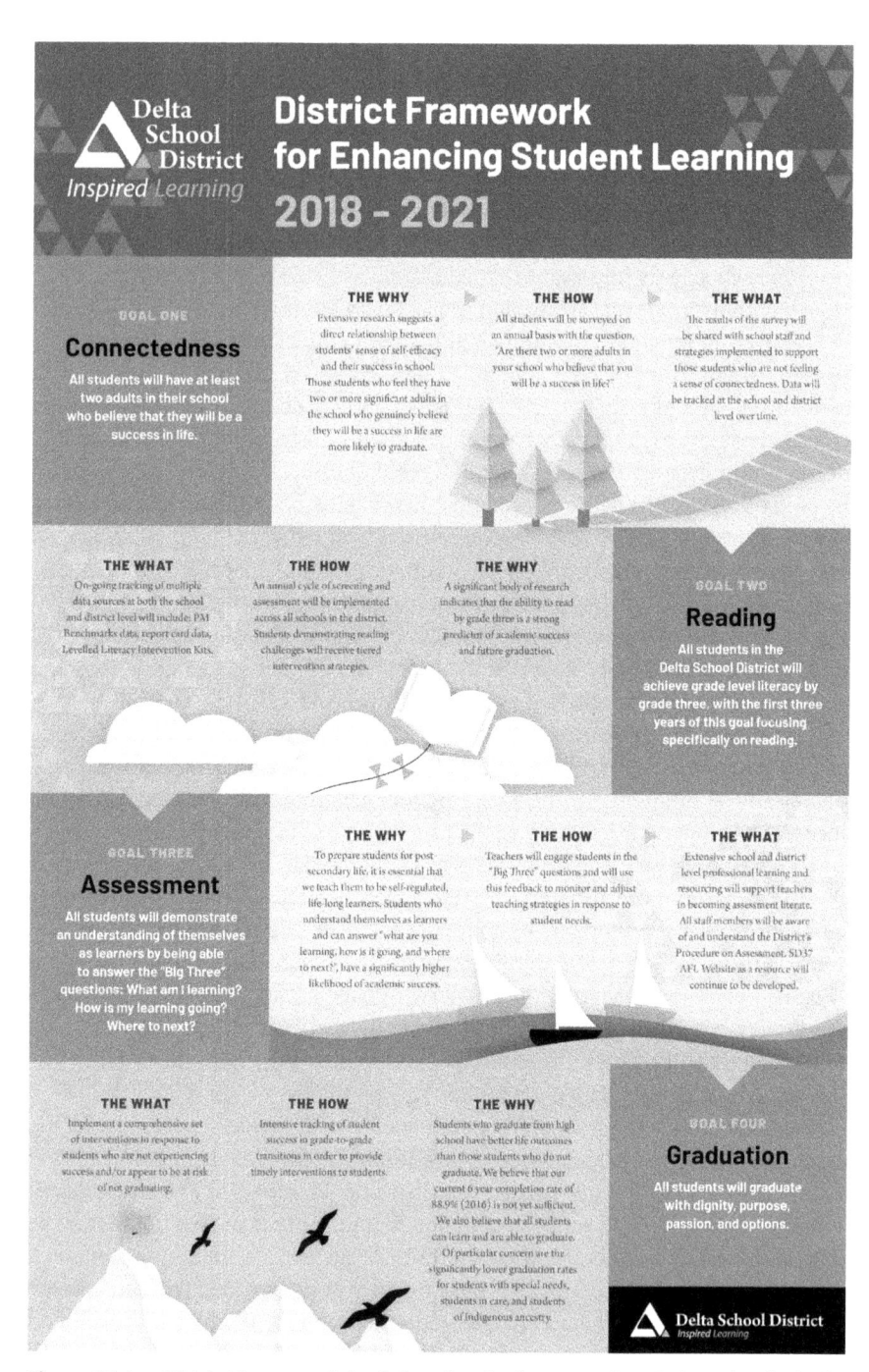

Figure 13.4. District Framework for Enhancing Student Learning. *Delta School District*

graduation rates would be maximized. This *hunch* required new learning for not only the district support staff, but also for classroom teachers, as recent research in early reading was pointing to some findings that would definitely provoke debate and discussion. Even though the new learning might question the status quo, a decision was made to move forward and take action by piloting some specific instructional techniques in a few schools showing the greatest learner need. In the *checking phase*, improvements in students' reading level were analyzed and the spiral begins anew. Continuous improvement is the goal.

Using the phases of the *Spiral of Inquiry*, a new strategic plan was developed that will carry the district forward through to 2024. Through the *checking* phase of the spiral, data was gathered related to the four goals of the FESL and based on *checking and scanning*, the learning goals were revised to be Graduation for All, Powerful Learning Environments, and Strong Foundations in Literacy and Numeracy (see figures 13.5, 13.6, and 13.7).

It is clear that district goals in Delta have evolved to recognize and focus on areas related to Powerful Learning Environments on a much broader level than in the past. By broadening the district goals that impact instruction, relationships, and physical space, long-term goals such as all students graduating with dignity, purpose, and options become much more realizable. These learning goals were founded on the guiding principles that had emerged from Vision 2020 (see figure 13.8).

These guiding principles, or transversals, are foundational to all of the learning goals:

- **Equity:** A commitment to equitable outcomes requires that we recognize and respond to differences in strengths and needs. We will seek to ensure that *all* Delta students have the opportunities required to reach their full potential.
- **Well-Being and Connectedness:** We know that the well-being of staff has a direct impact on student well-being, which is directly correlated to their learning (Oberle & Schonert-Reichl, 2016). As such, we will prioritize social, emotional, and physical well-being and a sense of belonging for all students and staff, with a particular focus on mental wellness.
- **Diversity:** Diversity is a defining aspect of the Delta School District. We recognize the need for continued learning and engagement in this regard and will actively respect, appreciate, embrace, and learn from the valuable diversity within our district.
- **Core Competencies:** Thinking, Communication, Personal, and Social. We will support students in their growth as educated global citizens by helping them achieve proficiency in the intellectual, personal, social,

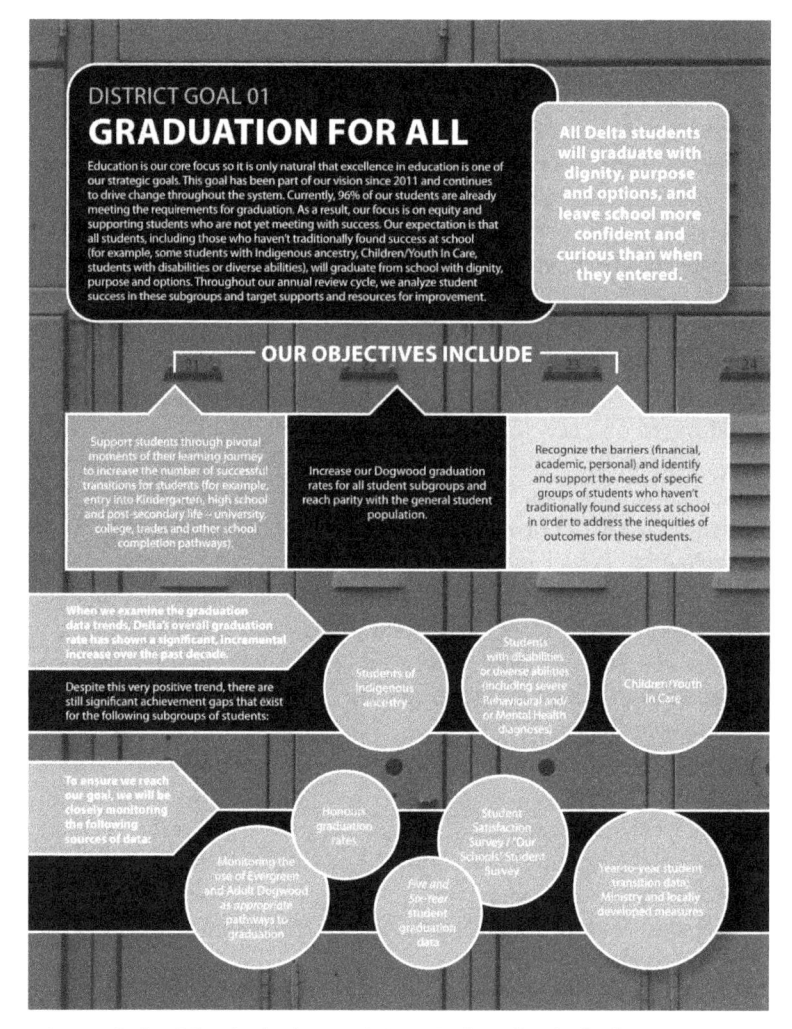

Figure 13.5. Delta School District Goal One. *Delta School District*

and emotional knowledge, skills, and processes associated with the three core competencies.
- **Indigenous Worldviews and Knowledge:** We will seek a deeper understanding and appreciation of the Indigenous histories, cultures, and Principles of Learning through our learning and working practices. We will foster stronger relationships with local First Nations communities through collaboration and consultation. We will implement the Truth and Reconciliation Commission calls to action related to education.
- **Universal and Inclusive Approaches/Practices:** We will account for the uniqueness and variability in learners when designing and delivering

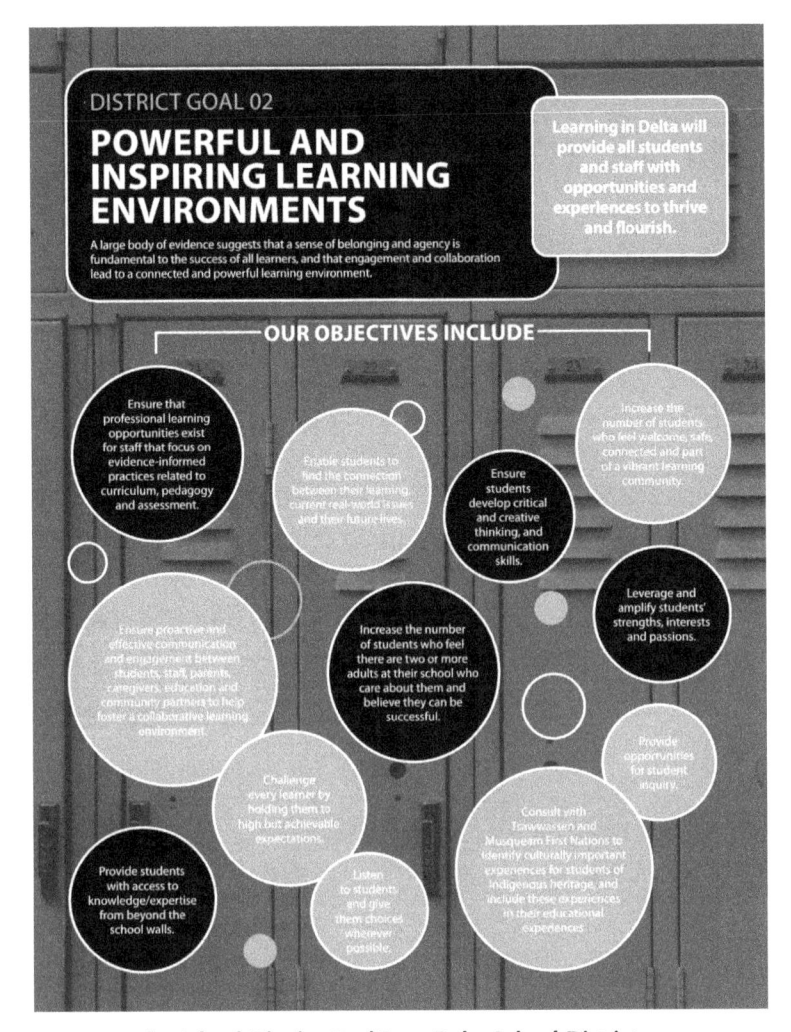

Figure 13.6. Delta School District Goal Two. *Delta School District*

education to help make space for a strength-based, innovative, and individualized approach, and reduce the need for specific accommodations for students with disabilities and/or diverse abilities.

These guiding principles emerged as being critical to Vision 2020. As a result, they became a central focus of moving the district forward. Being more declarative at the district level as to what matters in strong learning environments increases the likelihood that classrooms in Delta will incorporate what makes a positive difference to student learning.

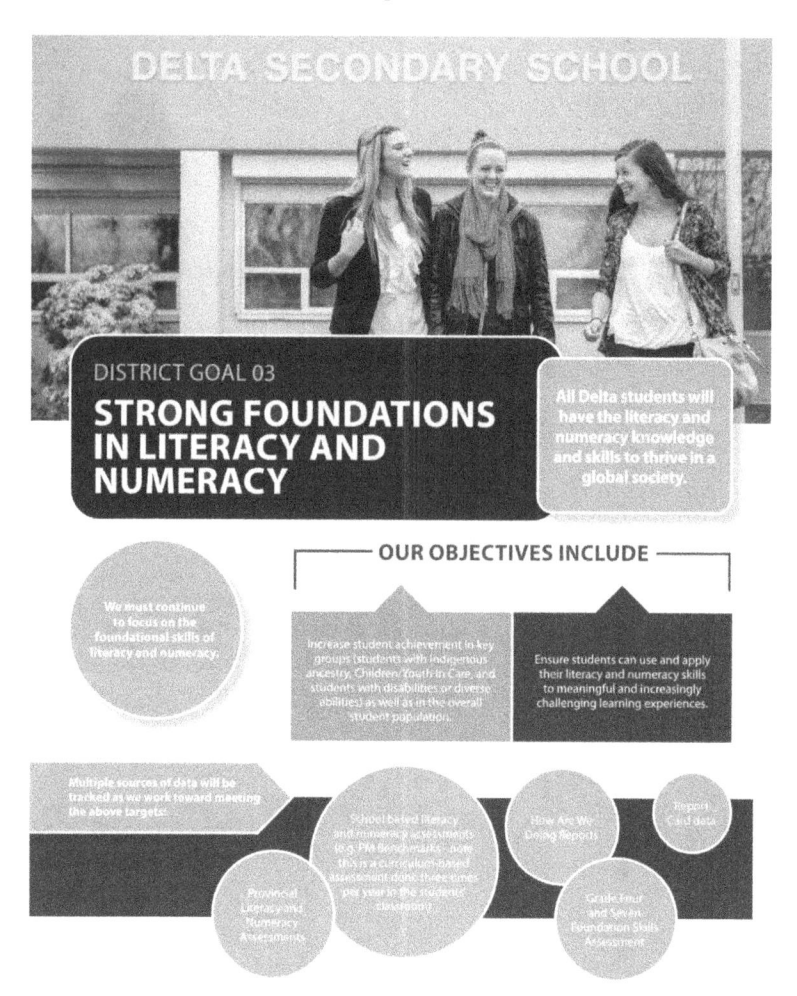

Figure 13.7. Delta School District Goal Three. *Delta School District*

Through the *scanning* phase of the *Spiral of Inquiry* it was recognized that for many years there had been a strong focus on curriculum and assessment. However, a deeper discussion related to classroom instruction was needed. A large body of evidence suggests that a sense of belonging and agency is fundamental to the success of all learners, and that engagement and collaboration lead to a connected and powerful learning environment.

These characteristics of a Powerful, Inspiring Learning Environment, taken from the Delta School District Strategic Plan (2021–2024), help to define the components of what make a learning environment effective:

Strong Learning Environments 145

Figure 13.8. Delta School District Guiding Principles. *Delta School District*

- Ensure that professional learning opportunities exist for staff that focus on evidence-informed practices related to curriculum, pedagogy, and assessment.
- Enable students to find the connection between their learning, current real-world issues, and their future lives.
- Ensure students develop critical, creative-thinking, and communication skills.
- Increase the number of students who feel welcome, safe, connected, and part of a vibrant learning community.
- Ensure proactive and effective communication and engagement between students, staff, parents, caregivers, and education and community partners to help foster a collaborative learning environment.
- Increase the number of students who feel there are two or more adults at their school who care about them and believe they can be successful.
- Leverage and amplify students' strengths, interests, and passions.
- Challenge every learner by holding them to high but achievable expectations.
- Provide opportunities for student inquiry.
- Provide students with access to knowledge/expertise from beyond the school walls.
- Listen to students and give them choices wherever possible.

- Consult with local Indigenous communities to identify culturally important experiences for students of Indigenous ancestry, and include these in the educational experiences for all.

These bullets demonstrate the holistic approach that Delta has taken toward learning. The intellectual components of a learning environment cannot be separated from the affective domain. Over the coming years, these elements of a powerful learning environment will be delved into in greater depth across the school district. Using the *Spirals of Inquiry* once again to guide this next part of the journey, the *hunch* is that if attention is paid to all levels of these elements, student engagement in their learning will increase, their satisfaction with learning will be enhanced, and ultimately, student achievement and outcomes will be further improved.

It is important to note that the three goals of the strategic plan are interdependent. When learning environments are as impactful as possible and teacher pedagogy is as effective as possible, literacy and numeracy results will improve and graduation rates will be as high as possible.

The strategic plan of the district will further develop the instructional coherence that Leithwood (2013) states will contribute to a strong school district. A sustained focus on the learning goals of the strategic plan and the district's underlying guiding principles, coupled with the vision, will result in even greater coherence across classrooms, schools, and the district.

LESSONS LEARNED

- *Powerful Learning Environments is a complex term.* The research in this area is continually evolving. To fully realize how to improve the effectiveness of a learning environment, continuous learning for educators is required in this area.
- *Effective teaching matters, but so does the relationship with the student.* One of the number-one predictors of student success is the relationship between the student and the teacher.
- *Physical space and design are important.* Individuals tend to learn more readily in an environment that is calming, comfortable, and safe.
- *Student voice and choice matter.* It is not possible to maximize student learning without listening to the learners. Knowing their interests, curiosities, and goals not only helps to foster positive relationships and shows the student that they matter, but it aids in effective delivery of the curriculum. When student interests can be connected to and incorporated into the learning goals there is an increased likelihood of student engagement in the learning.

- ***The quality of teachers' instructional practices is critically important.*** Like any profession, it is vital that all educators continue to hone their skills and stay abreast of the latest research findings. It is no longer acceptable to teach as we have always taught.

CONNECTING YOUR LEARNING

1. How does your jurisdiction ensure that high expectations are held for every learner—especially those who need the most support?
2. How well embedded is Assessment for Learning in your district? Is feedback for learning the norm or is your current assessment model based solely on percentages or letter grades? What questions do you have about how best to assess students?
3. Are conversations taking place about what effective teaching looks like? How often is curriculum, instruction, and assessment talked about? If not, what are the barriers to these learning conversations?
4. Does student data inform teaching practice? For instance, when a deficit in student learning is observed, what actions do teachers take to remedy the situation?
5. How is student voice taken into consideration when planning the learning environment?
6. How might you use the *Spiral of Inquiry* to make decisions related to the physical, emotional, and instructional aspects of your classroom?

Part 3 focused on some of the work that is emerging in the Delta School District related to strong learning environments—environments that are centered around equity and excellence. Part 4 of the book will provide a summary of key actions that contributed to continuous improvement in the Delta School District, along with testimonials from educators regarding improvements in the district. It will also outline the specific qualitative and quantitative data that demonstrates what long-term, deliberate actions can achieve within a school system. Further comments are made regarding how the district handled the crisis of the COVID-19 pandemic and the disruption that took place as a result of the pandemic, both globally and locally. Finally, the conclusion will describe how the Delta School District has come full circle. The *Spiral of Inquiry* that the district engaged in to achieve Vision 2020 has concluded, however, the *checking* phase has led seamlessly into a new *Spiral of Inquiry*—that of Vision 2030.

PART 4

A Summary of What Made a Difference

Chapter 14

A Summary of What Made a Difference

There have been several key drivers of transformation in the Delta School District. Although there are numerous actions and innovations that have taken place across the school district since Vision 2020 was created, we believe there are at least nine key foundational elements which have contributed to the success the district has realized:

1. First and foremost was **the creation of Vision 2020.** The highly collaborative, appreciative inquiry process that was utilized in the development of the vision was pivotal. It set direction and became the guiding North Star for the district. Because the process used to develop the vision was highly collaborative, including every school and worksite in the district, it resulted in strong ownership and buy-in, which in turn encouraged engagement in actions to achieve the vision.
2. Second, **using the *Spiral of Inquiry*** as a framework for professional learning was instrumental in actions taken for improvement and transformation. It formed the basis of the development of school and district goals, professional learning and professional growth plans, and was instrumental in determining the learning needs for students, teachers, vice-principals, and principals. Related to the use of the *Spiral of Inquiry* was the creation of Coordinators of Inquiry in each school throughout the district. Establishing this new role highlighted the district's commitment to using inquiry as a vehicle for district transformation and has had a strong influence on development of inquiry mindedness.
3. A third key foundational element that contributed to transformation in Delta was the **provision of teacher collaboration time** in every school. The addition of this time contributed to building teacher capacity in the areas of curricular understandings, pedagogy, and assessment for learning practices and moved teachers toward stronger collective efficacy.

4. A fourth foundational element that made a significant difference to the district's transformation was **purposeful professional learning** that aligned with the vision as well as school and district goals. The district's focus on professional learning created a culture that recognized the need for continuous improvement within the teaching profession. Delta's strong focus on curriculum, instruction, and assessment was powerful in moving system learning forward across the district. Each year since the inception of the vision, the district created an organizational template of professional learning opportunities that connected to school goals, district goals, and professional growth plans. It helped organize district teaching and learning through the lens of the district's work and it helped to maintain clarity and alignment of the initiatives happening in the district. Whenever professional learning opportunities were being considered for the district, the scanning phase of the *Spiral of Inquiry (*Kaser & Halbert, 2017) was used to determine the learner needs at all levels in the system. This ensured that professional learning opportunities were aligned with the school's goals and the district's vision and goals.
5. Fifth, there was a **continuous, purposeful focus on storytelling** to increase opportunities for networking and capacity-building across the district. Deliberately sharing stories of success (and failure) helped transfer the learning in the district across school sites.
6. Sixth, using appreciative inquiry and the storytelling process, the district engaged in a **reflective check-in process at the halfway mark** of the 10-year vision cycle. Using the results that emerged from that reflective check-in, the district was then able to adapt new strategies to help achieve the goals that came from the original vision process.
7. Seventh, the district focused on **building leadership capacity** through the creation of a differentiated, six-strand model titled *Leading for Learning.*
8. Eighth, there was **a coherent approach across the district** to help attain the Vision 2020. Individuals who work in finance, human resources, information services, facilities, and education programs were all committed to achieving the vision. Most importantly, the Delta Board of Education structured their work around the district's vision. Every decision made in the district was filtered through the lens of Delta's vision—including the contents of the district's policy and administrative procedures.
9. Finally, in Delta there was **a significant change in the way educational research was viewed and used** and, as a result, district educators made meaningful contributions to educational knowledge creation. Leading researchers and global scholars helped influence the way the

A Summary of What Made a Difference 153

school district approached strategies for improvement, and, as a result, both directly and indirectly, they have made important contributions toward Delta becoming a leading district for innovative teaching and learner success.

CONNECTING YOUR LEARNING

1. From the perspective of your current context, reflect on these nine points. What is going well?
2. Which areas, if any, require further attention? What steps might you take?

IMPACT ON STUDENT LEARNING

We would be remiss if we did not mention the improvements in student achievement realized over the 10 years of Vision 2020. Although it is challenging in education to attribute causality of outcomes to any one variable, the results over the past 10+ years have been noteworthy. Historically, school completion rates for all residents in Delta have been high. Over the course of Vision 2020, the Delta School District realized further improvement in completion rates, particularly for students of Indigenous heritage and students with special needs (see figures 14.1 through 14.5).

Completion Rate Over Time
● B.C. Residents ● Diverse Needs ● Indigenous

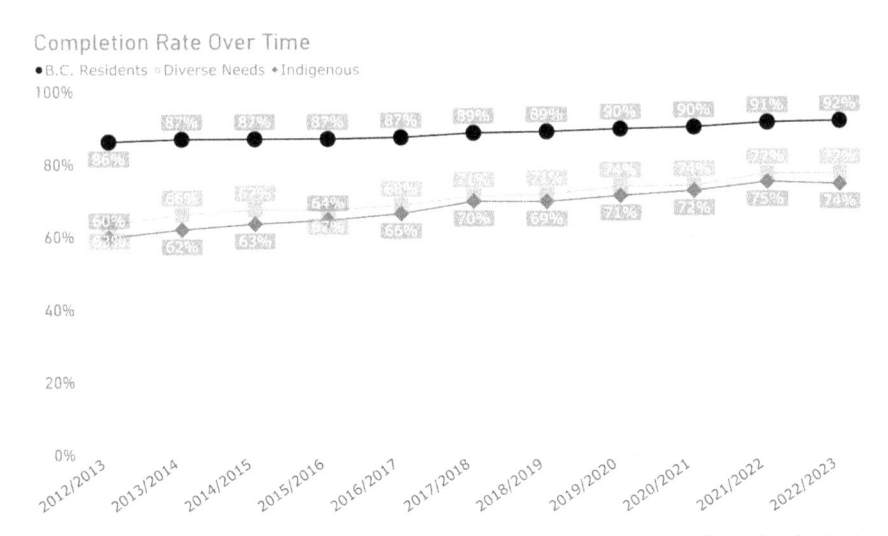

Year	B.C. Residents	Diverse Needs	Indigenous
2012/2013	86%	50%	—
2013/2014	87%	66%	62%
2014/2015	87%	67%	63%
2015/2016	87%	64%	64%
2016/2017	87%	68%	66%
2017/2018	89%	74%	70%
2018/2019	89%	72%	69%
2019/2020	90%	74%	71%
2020/2021	90%	75%	72%
2021/2022	91%	77%	75%
2022/2023	92%	77%	74%

Figure 14.1. Delta School District Completion Rates Over Time. *Delta School District*

Completion Rate Over Time for Indigenous and BC Residents

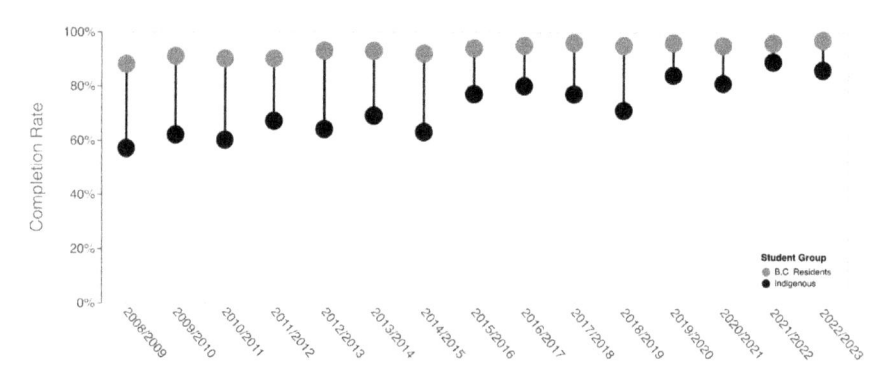

Figure 14.2. Completion Rates for Delta School District Indigenous Students. *Delta School District*

Completion Rate Over Time for Students with Diverse Abilities and BC Residents

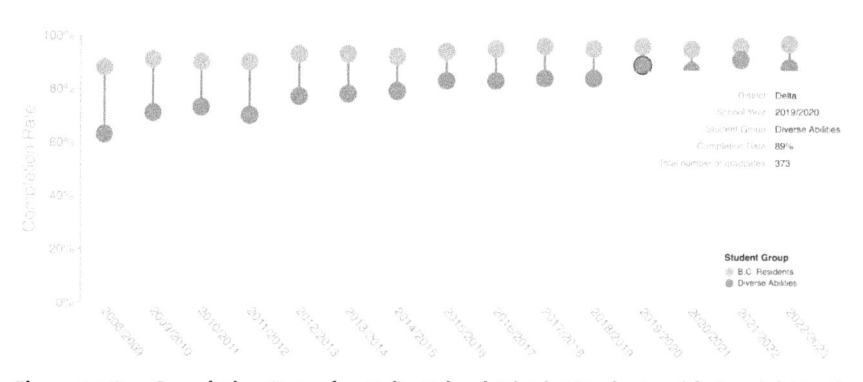

Figure 14.3. Completion Rates for Delta School District Students with Special Needs. *Delta School District*

When considering the completion rates of Indigenous students in Delta (see figure 14.6), it must be noted that due to the small size of the population, significant variation is to be expected.

These graphs demonstrate improvement over time not only for the grade-to-grade transitions since 2011 when Vision 2020 was introduced, but they also show success in narrowing the gap in school completion rate for both students with Indigenous ancestry and students with disabilities

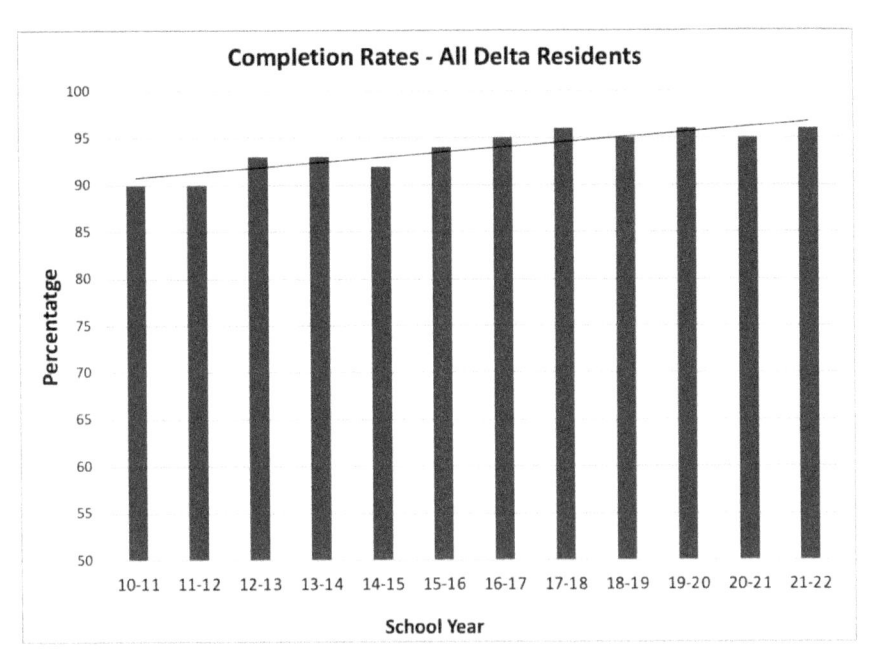

Figure 14.4. Trend Over Time: Completion Rates for Delta Students. *Delta School District*

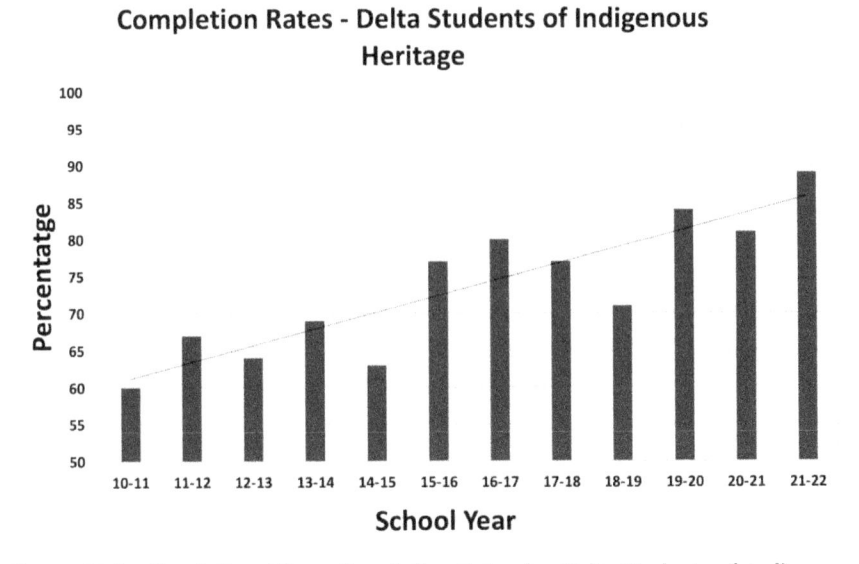

Figure 14.5. Trend Over Time: Completion Rates for Delta Students of Indigenous Heritage. *Delta School District*

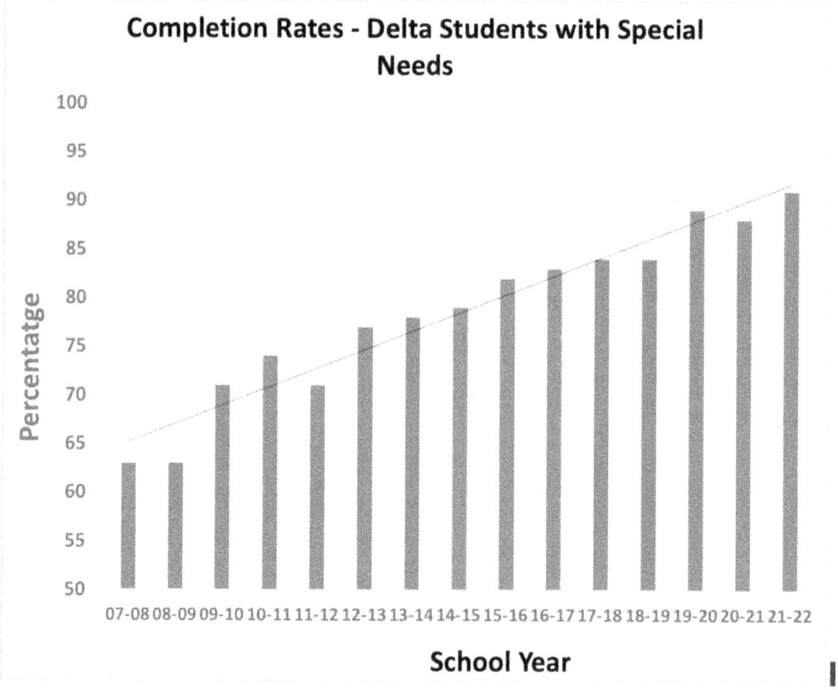

Figure 14.6. Trend Over Time: Completion Rates for Delta Students with Special Needs. ***Delta School District***

and diverse abilities. Although it would be impossible to draw a direct link between the introduction of Vision 2020 and the positive results, we believe that improvement in outcomes, especially for our most vulnerable students, is likely due in large part to the clear direction that Vision 2020 set.

> The increased focus on vulnerable students has shown very positive results. Additional funding was put into supporting literacy programs for Indigenous students and primary students who were struggling. Educators had the opportunity to participate in workshops that enhanced their teaching practice, ultimately benefiting their students. Learning was more focused.
>
> Val Windsor, Delta Board of Education trustee

In addition to the quantitative data provided, there is an abundance of qualitative data to indicate that Vision 2020 had a positive impact on the district. Some of the key indicators that district leaders commented upon are the shift from competition to cooperation between schools, an increase in the amount of teacher collaboration occurring, increased district support for teachers in key areas of instruction (especially in the areas of assessment, inquiry, and literacy), which has resulted in more risk-taking and innovation in teaching. This is captured below in quotes from district leaders who have provided outstanding commitment and leadership to Delta:

> Vision 2020 had a wide and impactful reach across the district that is still felt today. The process alone is singularly the most unifying event the district has ever been a part of. It's difficult to even disentangle the Delta School District in its current form without seeing it through the vision. I look at all the department growth, staff excitement, district initiatives, strengths, successes, and achievements in the last 10 years and can see their roots and development through Vision 2020. It truly is the backbone of the district.
>
> The macro-outcomes of the vision: A district that is connected more deeply (alignment—language, structures, process). A district that has a North Star. A district that stands for something and follows through on those values.
>
> There are so many micro-outcomes. It's literally impossible to list all the initiatives and efforts that trace their beginnings to the vision. The obvious outcomes include coordinator positions, COIs, professional development initiatives, and so on. But they just scratch the surface. The number of meetings (school-based and district level) that I have been a part of where we have used the vision, or addressed the vision, are innumerable. The vision truly is embedded at every level in the district.
>
> Niels Nielsen, elementary principal

> Over the years, the vision has served as a North Star for each of us as individuals and for the district as whole. We may not refer to the vision on a daily basis but more importantly because of the values represented in the vision, we live the vision every day. The vision ensures that collectively each of us from across the district shares something in common with each other, it provides a foundation for decision-making and a guide for our learning.
>
> Aaron Akune, secondary principal

Testimonial: Brief thoughts on Vision 2020 by Don Younger, secondary school principal

> [Being] new to the Delta School District in 2006 or 2007, I often heard of "the Delta way" but was unable, after much questioning, to get a clear understanding as to what this meant. As a secondary principal, what I witnessed were schools not only working in isolation from each other but also in competition with each other. We all had goals for our schools, but were lacking a widely held vision. For me this came to the forefront at a conference in Winnipeg where our district team was asked to speak of our school district's vision and we were unable to clearly arrive at the vision. The strength in the creation of Vision 2020 is that it brought all stakeholders together to share their goals and wishes for Delta.

Having the vision provided a lens to examine new ideas and a screen to pass ideas and initiatives through and filter how they fit with the broader district goals. The vision, through the values, also highlighted the expectations in how we interact with others and the standards we hold ourselves to. For me the effect of the vision was:

- A move to focus on *all* learners—not just those university bound.
- A kickstart to get initiatives moving and a means to share with others how these fit in with the district goals. With some earlier initiatives (e.g., change in assessment practice) I had been asked if I would support the teachers when parents questioned what we were doing. No longer were we on our own.
- An opening to discuss with others initiatives occurring in their schools and how to take these across the district. What was working and why?
- The development of district resources/supports—Learning services to better develop our teachers.
- The focus on the values and the need to keep these at the forefront of our conversations when we are: discussing courses, teaching and assessment strategies, and especially when we are discussing students who may not be meeting our expectations.
- Uniting our schools with a common focus and greatly lessening the competition, for students, achievement, between schools—a much greater attitude of working together to better serve all schools and the full community.

District leaders believe that this observation, of less competition and more collaboration, has been a critical element in realizing improvements in Delta, not only in student achievement, but also in school and district climate and culture.

Disruption

Just as the Delta School District was beginning to move toward establishing a framework for Strong Equitable Learning Environments, the work was forced to stop. In March of 2020, a global pandemic brought the world, and much of the district work, to a halt. COVID-19 forced schools in Delta, and around the world, to close for face-to-face learning. This meant that all of the progress on system alignment that the district had been engaging in paused while staff coped with the impact of maintaining student learning in the middle of a pandemic. Educators were forced to adapt quickly, and, within a week, become adept at offering remote learning to students. This could have resulted in chaos, but in Delta several key factors played a role in making a very positive difference.

First and foremost, anchoring the work in the district goal to the *School as a Learning Organization* (SLO) transversal of Connectedness helped the educators in Delta ease into the change by ensuring that connecting with students was the first priority. By the end of the first week of moving to remote learning, every student received a personal phone call from their teacher to touch base and check in on how students and their families were doing. This was important as the closure for the COVID-19 pandemic began immediately following two weeks of Spring Break vacation, so teachers had not had contact with their students for 16 days. The personal connections helped to establish a sense of reassurance and a mindset that "together, we will get through this." Several teachers commented that these phone calls with students and families were some of the best they had experienced in their careers.

> All in all, it was a good day that made me remember what is at the core of our "jobs"; connecting and caring about families. Hopefully, we can all appreciate the time that has been given to us in order to send home meaningful, reasonable and intentional tasks. Talking to the families gave me a powerful lens to see through. We have the luxury of time. The families know that we care and can feel it when we take the time to just talk to them and listen.
>
> Delta teacher

> There is no need to panic! Enjoy the kids when you talk to them, and just enjoy "listening." Often the students are so excited to share their lives with us in stories while at school and we seem to be lacking the "time" to stop and just listen; now we have it!
>
> Delta teacher

These quotes speak volumes about the approach taken across the Delta School District during the early phase of the pandemic. Focusing on connectedness allowed teachers to get an inside look at their students and their families so that they could anticipate where struggles might occur and work proactively to help solve them. In addition, the Schools as Learning Organizations dimension of compassion emerged as a critical factor in successfully navigating the pandemic. District leaders regularly collaborated with the leaders of the teachers' union and the union representing support workers. There was continuous collaboration with the principals and vice-principals who in turn collaborated with educators. Powerful collaboration became the norm between school leaders, with principals and vice-principals discussing challenges and helping one another arrive at solutions.

Secondly, the Ministry of Education set out four clear priorities for districts moving to remote learning during the COVID-19 pandemic. These priorities became the drivers for implementing remote learning in British Columbia.

- Maintain a healthy and safe environment for all students, families, and employees
- Provide the services needed to support the children of our essential workers (ESWs)
- Support vulnerable students who may need special assistance
- Provide continuity of educational opportunities for all students

In Delta, this meant that as employees had to shift to working remotely from home, there was a need to put structures in place through WorkSafe BC[1] to protect those who were working alone. The district also needed to quickly establish daycare support in schools to provide for frontline workers in emergency services so that they could continue to go to their worksites. Vulnerable learners in every school were identified and their needs were focused on either remotely, or by bringing them into schools to work one-on-one with educational assistants. This was an important step as a critical goal was, as much as possible, to prevent the equity gap from widening. After these priorities were addressed, the goal became to provide a worthwhile educational program for students who were learning from home. This was certainly no small task as many teachers had to learn new computer programs such as Google Classroom, Google Hangouts, Zoom, Microsoft Teams, and WebEx, among others. While there were some differences across classes in the amount of work provided, the approaches used, and the amount of face-to-face presence, for the most part the parent community was appreciative and grateful for the efforts made by teachers. The quotes below speak to the level of commitment that teachers provided, especially to the most vulnerable learners:

> The question of how teachers can best support parents arose recently. The challenge is that none of my children speak, read, watch TV nor are they remotely capable of accessing online educational assistance. Most activities are learned through serendipitous experiential moments or hand over hand repetition; all at a 1:1 ratio of instructor to student.
> The first thing the teacher did was set up a Zoom meeting of classmates.
> To sit beside my teens, all with varying levels of cognitive aptitudes and a multitude of challenges, it was amazingly inspirational to see the gallery of their classmates, speaking names of the kids in their class or simply reaching out and touching the faces of their friends on the computer screens. I seldom cry but I did "tear up" at the sight of these students connecting virtually.

The teacher followed this up with a socially distanced home visit with my kids. She delivered a parcel of individualized packets of art supplies and a COVID Crisis Time Capsule workbook. Students received calming t-shirts, sketchbooks, and collections of tactile objects.

Delta parent

I have always maintained that the Delta School system is the Cadillac of learning opportunities.

I just wanted to share that you are fortunate to have teachers and support staff who raise the bar EVERY day and they set an example for all other districts to emulate.

I'm now at home with an ecstatic group of teens who are smiling, excited and feeling very "special" indeed!

Delta parent

During the beginning of the pandemic, remote learning continued for several weeks. Educators, leaders, and support staff all had to adjust rapidly to a new way of delivering education.

Once face-to-face learning returned in schools, physical distancing became a priority along with continuous hand washing and sanitizing. Everyone in the system needed to adjust to significant new practices, including meetings held on Zoom. Two actions in particular that made a positive difference were a strong focus on regular communication with the local unions, and ongoing, clear communication with school leaders. Initially, the superintendent arranged daily conversations with the Delta Teachers' Association (DTA) and the Canadian Union of Public Employees (CUPE) Local 1091. Eventually, as time passed during the pandemic, these conversations took place weekly. This helped to keep the union presidents informed and aware of important updates about what was happening in the district and the province, and therefore it helped to eliminate surprises. In addition, initially, there was almost daily communication via Zoom between district leaders and school leaders. This allowed them to know what was being proposed, to provide input, and to help the system move forward with consistency across sites and still have the necessary flexibility to address the site-based nuances of each school. As could be imagined during that crisis, there was a lot of uncertainty and many questions, but attempting to stay on top of the issues and address the queries quickly was a helpful approach.

The pandemic came along at a time when Delta was about to begin reflecting on where the district was at with Vision 2020 after 10 years. It was almost time for the Delta School District to go through a new visioning process, so the fact that district initiatives had to stop moving forward for the time being during the pandemic was not altogether a bad thing. In fact, taking a pause actually helped to uncover some things that likely would not have otherwise been discovered.

The pandemic pushed district leaders to not only reflect on what the Delta School District had achieved since 2011 but also to consider where the district was currently at. Additionally, it helped to encourage educators to pause and consider what was lost during the COVID-19 pandemic, what positives had come from the shift to remote learning, and what should be kept and continued as the district moved through and eventually out of the pandemic. Figure 14.7 depicts where the district was at that point.

The five Rs, seen in the graphic, are adapted from a McKinsey & Company presentation "Coronavirus COVID-19: Perspectives for School Leaders" (2020). While the initial steps of Resolve, Resilience, and Return are more universal, the real opportunity lies in the final steps of Reimagine and Reform. In the words of Klaus Schwab, the founder of the World Economic Forum, "The pandemic represents a rare but narrow window of opportunity to reflect, reimagine, and reset our world" (2020). This also applies to education. Delta's leaders believe that the two steps of reimagine and reform hold incredible potential for system improvement as educators consider what has been learned from the impact of the pandemic (both the negatives and the positives). Reimagining what education could look like moving forward, and reforming the current educational reality in new and creative ways, is a rare opportunity. Resetting education would involve input from all levels of the system.

As the Delta School District moves forward, careful consideration will be given to the discoveries gleaned from the pandemic that would be beneficial to continue while moving toward the future. These discoveries will inform planning as the Delta School District creates and finalizes the district's

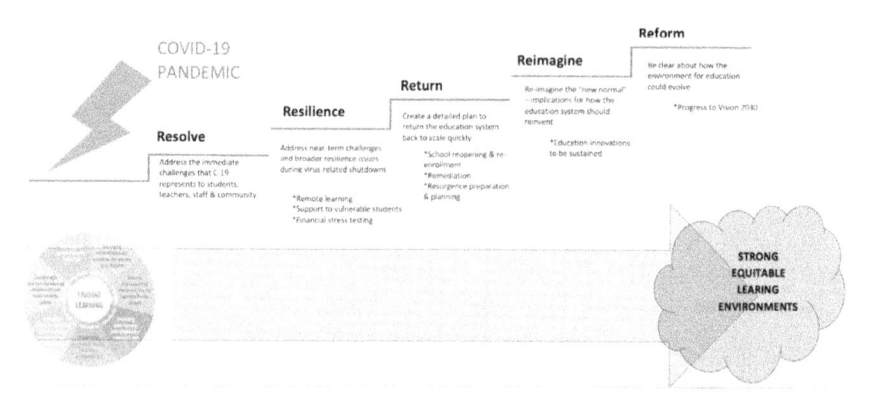

Figure 14.7. The Five Rs for Consideration Post COVID. *McKinsey & Company (2020)*

framework for Strong Learning Environments for Equity and Excellence. Had the district moved into the creation of this framework prior to experiencing the pandemic, it would very likely have been incomplete. A great deal has been learned about how best to support students with diverse learning needs, which secondary timetable best meets the needs of teenage learners, the importance of technology as a tool to engage parents, and the importance of connectedness for everyone in the education system. Further, these findings helped to ground the process of establishing a new district vision—Vision 2030. And thus the Delta School District will have come full circle as in 2022 the district was poised to launch a new 10-year journey of inquiry, learning, and continuous improvement, all grounded on a foundation of inquiry.

LESSONS LEARNED

- *In every successful change process there are foundational elements and key factors that contribute to the change.* Be sure to recognize what those key factors are and acknowledge them and use them in working toward future improvement efforts.
- *Outcomes in student achievement should be regularly referred to in order to help make decisions* about where additional support and resources are required to make further improvements.
- *Communication is critical when managing disruption.* In times of system chaos, such as COVID-19 presented, it is critical to increase communication to ensure that those leading the system clearly understand the nature and the demands of the disruption.
- *Involve stakeholders in decisions that impact them.* Providing time for those most likely to be affected by decisions to engage in discussion will increase cooperation and buy-in. Making sure that people feel heard is important.
- *A clear, shared vision serves as an anchor during times of change.* When managing change, having cocreated values, a well-understood mission, and a shared vision for the future serves as a reference to help guide decisions.
- *In every crisis, there is an opportunity. Make time to reflect on new learnings.* Even when change is forced upon us it is important to take the time to ask, "What did we learn and why does it matter?" Sometimes forced disruption can lead to new, creative outcomes.

CONNECTING YOUR LEARNING

1. How well did your organization navigate the global pandemic? What did you learn and what might you do should another similar situation arise?
2. What role does communication play during times of crisis? What structures are currently in place that work well? How might you strengthen lines of communication?
3. How do you involve stakeholders, including students, parents, educators, and leaders, in the decisions that impact them? Is there any group that might benefit from greater attention?

NOTE

1. An organization in British Columbia that consults with and educates employers and workers about safe work practices. It enforces the Occupational Health and Safety Regulation and the Workers Compensation Act.

PART 5

Full Circle: Where to Next?

Chapter 15

Full Circle: Where to Next?

In the spring of 2021, the Delta School District elected to once again engage in a visioning process. Vision 2020 had been in place for 10 years, and it was time to redefine the values, mission, and the vision of the district. Proposing to engage in a visioning process at that time was not without controversy. The global pandemic had been in existence for over a year and many educators and leaders felt that the visioning process should be put on hold until there was a "better time." After careful consideration and a great deal of listening and consideration, the senior leadership team made the decision to explore how a visioning process could unfold in the midst of COVD-19. The original visioning process in 2011 involved multiple in-person facilitated meetings. During the early phase of the pandemic, this would not be possible. One of the silver linings of COVID-19 was the discovery that effective meetings could still be held virtually. Thus, the decision was made to explore a revisioning process in a novel fashion.

Similar to the process used in the first visioning process, external facilitators were contracted by the district to lead the visioning exercise. In fact, one of the facilitators was the same graphic designer who created the original Vision 2020 graphic illustration with the working committee in 2011. Much like Vision 2020, there was a tight timeline for the process. Creating Vision 2030 was a multistep process. It began with a large virtual meeting of over 300 participants that included staff, students, parents, and community members. Through a series of guided discussions and breakout sessions, a great deal of information was gleaned. Of particular importance was the information that students shared regarding what they valued in their education.

The virtual session was followed by a series of surveys that went to students, staff, parents, and community members. Almost 3,000 surveys were completed, providing approximately 10,000 data points. In compiling the data, common themes were identified with regard to the values that the district should adhere to, as well as what needed to be included in the mission and the vision statements. In addition, 10 success indicators were identified

168   Chapter 15

and included in Vision 2030. A recommendation made to the vision planning team was for the new vision to appear less "cluttered" than Vision 2020. The feedback on Vision 2030 suggests that the new vision met the criterion (see figure 15.1).

Vision 2030 was unveiled in the fall of 2021 and it was met with enthusiasm.

> We feel very proud to be a part of District 37! Thank you for all of your hard work in bringing our ideas together to make this vision a reality.
>
> Elementary school staff

Since that time, Vision 2030 is referred to regularly in all district operations. As with the first vision, the image is evident everywhere throughout the district. Large posters of Vision 2030 are on display in every school and worksite, and each classroom teacher has been provided with smaller versions of the image for their reference. In particular, the new vision is referenced in meetings with school leaders who have been provided with strategies to delve into all aspects of Vision 2030. Following those meetings, school leaders were asked to return to their schools and sites to replicate these strategies with

Figure 15.1.   Delta School District Vision 2030. *Delta School District*

their staff. In addition, student leadership groups that exist in the district's seven high schools have examined the vision to discuss and make meaning of it. One student group used the 10 success indicators in the center of the vision to find examples of each in their school. Teachers are encouraged to refer to the Vision 2030 posters in every classroom and to draw attention to how student learning aligns with the vision. Time has been set aside for events such as vision awareness week where a social media contest and a range of school and district activities were planned to keep the vision alive.

> I feel that Vision 2030 has taken underpinnings to a new level in that senior leaders brought the process directly into the schools and created a vision that is very much grown from a grassroots level. Vision 2030 is very much our North Star as we move beyond a pandemic toward greater expectations.
>
> Keri Hanlon, elementary principal

The visioning process, and the journey to achieve the vision, in the Delta School District is an example of long-term system inquiry, with multiple embedded subinquiries. Every step along the way has been guided by beginning with the scanning question: "What does the district need to focus on in order to move forward in the strongest manner possible?" The 10-year process began with the realization that the district needed a guiding sense of direction or vision. The creation of Vision 2020 led to continuous improvement throughout the district. Further, because the story of the visioning process was shared regularly both within and beyond the district, the visioning process had impact beyond Delta:

> Throughout vision 2020 and 2030, I have been amazed and impressed at the reach of the vision beyond the district. It was incredible that in many of the conversations I had with educators from outside of Delta, they would reference the vision in some way. In many ways, I feel as though the vision put Delta on the map. Clearly, the vision has helped attract countless teachers to Delta as they have seen the progressive and innovative work that we have all been doing.
>
> Aaron Akune, secondary principal

As noted, Delta's visions have had impact within the district and beyond. Through the International Student Program, we have seen how it has garnered interest abroad, as figure 15.2, from Japan, demonstrates.

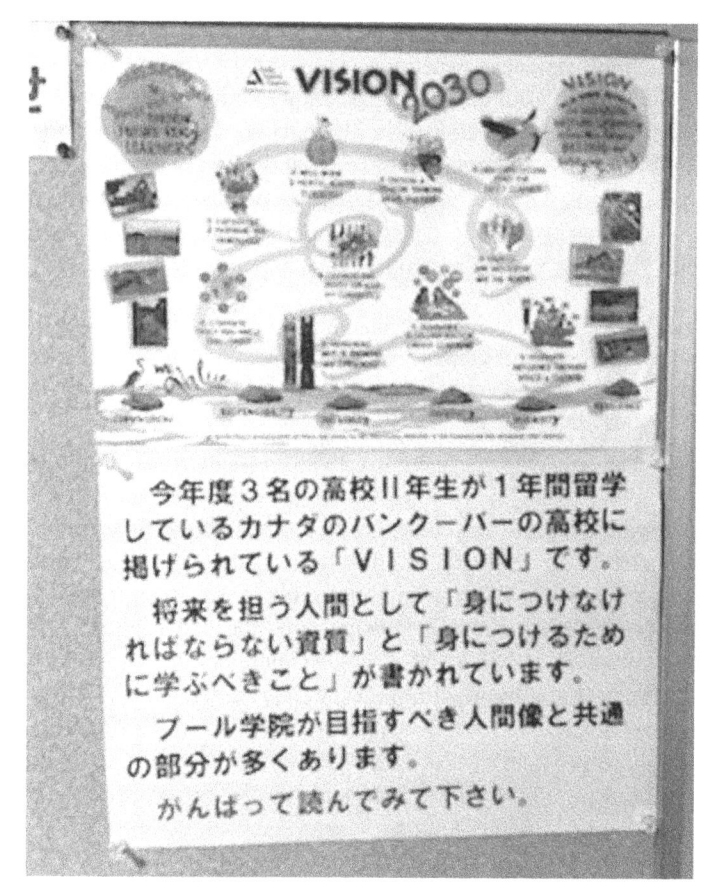

Figure 15.2. Delta School District Vision 2030 as seen in Japan. *Delta School District*

It is clear that the networking and sharing that we refer to as being critical to developing a strong district have been impactful.

> The Delta School District has long been regarded as a lighthouse district. With Vision 2020 and now, Vision 2030, other school districts have seen the success of the programme and are now creating their own visions.
>
> Val Windsor, Delta Board of Education trustee

The Delta School District is now back at the place where it began 10 years ago, with a new vision, cocreated by all stakeholder groups, of being *"an innovative, inclusive community where all learners belong and everyone soars."* Over the next 10 years, the district will continue to purposefully move forward through inquiry-mindedness to become the strongest learning community possible for learners at all levels in the system—classrooms, schools, and the district. Within only a few months, Vision 2030 was already having an impact on professional learning, student outcomes, and collaboration in the district:

TESTIMONIAL

I am realizing that Vision 2030 is the root from which our learning blooms. Back in December, we asked our staff to reflect on the 10 strands and comment on how they were engaging in each. This provided us with a sense of what we were doing and where we needed to focus. In February, we asked our staff to choose a strand that they had not spent much time exploring and use this as a springboard to engage in a learning burst with their students. We did this using the Jamboard platform (attached are three examples of teacher responses). By circling back to the strands or values embedded in the vision, we are developing common language and a cohesive lens for leaning into new, and sometimes uncomfortable, learning.

Moving to a new school this Fall meant a range of experiences for me. I chose four values, from Vision 2030 to integrate in a Four-Corners exercise with Staff (see figures 15.3a and 15.3b). By using Vision 2030, I knew there would be familiarity in the language and that staff would be able to engage in the process of relating this to their current experience. This was our starting point, from here we will grow.

The formation of Vision 2030 brought us together during a time when we were very isolated. I have realized Vision 2030 was not just a process to create, it is a living understanding. It is a common ground to begin new learnings and a third point to access when ideas become too broad. I hadn't really considered how I would access Vision 2030 over time—how malleable it would be, at the same time providing such a clear structure.

Toshi Carleton-Gaines, elementary principal

Further, the same school began a deep exploration of the values embedded in Vision 2030 by asking staff to address questions—figure 15.4—for each of the six values.

The power in these reflective questions is that it not only provides baseline data for where the school is at in achieving the values, but it inspires staff and families to take action toward the acquisition of these values.

The Delta School District's journey is certainly not complete by any means. Vision 2030 is now driving the work across the district and although transformation has taken place over the past 10 years, more improvements will continue to take place over the next 10 years.

One new area that emerged during the Vision 2030 process that the district believes can be leveraged to make a further positive difference for student

Chapter 15

- ✷ INDIGENOUS WAYS OF KNOWING ARE EMBRACED
- ✷ TEAMWORK & COLLABORATION ENRICH LEARNING
- ✷ STUDENTS TACKLE REAL-WORLD CHALLENGES
- ✷ WELL-BEING & MENTAL HEALTH FLOURISH

→ Using Thinking Classrooms textbook to engage students in math and enrich their learning by using vertical surfaces, whiteboards, open ended questions, and random groupings.

Figure 15.3a.

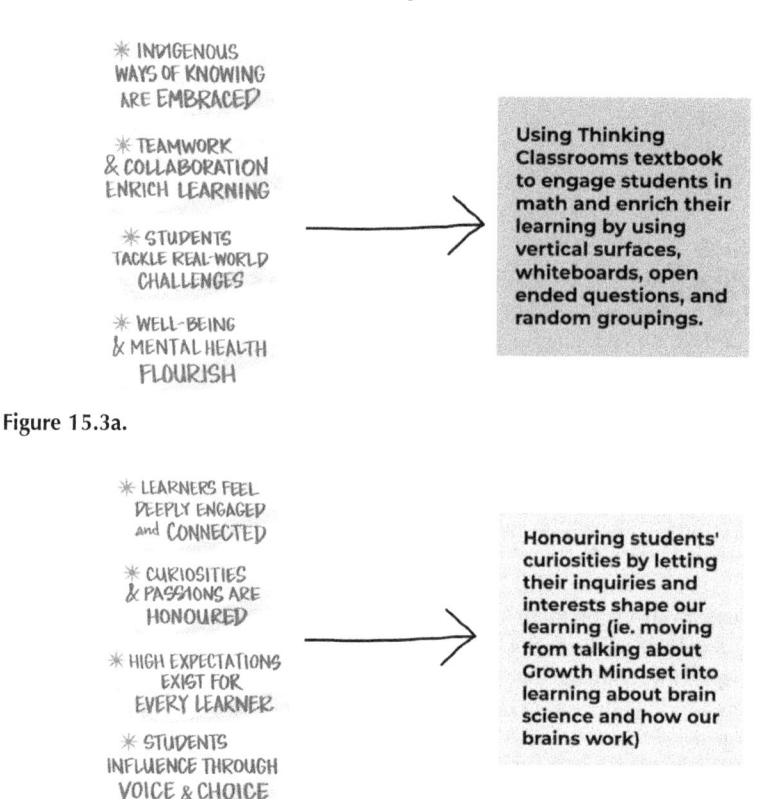

- ✷ LEARNERS FEEL DEEPLY ENGAGED and CONNECTED
- ✷ CURIOSITIES & PASSIONS ARE HONOURED
- ✷ HIGH EXPECTATIONS EXIST FOR EVERY LEARNER
- ✷ STUDENTS INFLUENCE THROUGH VOICE & CHOICE

→ Honouring students' curiosities by letting their inquiries and interests shape our learning (ie. moving from talking about Growth Mindset into learning about brain science and how our brains work)

Figure 15.3b. Samples of Jamboards where teachers created personal goals based on the indicators of success from Vision 2030. *Carleton Gaines*

outcomes is parent engagement—especially as the district emerges from the isolation of the pandemic. In 2020, an invitation came from the Brookings Institute for Delta School District to take part in a formal study on family engagement. Although the entire system was dealing with a global pandemic and the timing of the study was less than optimal, the Delta School District made it a priority to become involved. The topic of family engagement as a leverage to improve results for students aligned well with the direction of the district. Delta was focusing on revising its vision and the strategic plan, as well as moving the framework of *Schools as Learning Organizations* forward in schools. These priorities, all foundational to the district's plans for improvement, support the need to ensure that family engagement becomes a higher priority.

The findings from the Brookings study (Winthrop et al., 2021), which included jurisdictions from around the world, were fascinating in that there were vast differences between the results from the countries that took part in

1. What does **COMPASSION** look like at EB?

2. How do we know?

3. Whose job is this?

4. What supports could be called upon?

5. Ideas to grow in this area?

Figure 15.4. Sample School Assessment of the Vision's Core Values. *Carleton Gaines*

the study. These discrepancies were similar to some of the differences that Delta noticed when undertaking the visioning process for Vision 2030. For example, the variation in how families viewed the priorities of education versus how teachers ranked the priorities told us that building common understandings between home and school with regard to the purpose of education needed to be a district focus. Further, the distinction that Brookings has drawn between family "involvement" versus "engagement" has shown that while schools may be very good at family *involvement*, globally there is much work to be done when it comes to creating true family *engagement*.

As the Delta School District moves forward with Vision 2030, it makes sense to ensure family engagement, in its truest sense, is a priority. The new vision, unveiled in October of 2021, was developed with family engagement at its core. Parents, students, staff, and community members provided feedback through the development process by participating in Zoom meetings and completing surveys. Much the same as the findings from the Brookings Institute's study, Delta discovered that while there were common understandings between parents and staff on what they valued in education for their children, there were also some significant discrepancies between home and school in the values prioritized as important. Engagement in conversations between home and school related to Vision 2030 would help to align goals and expectations and thus result in greater cohesion between educators and families. Further, similar to new staff coming into the district, as families of kindergarten students enter the system for the first time, it is important to ensure that regular conversations related to Vision 2030 occur in order to ensure that everyone shares a common understanding and commitment to the district's vision.

The Delta School District has shared results of the Brookings study with school and district leaders. Co-planning how to work with the structures that exist in the system, or even develop new frameworks to strengthen the relationship between home and school, would likely further strengthen the school district. For example, Parent Advisory Councils at both the school and district levels can do a much more comprehensive job of creating opportunities that allow for the deep conversations that are necessary to create shared understandings. Common definitions, priorities, and expectations will ultimately lead to improved outcomes for students. Only through establishing a common vision for the future of education will home and school be able to achieve the shared goal of maximizing outcomes for children. One school in Delta initiated "chai chats" with Punjabi-speaking parents. Once a week an interpreter was brought in to facilitate conversations between parents and the school leaders. By focusing on the education that parents experienced in India, trust was built between the home and the school. The stories shared by the parents helped the school leader to better understand the experiences and expectations of the parents, and, ultimately, to develop greater compassion for the parents of the students. The supportive partnership that developed between parents and educators in the school ultimately resulted in improved outcomes for the students.

LESSONS LEARNED

- *Times of greatest challenge can present opportunities for innovation.* Einstein said "in the middle of difficulty lies opportunity." The challenges faced during the pandemic resulted in some changes in the education system that could be viewed as improvements, such as the realization that technology could provide an alternative means of conducting meetings and the collaboration that resulted among school leaders when making educational decisions.
- *Once a shared, cocreated vision is established, the system comes to expect it.* When all stakeholders have had the opportunity to provide input into a school district's long-term vision for the future, inclusion becomes the norm and those parties impacted by the vision will expect to have their voices heard.
- *Referencing the vision on a regular basis keeps it alive.* Senior district and school leaders need to take the lead in highlighting the links between district and schools' goals and the vision.
- *Student voice matters.* The vision exists to improve outcomes for all learners. As a result, students need to not only understand the vision, but see how the system is upholding the vision, mission, and values of it.

- ***Improvement takes time, focus, and effort.*** Don't give up on initiatives too soon. Rather, refer to the *Spirals of Inquiry* when checking to see if an initiative is making a difference and if it isn't, readjust your *focus* and *hunch* and try again.
- ***Storytelling is a powerful, effective tool for change.*** Telling the stories that exemplify the outcomes you are hoping to achieve helps to encourage more of the same actions.
- ***Courageous leadership matters!*** Leading change and transformation is not an easy task, and, often, challenging conversations are required.
- ***The involvement of all community stakeholders is important in education, especially for those closest to the student.*** When students, parents/guardians, and educators all are on the same page with their beliefs related to education, the opportunity for maximizing educational outcomes improves. Additionally, parents are the child's first teacher so the more they can understand and support the learning goals for the child, the more likely the students will realize them.

CONNECTING YOUR LEARNING

1. After reading this book, what are your key takeaways?
2. What made you curious? Why?
3. What were the most intriguing or challenging ideas in this book?
4. Now that you have read this book, what next steps will you take?

Chapter 16

Conclusion

The work of creating a strong district, a strong school, and a strong learning environment is continuous and never ends. There will always be more work to be done in improving outcomes for learners. The Delta School District has used Vision 2020 and Vision 2030 to help transform its culture by focusing on continual improvement and embracing the notion that everyone in the system is a learner, a teacher, and a leader. As stated by Dylan Wiliam in his keynote speech at the Schools, Students, and Teachers (SSAT) Conference in December 2013, "If we create a culture where every teacher believes they need to improve, not because they are not good enough, but because they can be even better, there is no limit to what we can achieve." Delta has embraced this philosophy and expanded it to include learners at *every* level—students, teachers, school leaders, and district staff.

The *Spiral of Inquiry* will continue to ensure that educators *scan*, *focus*, and *develop hunches* all the while *engaging in new learning*, *taking action*, and *checking* to see if they have made enough of a positive difference for learners. The *Spiral of Inquiry* will help to provide coherence to the improvement work in the school district as it follows an inquiry process that comes from people asking good questions that honestly and curiously focus on the needs of the learner. The iterative nature of the *Spiral of Inquiry* ensures that the district will continue to adopt "a fundamental mindset of seeking to get better all the time" (Breakspear, 2016a, p. 5) and isn't that what learning and education is all about—for everyone at every level?

To conclude, we are very hopeful that this book has told you a compelling story of the importance and power of having a shared vision and how it has made a remarkable impact on capacity building and improving outcomes for students in one school district. The lessons learned throughout the past 10 years have been shared with others many times, and often that sharing took place while the various processes and inquiries were still in progress. Just as Delta was learning from the research of others, it was hoped that by sharing what has been learned in Delta might be of help to other school districts, and, possibly, some of the lessons learned would be transferable from one district to another. The external networking Delta educators engaged in over the years has also provided opportunities for reciprocal learning between colleagues to be brought back to Delta and to contribute to the richness of professional learning taking place among educators. Feedback on many occasions showed that networking with other districts strengthened and enriched the work, and the learning became much more powerful.

On the evening in April 2011 when Vision 2020 was revealed, it was noted that the true impact of the vision would not be realized for many years into the future. Participants talked excitedly about the possibility of a book being written one day. They spoke of a book that would describe the Delta School District's journey and the strong influence a shared vision could have in district innovation and improvement. What is even more compelling and inspiring within this story about Delta is the true commitment of the dedicated people who engaged in the visioning exercises and inquiry processes over the 10-year period—because they knew instinctively that this vision would become the North Star and that it had the potential to create better outcomes for learners in the school district. That potential turned out to be powerful motivation for those who are dedicated to improving outcomes for children and youth! The power of a shared district vision, guiding coherent and important work taking place in the district, will have a long-lasting impact on the lives of the children, youth, and adults in the Delta School District and beyond.

Appendix A

Policy 1

DISTRICT FOUNDATIONAL STATEMENTS

The Delta Board of Education assumes its responsibility to provide leadership and direction to the school district. In so doing, the board is committed to Vision 2030, mission, values and goals.

Vision

The Delta School District is an innovative, inclusive community where all learners belong, and everyone soars

Mission

To inspire and nurture thriving, future-ready learners

Values

In fulfilling our mission, these core values guide our every decision, action and relationship:

- Compassion
- Responsibility
- Integrity
- Creativity
- Diversity
- Resilience

Figure 17.1a.

Policy 1

Key Goals

We will know we have achieved our vision when we have evidence that:

1. Students influence through voice and choice
2. Teamwork and collaboration enrich learning
3. Indigenous ways of knowing are embraced
4. Students tackle real-world challenges
5. Learners feel deeply engaged and connected
6. Curiosities and passions are honoured
7. Well-being and mental health flourish
8. Critical and creative thinking drive success
9. Equity and inclusion are the norm
10. High expectations exist for all learners

Strategic Plan 2021-2024

The district strategic priorities are:

1. Graduation for all
2. Powerful and inspiring learning environments
3. Strong foundations in literacy and numeracy
4. Engaged, empowered and healthy workforce
5. Strong governance and stewardship of resources

Delta School District Logo

Delta School District
Inspired Learning

Legal Reference: Sections 65, 74, 74.1, 75, 76.1, 79.2, 81.1, 82.1, 82.2, 85 *School Act*

Figure 17.1b. Appendix A. *Delta School District*

Appendix B

SLO Dimension	Elements
Developing a shared vision centred on the learning of *all* students	<ul><li>A shared and inclusive vision aims to enhance the learning experiences and outcomes of all students</li><li>The vision focuses on a broad range of learning outcomes, encompasses both the present and the future, and is inspiring and motivating</li><li>Learning and teaching are oriented towards realising the vision</li><li>Vision is the outcome of a process involving all staff</li><li>Students, parents, the external community and other partners are invited to contribute to the school's vision</li></ul>

Figure 18.1a.

SLO Dimension	Elements
Creating and supporting continuous professional learning for all staff	<ul><li>All staff engage in continuous professional learning</li><li>New staff receive induction and mentoring support</li><li>Professional learning is focused on student learning and school goals</li><li>Staff are fully engaged in identifying the aims and priorities for their own professional learning</li><li>Professional learning challenges thinking as part of changing practice</li><li>Professional learning connects work-based learning and external expertise</li><li>Professional learning is based on assessment and feedback</li><li>Time and other resources are provided to support professional learning</li><li>The school's culture promotes and supports professional learning</li></ul>

Figure 18.1b.

SLO Dimension	Elements
Promoting team learning and collaboration among all staff	• Staff learn how to work together as a team • Collaborative working and collective learning – face-to-face and through ICTs – are focused and enhance learning experiences and outcomes of students and/or staff practice • Staff feel comfortable turning to each other for consultation and advice • Trust and mutual respect are core values • Staff reflect together on how to make their own learning more powerful • The school allocates time and other resources for collaborative working and collective learning

Figure 18.1c.

SLO Dimension	Elements
Establishing a culture of inquiry, exploration and innovation	• Staff want and dare to experiment and innovate in their practice • The school supports and recognises staff for taking initiative and risks • Staff engage in forms of inquiry to investigate and extend their practice • Inquiry is used to establish and maintain a rhythm of learning, change and innovation • Staff have open minds towards doing things differently • Problems and mistakes are seen as opportunities for learning • Students are actively engaged in inquiry

Figure 18.1d.

SLO Dimension	Elements
Embedding systems for collecting and exchanging knowledge and learning	• Systems are in place to examine progress and gaps between current and expected impact • Examples of practice – good and bad – are made available to all staff to analyse • Sources of research evidence are readily available and easily accessed • Structures for regular dialogue and knowledge exchange are in place • Staff have the capacity to analyse and use multiple sources of data for feedback, including through ICT, to inform teaching and allocate resources • The school development plan is evidence-informed, based on learning from self-assessment, and updated regularly • The school regularly evaluates its theories of action, amending and updating them as necessary • The school evaluates the impact of professional learning

Figure 18.1e.

SLO Dimension	Elements
Learning with and from the external environment and larger system	• The school scans its external environment to respond quickly to challenges and opportunities • The school is an open system, welcoming approaches from potential external collaborators • Partnerships are based on equality of relationships and opportunities for mutual learning • The school collaborates with parents/guardians and the community as partners in the education process and the organisation of the school • Staff collaborate, learn and exchange knowledge with peers in other schools through networks and/or school-to-school collaborations • The school partners with higher education institutions, businesses, and/or public or non-governmental organisations in efforts to deepen and extend learning • ICT is widely used to facilitate communication, knowledge exchange and collaboration with the external environment

Figure 18.1f.

SLO Dimension	Elements
Modelling and growing learning leadership	• School leaders model learning leadership, distribute leadership and help grow other leaders, including students • School leaders are proactive and creative change agents • School leaders develop the culture, structures and conditions to facilitate professional dialogue, collaboration and knowledge exchange • School leaders ensure that the organisation's actions are consistent with its vision, goals and values • School leaders ensure the school is characterised by a "rhythm" of learning, change and innovation • School leaders promote and participate in strong collaboration with other schools, parents, the community, higher education institutions and other partners • School leaders ensure an integrated approach to responding to students' learning and other needs

Figure 18.1g. Appendix B. *Louise Stoll*

References

Barker, J. (1991). Discovering the future series: The power of vision (video). https://starthrower.com/products/power-of-vision-joel-barker?_pos=10&_sid=03c8a9193&_ss=r

Bascia, N. (2014). The school context model: How school environments shape students' opportunities to learn. In *Measuring what matters, people for education*. Toronto.

Bauman, B., & Gordon, N. (2021, Spring). Leading the learning: Leadership development pre-and during Covid-19. *Transformative Educational Leadership Journal*.

Blanchard, K. (2011). *Full steam ahead! Unleash the power of vision in your company and life* (2nd ed.). Berrett-Koehler.

Breakspear, S. (2016a). *Agile implementation for learning: How adopting an agile mindset can help leaders achieve meaningful progress in student learning* (Occasional Paper No. 147). Centre for Strategic Education. https://simonbreakspear.com/wp-content/uploads/2021/06/Dr.-S.Breakspear-Agile-Implementation-for-learning.pdf

Breakspear, S. (2016b). Embracing agile leadership for learning—How leaders can create impact despite growing complexity. *Australian Educational Leader*, *39*(3), 68–71.

Brown, J. (2006). *The imperfect board member: Discovering the seven disciplines of governance excellence*. Jossey-Bass.

Bryk, A., & Schneider, B. (2002). *Trust in schools: A core resource for improvement*. University of Chicago Press.

Bryk, A., Bender Sebring, P., Allensworth, E., Luppescu, S., & Easton, J. (2010). *Organizing schools for improvement: Lessons from Chicago*. University of Chicago Press.

Burkett, H. (2006, January). *The school improvement planning process*. The Centre for Comprehensive Reform and Improvement.

Butler, D. L., Schnellert, L., & MacNeil, K. (2015). Collaborative inquiry and distributed agency in educational change: A case study of a multi-level community of inquiry. *Journal of Educational Change*, *16*(1), 1–26.

Campbell, C., Fullan, M., & Glaze, A. (2006). *Unlocking potential for learning: Effective district-wide strategies to raise student achievement in literacy and numeracy.* Toronto: Ontario Ministry of Education.

Campbell, C., et al. (2016). *The state of educators' professional learning in Canada.* Learning Forward.

CAST (2018). Universal design for learning guidelines version 2.2 [graphic organizer]. Wakefield, MA: Author.

Cleary, J. A., Morgan, T. A., & Marzano, R. J. (2018). *Classroom techniques for creating conditions for rigorous instruction.* Learning Sciences International.

Cooperrider, D. L., & Whitney, D. (2005). *Appreciative inquiry: A positive revolution in change.* Berrett-Koehler.

Coristine, S., Russo, S., Fitzmorris, R., Beninato, P., & Rivolta, G. (2022, April 1). *The importance of student-teacher relationships.* Classroom Practice in 2022. https://ecampusontario.pressbooks.pub/educ5202/chapter/the-importance-of-student-teacher-relationships/

Costa, L., & Kallick, B. (1993). Through the lens of a critical friend. *Educational Leadership, 51*(2), 49–51.

Dervarics, C., & O'Brien, E. (2019). *Eight characteristics of effective boards.* Center for Public Education. https://www.nsba.org/-/media/NSBA/File/cpe-eight-characteristics-of-effective-school-boards-report-december-2019.pdf

DeWitt, P. (2019, January). 4 reasons educators use research and 4 reasons they don't. *Education Week.*

Donohoo, J. (2017). *Collective efficacy: How educators' beliefs impact student learning.* Corwin.

Doonohoo, J., & Velasco., M. (2016). *The transformative power of collaborative inquiry: Realizing change in schools and classrooms.* Corwin.

Failing, L., Gregory, R., Long, G., & Moore, B. (2019). *The decision playbook: Making thoughtful choices in a complex world* (Teachers' ed.). GutsNHeads Project.

Fichtman Dana, N., Thomas, C., & Boynton, S. (2011). *Inquiry: A districtwide approach to staff and student learning.* Thousand Oaks, CA: Corwin.

First Nations Education Steering Committee (FNESC 2006). The First Peoples Principles of Learning with permission of FNESC. First Peoples classroom resources: www.fnesc.ca

First Nations Education Steering Committee (FNESC 2020). https://www.fnesc.ca/

Fullan, M. (2002). The change leader. *Educational Leadership, 59*(8), 16–21.

Fullan, M. (2010). *All systems go: The change imperative for whole school reform.* Corwin.

Fullan, M. (2011). *Change leadership: Learning to do what matters most.* John Wiley and Sons, Inc.

Fullan, M. (2014). *The principal.* Jossey-Bass

Fullan, M., & Quinn, J. (2016). *Coherence: The right drivers in action for schools, districts, and systems.* Corwin Press.

Fullan, M., Rincón-Gallardo, S., & Hargreaves, A. (2015). Professional capital as accountability. *Education policy analysis archives, 23,* 15–15.

Gallo, C. (2011, January 18). Steve Jobs and the power of vision. *Forbes.* http://www.forbes.com/sites/carminegallo/2011/01/18/steve-jobs-and-the-power-of-vision/

Gittell, J. (2009). *High performance healthcare.* McGraw-Hill.

Gregory, R., & Moore, B. (2024). *Sorting it out: Supporting teenage decision making.* Cambridge University Press.

Gurr, D., & Huerta, M. (2013). The role of critical friends in leadership and school improvement. *Procedia—Social and Behavioral Sciences, 106,* 3084–3090.

Halbert, J., & Kaser, L. (2013). *Spirals of inquiry for equity and quality.* Vancouver: Principals and Vice-Principals' Association.

Hargreaves, A. (2018). *Collaborative professionalism: When teaching together means learning for all.* Corwin.

Harris, A. (2011). System improvement through collective capacity building. *Journal of Educational Administration, 49*(6), 624–636.

Hattie, J. (2010). *Visible learning: A synthesis of over 800 meta-analyses relating to achievement.* Taylor & Francis.

Hattie, J. (2012). *Visible learning for teachers: Maximizing impact on learning.* Routledge.

Hattie, J. (2016, July 11). *Third annual visible learning conference* (subtitled *Mindframes and maximizers*). Washington, DC.

Health Schools BC. (2014). *School connectedness: What does the evidence say?* https://healthyschoolsbc.ca/

Hendrix E. (2019, December 19). How your surroundings affect the way you study. Blog for the Universities and Colleges Admissions Service. https://www.ucas.com/connect/blogs/how-your-surroundings-affect-way-you-study

Honig, M. et al. (2007). *Central office transformation for district-wide teaching and learning improvement.* Paper commissioned by the Wallace Foundation. Center for the Study of Teaching and Policy, University of Washington.

Jensen, B. (2016). *Beyond PD: Teacher professional learning in high-performing systems.* The National Center on Education and the Economy (NCEE). Washington, DC.

Jerald, C. (2012). *Leading for effective teaching: How school systems can support principal success.* Bill & Melinda Gates Foundation.

Kaser, L., & Halbert, J. (2017). *The spiral playbook: Leading with an inquiring mindset in school systems and schools.* C21 Canada—Canadians for 21st Century Learning and Innovation.

Katz, S., Earl, L., & Ben Jaafar, S. (2009). *Building and connecting learning communities: The power of networks for school improvement.* Corwin Press.

Kools, M., & Stoll, L. (2016). What makes a school a learning organisation? OECD Education Working Papers No. 137. OECD Publishing. https://www.oecd.org/education/school/school-learning-organisation.pdf

Kouzes, J., & Posner, B. (1998). *Encouraging the heart: A leader's guide to rewarding and recognizing others.* Jossey-Bass.

Kouzes. J., & Posner, B. (2009). To lead, create a shared vision. *Harvard Business Review.* http://hbr.org/2009/01/to-lead-create-a-shared-vision

Leana, C. R. (2011, August 16). The missing link in school reform. *Stanford Social Innovation Review.*

Leithwood, K. (2013). *Strong districts and their leadership*. A Paper Commissioned by the Council of Ontario Directors of Education and the Institute for Education Leadership.

Leithwood, K., Seashore Louis, K., Anderson, S., & Wahlstrom, K. (2004). *How leadership influences student learning*. Paper Commissioned by the Wallace Foundation.

Macintosh, J. (2023). *The Spiral Notebook for Student Changemakers*. Network of Inquiry and Indigenous Education (NOIIE).

McGregor, C., Halbert, J., & Kaser, L. (2022, January). *Catalytic affiliation: Relational impacts in networks*. Paper presented at the International Congress on School Effectiveness and Improvement (ICSEI). Online conference.

McKinsey & Company (2020, April 24). *Coronavirus COVID-19: Perspectives for school leaders*. https://feaweb.org/wp-content/uploads/2020/05/McKinsey-COVID19-Reopening-Schools.pdf

Nanus, B. (1992). *Visionary leadership: Creating a compelling sense of direction for your organization*. Jossey-Bass.

NSW Department of Education (2020). *What works best: 2020 Update*. Centre for Education Statistics and Evaluation, NSW.

Oberle, E., Schonert-Reichl, K. (2016). Stress contagion in the classroom? The link between classroom teacher burnout and morning cortisol in elementary school students. *Social Science and Medicine, 159*.

Organisation for Economic Co-operation and Development—OECD (2010). *The nature of learning: Using research to inspire practice*. OECD Publishing.

Organisation for Economic Co-operation and Development—OECD (2013). *Innovative learning environments*. Educational Research and Innovation. OECD Publishing.

Organisation for Economic Co-operation and Development—OECD (2015). *Schooling redesigned: Towards innovative learning systems*. OECD Publishing.

Organisation for Economic Co-operation and Development—OECD (2016). *What makes a school a learning organization: A guide for policymakers, school leaders and teachers*. OECD Publishing. https://www.oecd.org/education/school/school-learning-organisation.pdf

Saatcioglu, A., Moore, S., Sargut, G., & Bajaj, A. (2011). The role of school board social capital in district governance: Effects on financial and academic outcomes. *Leadership and Policy in Schools, 10*(1), 1–42.

Schlechty, P. (2009). *Leading for learning: How to transform schools into learning organizations*. Jossey-Bass.

Schwab, K (2020). *World Economic Forum*. https://www.weforum.org/agenda/2020/06/now-is-the-time-for-a-great-reset/

Seely, D. S. (1992, April). *Visionary leaders for reforming public schools*. Paper presented at the Annual Meeting of the American Educational Research Association. San Francisco.

Sheninger, E. (2015). *Uncommon learning: Creating schools that work for kids*. Corwin.

Sinek, S. (2009). *Start with why: How great leaders inspire everyone to take action*. Penguin.

Stoll, L., & Kools, M. (2017). The school as a learning organisation: A review revisiting and extending a timely concept. *Journal of Professional Capital and Community*, 2(1) L 2–17.

Stoll, L. & Sinnema, C. (2021, March). *Realising curriculum change through schools as learning organisations in times of crisis and beyond*. Paper presented in the symposium Harnessing Schools as Learning Organisations to Realise System Change during and beyond Times of COVID-19 at the online ICSEI conference.

Talbert, J. E., & McLaughlin, M. W. (1999). Assessing the school environment: Embedded contexts and bottom-up research strategies. In S. L. Friedman & T. D. Wachs (Eds.), *Measuring environment across the life span: Emerging methods and concepts* (pp. 197–227). American Psychological Association.

Taylor, D. (2014). How do leaders get their organizations from vision to action? *Thinking Business*. https://www.thinkingbusinessblog.com/?s=How+do+leaders+get+their+organizations+from+vision+to+action%3F+&submit=Search

Timperley, H. (2011). *Realizing the power of professional learning*. Open University Press.

Timperley, H., Kaser, L., & Halbert, J. (2014). *A framework for transforming learning in schools: Innovation and the spiral of inquiry*. Victoria, Australia: Centre for Strategic Education.

Togneri, W., & Anderson, S. E. (2003). Beyond islands of excellence: What districts can do to improve instruction and achievement in all schools. https://files.eric.ed.gov/fulltext/ED475875.pdf

Wagner, T., & Kegan, R. (2006). *Change leadership: A practical guide to transforming our schools*. Jossey-Bass.

Wellman, B., & Lipton, L. (2004). *Data-Driven Dialogue: A facilitators guide to collaborative inquiry*. Miravia.

West-Burnham, J. (2009). *Rethinking educational leadership: From improvement to transformation*. Continuum International Publishing Group.

William, D. (2012). Keynote speech at the Schools, Students and Teachers Network (SSAT) National Conference, Liverpool, England. https://www.youtube.com/watch?v=r1LL9NX1hUw

Willms, D., Friesen, S., & Milton, P. (2009) *What did you do in school today? Transforming classrooms through social, academic and intellectual engagement*. First National Report, Canadian Education Association.

Winthrop, R., Barton, A., Ershadi, M., & Ziegler, L. (2021). *Collaborating to transform and improve education systems: A playbook for family-school engagement*. Center for Universal Education at Brookings.

Index

academies, xiii, xvn1
accountability, 32, 33, 99–100; external, 101–2; for goals, 55; professional inquiry and, 50–51
achievement gaps, resources for, 24
action, 3, 5, 16, 17
administrative procedures, 23, 34, 73
administrative transfers, 73
AFL. *See* assessment for learning
Agile Leadership, 54
AI. *See* Appreciative Inquiry
Akune, Aaron, 9, 157, 169
Appreciative Inquiry (AI), 7–9, 91, 124
assessment, 55, 138
assessment for learning (AFL), 45, 47, 49–50, 147
assessment practices: collaboration in, 27; Vision 2020 relation to, 47
assistant superintendent, 6–7
Australia, Learning First in, 90

Barker, Joel, 3
BCSSA. *See* British Columbia School Superintendents Association
BCTF. *See* British Columbia Teachers Federation
behavior, 136; intellectual engagement relation to, 62; severe designation for, 39, 42

belonging, for learners, 144
Ben Jaafar, Sonia, 18–19
Beyond PD (Learning First), 90
Blanchard, Ken, 4–5
boards of education, 26, 31, 35, 36; goals of, 32, 34; improvement relation to, vii; professional learning of, 33; trust in, 15; visioning process and, 7; vision statements of, 6
Bold Vision, of Delta School District, xiv, 9, 18, 34; innovation in, 46; resources for, 23; *Spiral of Inquiry* for, 13
Breakspear, Simon, 54
British Columbia: external research organizations in, 56; Vancouver, xiii
British Columbia Ministry of Education, 40
British Columbia School Superintendents Association (BCSSA), 90
British Columbia Teachers Federation (BCTF), 66
Brookings study, 172, 173
Brown, J., 34
Bryk, A., 82
budget, 23, 26; decision making for, 30; Learning Services Department

relation to, 45; for professional learning, 28–29
Building and Connecting Learning Communities (Katz, Earl, and Ben Jaafar), 18–19
Burkett, Hugh, 5
buy-in: cooperation and, 163; for vision, 3–4, 6; "Why?" relation to, 21

Campbell, C., 25
Canadian Educational Leadership (CEA), 5–6
Canadian Union of Public Employees (CUPE), 161
capacity: for improvement, 73; for instructional guidance system, 49; leadership, 152; of teachers, 51, 101
Carleton-Gaines, Toshi, 171
CEA. *See* Canadian Educational Leadership
Center for Public Education, Effective School Boards and, 32
central office staff: collaboration with, 81; as learners, 79
Central Office Transformation investigation, 74
chai chats, 174
Change Leadership (Fullan), 82
change processes, 163
checking phase, in *Spiral of Inquiry*, 71, 141, 147; for Vision 2020, 91–92, 96. *See also "How Are We Doing? Vision Review 2016"*
Christ, Nicola, 25
Chrona, Jo, 35–36
CIA. *See* Curriculum, Instruction, and Assessment
clarity, 8; of roles, 36–37; *Spiral of Inquiry* for, 39–40
Clarke, Todd, 84–85
classroom management, 62, 136; learning environment relation to, 138
Cleary, J. A., 136
climate, 32–33, 158; conversations relation to, 44; trustees relation to, 34

coherence: instructional, 48, 49, 50, 146; in professional learning, 45; social capital relation to, 18
Coherence (Fullan and Quinn), 20, 49, 99
COI. *See* Coordinator of Inquiry
collaboration, 18–19, 158; in assessment practices, 27; communication relation to, 81, 85; during COVID-19 pandemic, 159; culture of, 99–100; engagement and, 144; GAFE for, 28; *Spiral of Inquiry* and, 67; in *Strong Districts* research, 55–56; with superintendent, 74; among teachers, 51, 85, 139, 151, 156; time for, 126, 127; Vision 2030 and, 170
collaborative inquiry, 18, 19, 127; COI relation to, 26; collective efficacy relation to, 43; professional capital and, 85; professional learning and, 81–82, 89–90; of teachers, 46, 83; Vision 2020 relation to, 47
collaborative learning, 42, 75; educators and, 64
collective beliefs, learning environment relation to, 102
collective efficacy, 102, 103; collaborative inquiry relation to, 43
Collective Efficacy (Donohoo), 102
common language, 20, 21, 49, 72
communicating student learning (CSL), 100
communication, 16–17, 164; collaboration relation to, 81, 85; during COVID-19 pandemic, 163; engagement and, 145; among leaders, 161; with stakeholders, 22; transparency in, 82
community forum, for Vision 2020, *10*
Community Youth Centre, of TFN, 24
Compassionate Systems Leadership, professional learning in, 77–78
competition, 157, 158

Index

completion rates, 153, *153*, 154, 156; for Indigenous students, *154, 156*
connectedness, 43, 85; horizontal, 77, 87; SLO and, 158–59; of students, 55, 60, 132
consultants, 34, 72
continuous improvement, 42, 141, 147; culture of, 43, 79; goals for, 47–48, 69; learning and, 103; professional learning for, 70; *Spiral of Inquiry* and, 51; in Vision 2020, 169
continuous learning, xv, 83. *See also* professional learning
conversations, 72, 147; for goals, 50; improvement relation to, 82; with parents, 174; for professional learning, 44; with students, 137; trust relation to, 86
cooperation, 76, 163
Cooperrider, David, 7
Coordinator of Inquiry (COI), 19, 26, *133*, 151; professional learning and, 46
COVID-19 pandemic, 147, 158–59, 171, 172; communication during, 163; Vision 2020 relation to, 161–62; Vision 2030 relation to, 167; vulnerable learners during, 160–61
CSL. *See* communicating student learning
Cultivating Collaborative Cultures, 99–100
culture, 28, 83, 158, 177; of collaboration, 99–100; of continuous improvement, 43, 79; conversations relation to, 44; for innovation, 60; of professional learning, 86
CUPE. *See* Canadian Union of Public Employees
curriculum, 41, 47
Curriculum, Instruction, and Assessment (CIA), 47, 73, 109

data, 33, 97; goals relation to, 55; for "How Are We Doing? Vision Review 2016," 95; Ministry of Education relation to, 54, 56; outcomes relation to, 138; for SLO, 121; *Spiral of Inquiry* relation to, 41; for student learning, 53, 57; superintendent relation to, 39, 42; teachers relation to, 56–57; for Vision 2030, 167–68
Data-Driven Dialogue, 56–57
decision making, 21, 28, 35; for budget, 30; leaders and, 164; vision relation to, 29
The Decision Playbook (Failing et al.), 28
Deepening Learning, 99–100
Delta Access, xiii
Delta Board of Education, 26, 31; policies and, 34–35; trustees in, 36
Delta Learns, 28, 67, 88
Delta Principals' and Vice-Principals' Association (DPVPA), 74
Delta School District, xiv–xv. *See specific topics*
Delta Teachers' Association (DTA), 161
Dervarics, Chuck, 32–33
design, of learning environment, 131
Design phase, of AI, 8
Destiny phase, of AI, 8
Discovery phase, of AI, 8
District Parent Advisory Committee (DPAC), 85
District Principal of Inquiry and Innovation, 26
diversity, 42, 136, 141
Dixon, Laura, 15, 34, 91
Donohoo, Jenni, 102
DPAC. *See* District Parent Advisory Committee
DPVPA. *See* Delta Principals' and Vice-Principals' Association
DTA. *See* Delta Teachers' Association

Earl, Lorna, 18–19
educators: collaborative learning and, 64; connectedness of, 60; Finance Department relation to, 25;

professional learning of, 52, 178. *See also* teachers
Effective School Boards, Center for Public Education and, 32
elected boards, 31, 32; leaders relation to, 34
elementary schools, collaboration at, 18–19
emotions, 77, 136, 141, 142
engagement, 4; collaboration and, 144; communication and, 145; family, 172, 173–74; in learning environment, 76; student, 5–6, 43
enthusiasm, 43
environment. *See* learning environment
equity, 141; learning environment relation to, 147
Equity and Success, 109
evidence: practice relation to, 53; *Spiral of Inquiry* and, 49, 56, 68; for student learning, 57
exit ticket, 15–16
expectations: for learners, 147; for students, 138
explicit teaching, 138
external accountability, 101–2
external input, for system growth, 89
external research organizations, 56

facilitator, for visioning process, 7
family engagement, 172, 173–74
feedback, 138; for learning, 147
FESL. *See* Framework for Enhancing Student Learning
Fichtman Dana, N., 41
Finance Department, educators relation to, 25
First Nations: relationships with, 142; Tsawwassen, xiii, 24
First Peoples, viiin1; learning principles of, vii, viiin2
First People's Principles of Learning, 62, *63*, *64*, *65*, 70; *Leading for Learning* program and, 75
The Five Rs, 162, *162*

Focusing Direction, 99–100
Formative Assessment knowledge, 88
Four-Corners exercise, 171
Framework for Enhancing Student Learning (FESL), 40–41, 48, 53–54, 73, *140*; goals in, 139; graphic organizers and, 62; professional learning and, 68
FSA. *See* Provincial Foundation Skills Assessment
Fullan, Michael, 5, 18, 20, 25, 49, 99–100; on accountability, 101–2; *Change Leadership* of, 82; on knowledge sharing, 87, 88, 90–91
funding, 30

GAFE. *See* Google Applications for Education
Gallo, Carmen, 4
Gittel, J., 82
Glaze, A., 25
Goal One, of Delta School District, *142*
goals, 21, 31, 73–74; of boards of education, 32, 34; for continuous improvement, 47–48, 69; conversations for, 50; culture relation to, 43; data relation to, 53, 55–56; in FESL, 139; inquiry around, 82; on Jamboard platform, *172*; for learning, 100; for learning environment, 141; for professional learning, 70, 152; SLO and, 122, 127; SMART, 53; *Spiral of Inquiry* and, 40–41, 54, 57, 139; strategic plan for, 99; of Vision 2020, 39
Goal Three, of Delta School District, *144*
Goal Two, of Delta School District, *143*
Golden Circle model, 5, 17–18, 72
Google Applications for Education (GAFE), 28
governance: consultant on, 34; professional learning for, 37; student success relation to, 36–37; trustees relation to, 35

graduation, 55; of vulnerable learners, 122, 123
graduation rates, 14, 95; literacy relation to, 139, 141; severe behavior designation relation to, 39, 42
grants: Inquiry and Innovation, 26; technology, 27–28
graphic organizer, 60, *61*; for FESL, 62; School Connectedness, *61*
Greater Metro area, of Vancouver, xiii
growth mindset, 62
Guide for Policy Makers, of OECD, 108
Guiding Principles, of Delta School District, *145*

Halbert, Judy, xiv, 25, 49; leadership development by, 71–72; NOIIE and, 89; TELP relation to, 77. *See also Spiral of Inquiry*
Hanlon, Keri, 169
Hargreaves, A., 5
Hattie, John, 102, 136, 137
Healthy Schools BC, 60, 70n1
high-performing school systems, 4
hiring practices, 79
HomeQuest, xiii
Honig, Meredith, 73, 74
horizontal connectedness, 77; knowledge sharing for, 87
"How Are We Doing? Vision Review 2016," 91–92, *92, 93, 94, 95*, 96; data for, 95
human resources department, 30
hunches, 40, 108; literacy and, 139, 141; in *Spiral of Inquiry*, 146, 175

ICSEI. *See* International Congress for School Effectiveness and Improvement
improvement, 48, 131; capacity for, 73; conversations relation to, 82; goals for, 40; knowledge sharing for, 90; of outcomes, 42–43; in student learning, 69; transformation and, vii. *See also* continuous improvement

Inclusive Learning, 109
Indigenous Education, 36
Indigenous Knowledge and Perspectives, 123, *124*
Indigenous students, 146; completion rates for, *154, 156*; reading skills of, 24
Information Services Department, 56
initiative overload, 44
innovation, 4, 16, 174; culture for, 60; District Principal of Inquiry and, 26; risk-taking and, 156; in Vision 2020, 45–47
Innovative Learning Environments (OECD), 131
innovative teaching, 60–62
inquiry, 69, 84–85; appreciative, 7–9, *8*, 91, 124; hiring practices and, 79; professional, 50–51, 59; for professional learning, 71–72; students and, 145; in Vision 2030, 163, 169. *See also* collaborative inquiry; Spiral of Inquiry
Inquiry and Innovation Grants, 26
Inquiry celebration, 84
inquiry questions, 16
instruction, 144, 147; learning relation to, 137–38
instructional coherence, 48, 50, 146; in Vision 2020, 49
instructional guidance system, 45, 49, 51; SLO as, 123, 124
intellectual engagement, behavior relation to, 62
International Baccalaureate, xiii
International Congress for School Effectiveness and Improvement (ICSEI), 90, 107
International Student Program, of Delta, 91, 169
investments, of professional capital, 84

Jamboard platform, 171, *172*
Japan, 169; Vision 2030 in, *169*
Jensen, Ben, 90

Jerald, C., 41
job-embedded professional development, 59
Johnson, Ted, 18
Just One Thing, 88

Kaser Linda, xiv, 25, 49; leadership development by, 71–72; NOIIE and, 89; TELP relation to, 77. *See also Spiral of Inquiry*
Katz, Steven, 18–19
Kirincic, Tashi, 67
knowledge-building partnerships, for learning, 99
knowledge sharing, 91; for improvement, 90; learning and, 87–88; networking and, 97
Kools, Marcus, 107, 108
Kouzes, J., 4, 83

Ladner district, xiii
leaders, 72, *75*, 100; CIA and, 73; collaboration among, 55; communication among, 161; community relation to, 4; data relation to, 56; decision making and, 164; as learners, 125; learning of, 84; professional learning for, 79; senior, 25; SLO relation to, 89; *Spiral of Inquiry* relation to, 46, 71; teachers relation to, 83; trustees relation to, 34; union, 14, 159; Vision 2030 and, 168
Leadership, 100, 102
leadership capacity, 152
leadership development, 78; *Leading for Learning* program for, 75; for principals, 71–72
leadership succession, 72–73
A Leading District of Innovative Teaching and Learner Success, 16, 19
Leading for Learning program, 29, 68, 75, *76*, 76–77; leadership capacity and, 152

Leading the Learning series, 102
Leana, C. R., 83
learners, 77; belonging for, 144; central office staff as, 79; expectations for, 147; leaders as, 125; outcomes for, 175; vulnerable, 55, 122, 123, 154, 156, 160–61. *See also* students
learner success, 62
learning: assessment for, 55; continuous improvement and, 103; cooperation for, 76; culture of, 83; feedback for, 147; goals for, 100; instruction relation to, 137–38; knowledge-building partnerships for, 99; knowledge sharing and, 87–88; of leaders, 84; Reggio-Emilio approach to, 132; remote, 160–61, 162; Vision 2030 relation to, 171. *See also* professional learning
learning environment, *132*, 139; classroom management relation to, 138; collaboration in, 144; collective beliefs relation to, 102; design of, 131; engagement in, 76; equity relation to, 147; goals for, 141; physical spaces for, 132, 133–34, *135*, 146; relationships and, 134, 136–37; SLO relation to, 126, *126*
Learning First, in Australia, 90
Learning Forward Annual Conference, 90
learning principles, of First Peoples, vii, viiin2
Learning Services Department, 59, 73; budget relation to, 45; physical spaces in, 81; Stoll relation to, 109
Learning with and from the External Environment, of SLO, 121
Leithwood, Ken, 4, 99, 103; on continuous learning, 83; on governance, 35; on improvement, 40, 48; on innovation, 46; on instructional coherence, 146; on instructional guidance system, 45, 123, 124; on organizational

improvement practices, 39; on professional development, 59, 64–65; *Strong Districts* of, 23–24, 31–32, 33, 36, 55–56, 71, 77, 81
lighting, 134
Lipton, Laura, 56–57
literacy, 58n1; graduation rates relation to, 139, 141; for vulnerable learners, 156
long-term plan, strategic plan compared to, 39
Lymburner, Julie, 16

Macintosh, Joanna, 28
McKinsey & Company, 162, *162*
meetings: for principals, 41–42; virtual, 167, 173
mentoring program, 75; for teachers, 48, 65–66, 70
Ministry of Education, 47, 159–60; communication with, 81; data relation to, 54, 56
mission statements, 9
model of an inquiry cycle, 20, *20*
moral purpose, 99
motivations, in learning environment, 77
music education, 26
Musqueam Indian Band, xiii

Nanus, B., 3–4
networking, 81–82, 169; knowledge sharing and, 97; for professional learning, 67; storytelling and, 152
Network of Inquiry and Indigenous Education (NOIIE), 88–89
Nielsen, Niels, 46–47, 157
NOIIE. *See* Network of Inquiry and Indigenous Education
North Delta district, xiii
numeracy, 58n1

O'Brien, Eileen, 32–33
Occupational Health and Safety Regulation, 164n1

OECD. *See* Organisation for Economic Co-operation and Development
180 Days of Learning (blog), 67, 87
Organisation for Economic Co-operation and Development (OECD), 90; *Innovative Learning Environments* by, 131; Principles of Learning of, 62, *63–64*, 70, 75; *What Makes a School a Learning Organisation* of, 107–8
organizational improvement practices, 39
orientation opportunities, 32
outcomes, 177; data relation to, 138; improvement of, 42–43; for learners, 175; pedagogy relation to, 49; for students, vii–viii, 24, 26–27, 31, 153, 154, 156, 163, 174; Vision 2030 and, 170; vision relation to, 3, 8; for vulnerable learners, 154, 156
outdoor learning opportunities, 94
ownership: stakeholders and, 21; of vision, 16

Parent Advisory Councils, 174
parents: conversations with, 174; decision making and, 164; teachers relation to, 160
participation, of stakeholders, 22
PBIS. *See* Positive Behavior Interventions and Supports
pedagogy: outcomes relation to, 49; precision in, 100–101
personnel policies, 24
physical distancing, 161
physical spaces: for learning environment, 132, 133–34, *135*, 146; in Learning Services Department, 81
policies, 32; Delta Board of Education and, 34–35; personnel, 24
Policy and Procedures Manual, 23
Policy Number One, 23
policy revision, in Vision 2030, 35–36
Positive Behavior Interventions and Supports (PBIS), 62

Posner, B., 4, 83
poster board template, 9
practice: assessment, 27, 47; evidence relation to, 53; hiring, 79; organizational improvement, 39; problems of, 41; research relation to, 103
precision, in pedagogy, 100–101
pride, 16, 17; stakeholders and, 21
Principal and Vice-Principal Association, 71
principals: leadership development for, 71–72; *Leading for Learning* program for, 75; meetings for, 41–42; professional growth plans for, 73; professional learning for, 68; SLO and, 111; vision relation to, 6. *See also* leaders
Principles of Learning, of OECD, 62, 63–64, 70; *Leading for Learning* program and, 75
"problems of practice," 41
professional capital, 5, 83; collaborative inquiry and, 85; investments of, 84
professional development, 19, 64–65; boards of education relation to, 33; job-embedded, 59
professional growth plans, 68, 73
professional inquiry, 59; accountability and, 50–51
professional learning, xiv–xv, 42, 62, 145; AFL for, 49–50; of boards of education, 33; budget for, 28–29; coherence in, 45; COI and, 46; collaborative inquiry and, 81–82, 89–90; in Compassionate Systems Leadership, 77–78; for continuous improvement, 70; conversations for, 44; culture of, 86; of educators, 52, 178; FESL and, 68; goals for, 69, 152; for governance, 37; inquiry for, 71–72; for leaders, 79; *Leading for Learning* program for, 75; networking for, 67; for principals, 68; for secretary treasurer, 25;

Spiral of Inquiry and, 62, 67, 151; student learning relation to, 19–20; trust relation to, 83; Twitter and, 88; in Vision 2020, 59–60; Vision 2030 and, 170
professional literacy communities, 24
Provincial Foundation Skills Assessment (FSA), 53, 58n1
Provincial Privacy Commissioner, 28

Quinn, Joanne, 20, 49, 99–100; on accountability, 101–2

RAG. *See* red, amber, or green
reading instruction, 50
reading skills, 55; of Indigenous students, 24. *See also* literacy
Realizing the Power of Professional Learning (Timperley), xiv, 19
red, amber, or green (RAG), 111, *112–20*, 125; SLO and, 121
Reggio-Emilio approach, 132
relationships: with First Nations, 142; learning environment and, 134, 136–37; in *Strong Districts* research, 81; student-teacher, 136–39, 146, 159; trust in, 82–83, 85
reluctance, 14, 15
remote learning, 160–61, 162
research, 99, 103, 152–53, 177–78; on learning environment, 146. *See also Strong Districts* research
Resource Investment investigation, 74
resources: for achievement gaps, 24; for Bold Vision, 23; *Spiral of Inquiry* relation to, 50; for "Vision Achievement," 25
Rethinking Educational Leadership (West-Burnham), 87
Rincón-Gallardo, S., 5
risk-taking, 87, 156–57; support for, 28; by teachers, 43, 46, 68
roles, clarity of, 36–37
Rubric Development Process, *121*

Saatcioglu, A., 36
Sample School Assessment of the Vision's Core Values, *173*
scanning phase, in *Spiral of Inquiry*, 41, 54, 56, 71, 107, 144; professional learning and, 152
Schleicher, Andreas, 131
Schneider, B., 82
"The School as a Learning Organisation" (Kools), 107
School Connectedness graphic organizer, 61
School Leadership investigation, 74
school ratings, 121, *122, 123*
Schools, Students, and Teachers (SSAT), 177
Schools as Learning Organisations (SLO), 78, *78, 109, 111, 124*; connectedness and, 158–59; data for, 121; goals and, 122, 127; as instructional guidance system, 123, 124; leaders relation to, 89; learning environment relation to, 126, *126*; principals and, 111; *Spiral of Inquiry* and, 108, 109, 122, 125; strategic plan for, 172
Schwab, Klaus, 162
secondary schools, collaboration at, 18
secretary treasurer, professional learning for, 25
Securing Accountability, 99–100, 101
Seeley, D. S., 3
Senge, Peter, 78
senior leadership team, 25
senior staff, 31, 45, 71
severe behavior designation, 39, 42
Sheppard, Doug, 17
Sinek, Simon, 5, 17–18, 72
Sinnema, Claire, 78
skepticism, 15
SLO. *See Schools as Learning Organisations*
SMART goals, 53
social capital, coherence relation to, 18
social-emotional skills, 136, 141, 142

Sorting It Out (Gregory and Moore), 28
spatial redesign, 131
special needs, students with, *154*
The Spiral Notebook for Student Changemakers (Macintosh), 28
Spiral of Inquiry, vii, xiv–xv, 39, *110*, 177; accountability and, 101; for Bold Vision, 13; *checking phase* in, 96, 141, 147; continuous improvement and, 51; evidence and, 49, 56, 68; FESL relation to, 48; goals and, 40–41, 54, 57, 139; graphic organizers and, 62; *"How Are We Doing? Vision Review 2016"* and, 91–92; hunches in, 146, 175; leaders relation to, 46, 71; NOIIE and, 88–89; professional learning and, 62, 67, 151; resources relation to, 50; *scanning phase* in, 41, 54, 56, 71, 107, 144, 152; secretary treasurer relation to, 25; SLO and, 108, 109, 123, 125; for student learning, 53; teacher mentoring and, 67; trustees relation to, 34; Vision 2020 and, 42
SSAT. *See* Schools, Students, and Teachers
stakeholders: decision making and, 164; ownership and, 21; participation of, 22; for Vision 2020, 157–58; in visioning process, 16
Start with Why (Sinek), 5, 17–18
Steve Jobs and the Power of Vision (Gallo), 4
Stoll, Louise, 78, 103, 108; Delta School District relation to, 109, 121, 126; at ICSEI conference, 107. *See also Schools as Learning Organisations*
storytelling, 175; networking and, 152; transformation relation to, 87, 97
strategic plan, 33; for goals, 99; for SLO, 172; *Spiral of Inquiry* relation to, 39–40
Strive, 27

Strong Districts research, 23–24, 31–32, 33, 77; collaboration in, 55–56; leadership development in, 71; relationships in, 81; trustees relation to, 36
Student Engagement, 5–6, 43
student learning: data for, 53, 57; improvement in, 69; professional learning relation to, 19–20. *See also* learning
students: connectedness of, 55, 62, 132; expectations for, 138; Indigenous, 24, 146, *154*, *156*; inquiry and, 145; outcomes for, vii–viii, 24, 26–27, 31, 153, 154, 156, 163, 174; relationships with, 136–39, 146, 159; with severe behavior designation, 39, 42; with special needs, *154*; well-being of, 32, 138
student success, governance relation to, 36–37
student-teacher relationships, 136–39, 146, 159
student voice, 146, 147
success, 3, 109; learner, 62; relationships and, 136; vision relation to, 4–5
superintendent, 6–7, 32; boards of education relation to, 33; collaboration with, 74; data relation to, 39, 42; DTA and, 161; trustees relation to, 34
support: for risk-taking, 28; for teachers, 50
system growth, external input for, 89
systemic change, 99–100
Systems for Collecting and Exchanging Knowledge, of SLO, 121
system transformation, 3
system-wide change, 15

Taylor, David, 16–17
teacher inquiry, 51, 174
teachers: capacity of, 51, 101; collaboration among, 51, 85, 139, 151, 156; collaborative inquiry of, 46, 83; data relation to, 56–57; mentoring program for, 48, 65–66, 70; parents relation to, 160; professional learning for, 45; risk-taking by, 43, 46, 68; support for, 50; Vision 2030 and, 168, 169
teacher-student interaction, 136–37
teaching: conversations for, 147; explicit, 138; innovative, 60–62; technology in, 27–28
team development, 33
technology, 163; in teaching, 27–28
TELP. *See* Transformative Education Leadership Program
TFN. *See* Tsawwassen First Nation
time, for collaboration, 126, 127
timetable model, 27
Timperley, Helen, xiv, 19–20, 79, 101
Toolkit Series, 29
transformation, 151–52; *Focusing Direction* and, 99–100; improvement and, vii; professional learning for, 59; storytelling relation to, 87, 97; system, 3
Transformative Education Leadership Program (TELP), 77, 80n1
transparency: in communication, 82; in visioning process, 4
transversals, SLO, 125
trust, 51; conversations relation to, 86; in relationships, 82–83, 85; vision statements relation to, 15
trustees, 34; in Delta Board of Education, 36; governance relation to, 35
Truth and Reconciliation, 36
Tsawwassen district, xiii
Tsawwassen First Nation (TFN), xiii; Community Youth Centre of, 24
Twitter (X), 87–88, 91, 95, *96*

UBC. *See* University of British Columbia

UDL. *See* Universal Design for Learning
UNDRIP. *See* United Nations Declaration on the Rights of Indigenous Peoples
union leaders, 14, 159
United Nations Declaration on the Rights of Indigenous Peoples (UNDRIP), 36
Universal Design for Learning, 62, *66*, 70; *Leading for Learning* program and, 75
Universal Design for Learning (UDL), 62
University of British Columbia (UBC), 77, 80n1

values, 8–9
Vancouver, British Columbia, Greater Metro area of, xiii
vice-principals, 6; *Leading for Learning* program for, 75; meetings for, 41–42; professional growth plans for, 73. *See also* principals
virtual meetings, 167; family engagement in, 173
vision. *See specific topics*
Vision 2020, 15–17, *96*, 143, 151–53, 156, 178; community forum for, *10*; continuous improvement in, 169; COVID-19 pandemic relation to, 161–62; culture and, 177; District Principal of Inquiry and Innovation relation to, 26; goals of, 39; *"How Are We Doing? Vision Review 2016"* and, 91–92, *92*, *93*, *94*, 95, *95*, 96; innovation in, 45–47; instructional coherence in, 49; knowledge sharing and, 87; professional learning in, 59–60; *Spiral of Inquiry* and, 42; stakeholders for, 157–58; teacher mentoring and, 65–66;
technology relation to, 28; Truth and Reconciliation in, 36; vision statements for, 10, 11, *11*, 12, *12*, *13*, 14, *14*
Vision 2030, xv, 147, *168*; collaboration and, 170; COVID-19 pandemic relation to, 167; culture and, 177; data for, 167–68; family engagement in, 172, 173–74; inquiry in, 163, 169; in Japan, *169*; learning relation to, 171; policy revision in, 35–36; teachers and, 168, 169
"Vision Achievement," resources for, 25
visioning process: of AI, 7, 8–9; stakeholders in, 16; transparency in, 4
vision statements, 9; community relation to, 6; trust relation to, 15; for Vision 2020, 10, 11, *11*, 12, *12*, *13*, 14, *14*
vulnerable learners, 55; during COVID-19 pandemic, 160–61; graduation of, 122, 123; outcomes for, 154, 156

well-being, 141; of students, 32, 138
Wellman, Bruce, 56–57
West-Burnham, John, 87
What Did You Do in School Today, of CEA, 5–6
What Makes a School a Learning Organisation (OECD), 107–8
What Works Best (NSW Department of Education), 137–38
"Who Is My Class," 101
"Why?," 21
William, Dylan, 177
Windsor, Val, 14, 156, 170
Workers Compensation Act, 164n1
WorkSafe, BC, 160, 164n1

X. *See* Twitter

Younger, Don, 157–58

Printed in the USA
CPSIA information can be obtained
at www.ICGtesting.com
LVHW021311100924
790553LV00001B/1

9 781538 195611